W9-BZG-924

Cambridge Studies in Social Anthropology

General Editor: Jack Goody

43

THE POLITICAL ECONOMY OF
WEST AFRICAN AGRICULTURE

The political economy of West African agriculture

KEITH HART

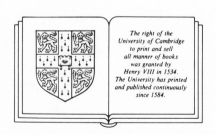

The right of the
University of Cambridge
to print and sell
all manner of books
was granted by
Henry VIII in 1534.
The University has printed
and published continuously
since 1584.

CAMBRIDGE UNIVERSITY PRESS
Cambridge
London   New York   New Rochelle
Melbourne   Sydney

Published by the Press Syndicate of the University of Cambridge
The Pitt Building, Trumpington Street, Cambridge CB2 1RP
32 East 57th Street, New York, NY 10022, USA
10 Stamford Road, Oakleigh, Melbourne 3166, Australia

First published 1982
Reprinted 1986

Printed in the United States of America

Library of Congress Cataloging in Publication Data

Hart, Keith.

The political economy of West African
agriculture.

(Cambridge studies in social anthropology;
no. 43)

Bibliography: p.

Includes index.

1. Agriculture-Economic aspects - Africa,
West. 2. Agriculture and state - Africa, West.
I. Title. II. Series.
HD2140.H37   338.1'0966   81-18174
ISBN 0 521 24073 5 hard covers   AACR2
ISBN 0 521 28423 6 paperback

For all my teachers,
especially M.F. and J.R.G.

If you ask why they are not employed, they tell you because commerce is not in the country: they talk of commerce as if it was a man, who comes to reside in some countries in order to feed the inhabitants.

Sir James Steuart,
Principles of Political Oeconomy
(1767:I, 106)

Contents

Contents

Acknowledgments

This book started out life as a summary of the literature on the development of commercial agriculture in West Africa for the United States Agency for International Development (Purchase Order REDSO/WA/79/169). I am grateful to Stephen Reyna in particular for giving me the opportunity to tackle a question that I had previously neglected in my researches. Bill Sandiford, Jonathan Ross, Victoria Ebin, and Moussa Okanla were my helpers on that project. Linda Leitch did the typing.

Several people kindly gave me their written comments on this earlier draft: Louise Berndt, Jack Goody, Polly Hill, Wolfgang Stolper, and, especially, Allen Roberts, whose detailed and informative notes went beyond the call of friendship's duty. These readers pointed out errors of style, logic, and fact, many of which I have since made good.

This original version contained a substantial annotated bibliography for the benefit of newcomers to the West African literature, which I have kept in the present text. Consequently, there are two segments of the bibliography: an annotated compilation of major sources and a more complete list of references for the serious scholar, many of which are not mentioned in the notes or text references.

My two years in Ann Arbor have been a joy in many ways. I will always remember my friends there for helping to make my stay so productive. Of no one is this more true than Skip Rappaport, whose initiative brought me to Michigan and whose friendship and inspiration I cherish.

Many people have helped me concretely; but I would like to thank Martha Dawson and Elizabeth Lada, in particular, for typing the manuscript.

The eight epigraphs that begin the book and each of its chapters were chosen as much for the identity of their authors as for the sentiments that they contain. Together they form a kind of hagiology, by no means complete. Perhaps they will persuade some of my readers that I am not a Marxist or a Weberian or just another British liberal; but probably they will not. In any case, through the gift of the book, these men (all, bar one, long dead) have been among my significant teachers.

ix

1

Introduction

... the brave army of heretics ... who, following their intuitions, have preferred to see the truth obscurely and imperfectly rather than to maintain error, reached indeed with clearness and consistency and by easy logic but on hypotheses inappropriate to the facts.

J. M. Keynes, *The General Theory of Employment, Interest and Money* (1936:371)

Scope and history of the work

The topic of this book is the rise of commercial farming in West Africa. Specifically, I ask what the various forms of agricultural commodity production have been and how the social life and economic structure of the region's communities have been affected by these developments. Such questions are analogous to asking, "What has been the effect of the Industrial Revolution on Western Europe?" except that much less is known about West Africa, many of the forces shaping its history originate from elsewhere, and there is far more variation in indigenous culture there.

What can one say about sixteen countries, four colonial traditions, and hundreds of ethnic groups? To attempt a summary would appear to be an act of gross hubris. Yet the unity of West Africa's experience of the modern world is real enough, and it is probable that, unless a synthesis of its fragmented polities is achieved fairly soon, no internal solution to the region's massive development problems will be forthcoming. Accordingly, I have chosen to abandon the apparent safety of the ethnographic case study in search of a canvas appropriate to the size of West Africa's agricultural question.[1]

The book deals with commercial agriculture since the early nineteenth century, when West Africans first sold vegetable oils in bulk to the industrializing countries of Western Europe. Although I argue that this period should be treated as a unity, greater attention is paid to the two decades since most West African states won their independence from colonial rule. The global economic context for modern agricultural developments is obvious enough, and it continues to receive much publicity (e.g., Amin 1971; A. G. Hopkins 1973). But the emphasis here is

1

mainly on the organization of internal political and economic affairs. There are two reasons for this: First, even if metropolitan powers have exercised great influence over West African economies, any solution to the dilemmas of economic backwardness requires the mobilization of endogenous social forces; second, an undue focus on overseas factors leads West Africans to gloss over the massive impediments to their growth that originate in local material and social conditions. Hence the "political economy" of the book's title refers principally to the management of public affairs within West Africa and only secondarily to the region's involvement in an expanding global economy dominated by the advanced industrial countries.

I have written the argument as a discursive narrative, minimally interrupted by the niceties of scholarship. I refer to many cases, but introduce none in any detail. The few facts and references that I have consigned to the tables, notes, and text citations are intended to lead the interested reader to my most important sources; the bibliographies give some idea of the field as a whole. The consequence of using the main text principally as a vehicle for structured argument is that strangers to West Africa may be at a loss to judge the authenticity of my many claims. But, although it rests on fifteen years of intermittent scholarly work, this is not a work of authoritative scholarship. It is designed to make people think about old problems in new ways and to revive old ways of thinking about new problems. It paints a picture with bold strokes and scant detail. It is not an encyclopedia of reference; and those who would like instant information of a quantitative sort should consult the many digests and reports that are now published annually on the economy and demography of African states.[2] Above all, it contains a plea for a perspective on West African political economy that is anthropological, in the best, most comprehensive, definition of that word.

I came to the topic of this book by a roundabout route. My doctoral dissertation research was on migration from northeast Ghana to the slums of Accra, the country's capital city (Hart 1969). It seemed reasonable enough to me then (1965–9) that issues of social change and economic development could best be broached by intensive investigations of city life. I later published a piece drawing attention to the buildup of labor in what I called "the informal sector" of urban economies such as Accra's (Hart 1973). I had no idea what caused it or what could be done about it. I worked on the problem of employment as an advisor in the Cayman Islands, Papua New Guinea, and Hong Kong. This experience, along with my teaching on urbanization, reinforced a specialization in the organization of nonagricultural labor markets.

For some seven years after completing my Ph.D. I tried without success to write a monograph on my Ghanaian work in which general ideas on development were combined with ethnographic field materials. At last I recognized that part of the reason for my failure lay in the hazy notions I had of the concrete social history that underlies Western theories of economic development. So I abandoned the pretense of writing a monograph and read European social and intellectual

2

history for a few years. In retrospect, the decisive experience that turned me toward the viewpoint expressed in this book was my participation in a World Bank team appointed to draw up a development program for Papua New Guinea on the eve of its independence (World Bank 1973). The world has seen no starker example of the forced formation of a modern state made up of many primitive societies; but it was only some years later, in the light of my subsequent historical researches, that I came to realize, more or less for the first time, that the anthropological study of social evolution and development planning practice were truly addressing the same problems. Moreover, it now seemed to me that the political economy of today's Third World nations was in some ways analogous to that of preindustrial Europe. But I did not make immediate use of these insights.

My attempt to reduce the intellectual gap between what most people see as rather different enterprises was given an unforeseen boost when in 1979 I was asked by the United States Agency for International Development (AID) to write a report synthesizing the literature on West Africa's response to the rise of commercial agriculture (Hart 1979). The library search led me to works I had previously neglected in my capacity as an ''urban'' specialist, but I also discovered that I knew more about the topic than I had imagined. The report, on which this book is itself very substantially based, was written during the month of October. In the course of writing it I found out a number of things. Most important, I now knew why I had not been able to write a fieldwork monograph: First, the topic of development was too big to be contained by the specificities of my original research; and second, the key to the development of predominantly agrarian states lies in the countryside and not in the cities. Moreover, this study has become a way of synthesizing what I learned about European history with my more secure knowledge of West Africa. In the process, the ideas of Marx, Weber, and the great economists, which had been so much dead weight during my long struggle to write up my fieldwork data, came alive as my ideas embraced the panorama of all modern West African history.

Time and space in anthropological vision

The focus of this book is on West African agriculture in the present. But when is that and where is it? It is this year's groundnut plot belonging to a Malian farmer; it is an oil palm stand in Togo that first yielded a cash crop decades ago. Neither of these places is known to the other, and to say that West African export of vegetable oils is 150 years old would be meaningless to the participants. Human biology and social development set the limits to what our ordinary perceptions of time and space can include. But physics has taught us to extend our vision of matter beyond the range of normal human experience, as far as the galaxies and as deep as elementary particles. Radio telescopes, satellite photography, electron microscopes, and nuclear accelerators allow us to observe matter in its largest and smallest forms. Moreover, there seems to be a correlation between the magnitude

3

of a phenomenon and the length of time that marks a significant period in observing it. Events are slower, take longer, when viewed in the large and from a distance.

So, if now is a moment, what is the appropriate framework within which to observe it? Is it a day, a year, a millennium? Does the event take place in many separate localities or in a region as a whole; or is it worldwide? The capacity of the human memory (with the aid of written records) to store information beyond the limits of one person's lifetime offers us the chance to look at ourselves in the large and from a distance. The study of classical antiquity once performed this function, and anthropological prehistorians carry on the task today. Geographers scan whole regions with the aid of satellites and computers. In the social sciences, however, we remain trapped in a division of labor that draws ever-narrower limits around each investigation: The result is that we live in a foreshortened present established by experimental time and the daily news. Americans especially are blind to history, not least because an abundant environment, technological inventiveness, and the work of building life from scratch in a new world helped them to escape from history. But this escape does not serve them well when it comes to solving the major, long-run dilemmas of our times.

Soon after beginning this study, I consulted a computerized bibliography on agricultural economics and learned that it contained no references to works written before 1975! This was clearly absurd, because few reliable statistics existed for the period *after* 1975, and the best information we have on many topics was written in the 1940s or before. I contrasted the myopia of expatriate consultants with the long-range vision of West Africa's savannah Muslims, some of whom still think of the pattern of coastal dominance that was introduced by European mercantilism as a momentary hiccup in the rhythm and shape of the region's history. Any vision of West African development that we may aspire to will evaporate if we remain anchored in a scientific present that resembles nothing so much as a child's-eye view of the world. Only a far-reaching telescope can take in the contours of agricultural commercialization, a process that began long ago in West Africa and that, over the last five centuries, has become part of a unified global movement.

Seen in this way, 1883 is not history but a point on the analogical continuum that contains the present. The digital extremes that denote the "before" and "after" of our moment in evolutionary time are a past human population devoted overwhelmingly to agriculture (in 1800 less than 3 percent of humanity lived in cities) and a future world in which direct agricultural producers will constitute less than 10 percent of the total population (probably somewhere around the year 2100; see Cipolla 1978; Davis 1969). Before this three-hundred-year period of hectic disengagement from the soil, a process I call "global industrialization," human populations had spent ten thousand years building societies suited to agriculture, half of that time being dominated by civilizations that were in some

4

small part urban. And at the end of this period, nine-tenths of the world's population will live in cities, most of them huge. (Mexico City will contain 30 million people by the year 2000.) So although it is conventional to think of the Industrial Revolution as a past event, as a few factories in Lancashire at the end of the eighteenth century (see Smelser 1959), it would be best to recognize industrialization as a worldwide transition that is entering its maximum rate of expansion during the second half of our century. The recent emergence of such industrial powers as Brazil, Mexico, India, Korea, and Taiwan attests to this ongoing process. The decisive phase of industrialization, affecting that majority of the human population which is Asian (principally Chinese and Indian), is as yet barely begun.

And what of Africa in all this? Industrialization draws in raw materials from everywhere and spawns world markets for manufactured goods and human labor. West Africa, as the nearest tropical region to Western Europe, was involved in industrialization soon after the beginning, as a supplier of raw materials. Its role is similar today, 150 years after the trade in vegetable oils began on a serious scale. West Africa still exports raw materials, mostly agricultural; a fifth of its burgeoning population now lives in cities (see Table 1, in chapter 2). But its economy is only minimally industrialized. As an underdeveloped backwater in the global industrialization process, West Africa responds to developments elsewhere, but as yet is left out of the mainstream. The political economy of modern agriculture, then, can only be understood within a time frame that includes at least the last 150 years as a whole and on a canvas that views the region in a global context of industrial capitalist development. The future of commercial agriculture in West Africa thus becomes inextricably tied up with the question of the region's capacity to achieve a measure of industrialization within its own boundaries.

I have characterized the present period of a few centuries (say, 1800–2100) as an irreversible moment in human evolution, one in which ten thousand years of slow accumulation have been cast aside and the conditions for a new phase of human society set in train. From living on the land as the source of their subsistence, people will live in man-built environments where they can circulate the products of their specialized labor in the form of goods and, increasingly, services. Seen from the perspective of a paleoanthropologist, used to surveying the remote prehistory of the hominids, this transition would appear as fast as the blink of an eyelid, like the switch of a computer bit from 0 to 1. The time in between, negligible to the casual observer of the computer or to the future long-range historian of our day, can be blown up and treated as significant, even periodized and made into a sequence of discrete events. This is what we do, as we live through this brief transition and experience its every jolt and ephemeral promise. It is good that we can do this, because evolutionary time is not the best framework for getting piecemeal things done now. So, after we have established an extreme vantage point from which to view our problem – human social evolution on a global scale – the much more difficult task remains of narrowing down the focus to temporal and spatial dimensions that correspond more clearly to the world of normal experience. Ideally we should move continuously from one analytical pole to the other, stopping off at any intermediate level without losing the overall vision of a multilayered reality. This is harder than it sounds – hence the plethora of "macro" and "micro" theories that plague the social sciences.

The world does not look the same from down among the millet stalks as it does from a Boeing 747. Indeed, almost any observation made from high altitude can be shown by a reporter at ground level to be factually incorrect, partially selective, or grossly misleading. Ethnographers enjoy deflating the generalizations of social scientists with their own particular sources of knowledge. Now that I have taken on this broad study, my views must be reconciled with the thousands of empirical studies that are mounting up in the world's libraries. This is not just a matter of scholarly inadequacy. The problem lies even more in the very fragmentation of West African society, whose rural economies are embedded in a host of particular material and social arrangements that defy generalization as the evolved market economies of the West, for example, no longer do. There is discontinuity, therefore, between the aims of the study and the ways in which its subject can be known at this time.

I have suggested that anthropologists might be equipped to run the gamut from large-scale/long-run to small-scale/short-run investigations. This is because in archaeology and ethnography they possess concrete tools, each of which encourages vision of the opposite extreme type. Unfortunately, archaeologists rarely escape from the remote past, and ethnographers are usually trapped in the unchanging present of their field notes. Nevertheless, some anthropologists have thought about time and space with more imagination than most of their contemporaries in the social sciences and history.[3] They have understood, for example, that time is relative to the several forces shaping the meaningful events of people's lives.

Once we acknowledge that time is a succession of events of varying perodicity, it follows that we should consider the rhythm of life careers as a significant dimension of social time. Given that so much of West African agriculture is conducted within the framework of family-based groups, it is essential to recognize that the growth and decay of these groups is intrinsic to their social organization. The process whereby new domestic groups form, expand, contract, and are replaced has been called a "development cycle."[4] It is a cycle in that the reproductive chain is unbroken and each generation encounters a world much like that of its predecessor, so that assumed role identities are broadly continuous. Much of the internal differentiation of West Africa's rural societies is attributable to regularities arising out of development cycles; thus, as elsewhere, older

6

household heads tend to be more affluent than younger men with underproductive children to feed. Social conflict often takes the form of residential fission within a family group.[5]

Timing in much of the natural world appears to be cyclical, too. The rhythm of agricultural cycles is longer in underpopulated forest areas, where shifting cultivators slowly rotate within an extensive territory, than in a peri-urban market garden irrigated by diesel pump, where the same plot may yield two or three crops a year. Some phenomena that appear to be cyclical are not. Thus the annual yield of a tree crop may give out after thirty years unless its fertility has been extended or replaced by careful arboriculture. In West Africa, when regional populations have converted wholesale to a new kind of farming, the long-run life expectancy of plantations sets an underlying rhythm of growth and decay that has all too often been ignored by policy makers. All these considerations, of course, make a time schedule framed in terms of annual budgets and project accountability wholly unsatisfactory for grasping the phenomenon of commercial farming in West Africa.

Onto these essentially nonlinear time patterns we have to map the irreversible history of world time. The year 1980 can never be 1960, nor 1880. Thus world events like the Great Depression or the rise of the Organization of Petroleum Exporting Countries (OPEC) stamp an indelible mark on their decades, in West Africa as elsewhere. Yet a single cognitive link – between a very old man alive today and his grandfather – spans the whole of our 150-year period; and the works of anthropologists and historians allow us to detect movements and correspondences that transcend the orderly march of official time. We can see separate parts of the region experiencing similar developments at different times: A classical example is the tropical forest export boom experienced in the Gold Coast before World War I and repeated in the Ivory Coast after 1945 (Amin 1967). That is why nineteenth-century history may be relevant today, if only so that we can sort out specific differences within the larger uniformities. The global economic cycle of boom and bust has assailed West Africa twice this century – in the 1920s and 1930s and again in the last three decades. Clear-cut similarities may be seen not only in the economic tendencies themselves but also in the ideological justification given for political responses to these wild swings in the affairs of ordinary Africans.

This is not the place to insist on rigid canons of discrimination when referring to the temporal and spatial context of social observations. The present work draws eclectically and unsystematically on a number of perspectives, ranging from synchronic ethnographies plucked out of time to very long-run accounts of world history in the period since Europe discovered West Africa and later produced the means of its own global dominance. Nevertheless, a major task assumed here is to recognize and, where possible, keep separate the processes of evolution, historical sequence, and development that have structured West African agriculture in all its multilayered spatial dimensions. Recognition is a poor substitute for systematic application, but it is a first step toward improved comprehension of our problem.

Productivity and the evolution of commodity economy

Has the commercialization of agriculture in West Africa laid the basis for that unleashing of capitalist organization and labor productivity which marked the birth of the Industrial Revolution elsewhere? (see Kemp 1978). Implicit in the form of the question are the assumptions that preindustrial commodity economy is not usually capitalist, that transformation of productivity is more crucial than the mere accumulation of wealth, and that industrialization depends on the rise of capitalism (whether public or private). This section attempts to clarify my use of these key terms in the West African context.

A "commodity" is a thing or a service made available for sale.[6] The production and circulation (the term "circulation" is preferred here to "distribution and exchange") of commodities is "commodity economy." The evolution of commodity economy is synonymous with the expansion of the market. The market, in turn, both reflects and enhances the advance of the division of labor, whereby producers become progressively differentiated. Intensification of specialized production for an expanded market often requires increased inputs of capital. The associated technological innovations and gains in productivity have historically culminated in industrialization. When the bulk of workers buy what they need out of wages received from the owners of capital, we may speak of "industrial capitalism." This has been the main force for change in the modern world. Industrial capitalism (a phrase that embraces the mechanization of agriculture) is thus the most advanced phase of a process of economic development that begins with small-scale production and exchange of commodities.

In the evolution of commodity economy, therefore, it makes sense to discriminate between capitalist commodity production and those other forms of commodity production (precapitalist or noncapitalist) where it is *not* the case that people sell their own labor as a commodity. These latter forms of commodity economy may – and often do – coexist with organized capital in the shape of merchants, bankers, and industrialists both at home and elsewhere. Much of the West African literature hinges on the question whether wholesale conversion to export cash crops has unleashed a capitalist revolution at the heart of rural society. The distinction being drawn here between production of goods for sale and the direct sale of wage labor to capitalist production units is crucial if we are to find any coherent answers to such a question.

The antithesis of commodity economy is "self-sufficiency" or "subsistence economy" – both terms that have been freely used in Western accounts of traditional West African economies. The topic of this book could, therefore, be described as the transition from subsistence to commercial agriculture. But such a formula would be unfortunate. Commodity production was no stranger to traditional West Africa. Agricultural commodities were, however, in general extremely limited by low market value, high physical bulk, and difficult transport conditions in a sparsely populated region. There was therefore considerable pressure toward local self-sufficiency in foodstuffs. This obviously does not mean that agricultural production was organized exclusively as a subsistence activity. In areas such as Hausaland (northern Nigeria), all foods entered the market as commodities and cotton was grown extensively for textiles (M. G. Smith 1955; Hill 1972). Even in remote areas, where the division of labor was less developed, mechanisms usually existed for the circulation of foodstuffs, including local marketplaces. Yet it could be said then – and may still be said for many places today – that the bulk of agricultural production was undertaken by small groups with a view to providing for their own food needs. Again, this does not mean that such groups were "households" or "families": Although domestic units formed around marriage and reproduction were usually the most intensively cooperative groups, agricultural production and distribution invariably involved higher-order collectivities based on common descent, age grades, slave estates, and so on. Indeed, families could never aspire to be self-sufficient, because they did not replicate within each unit all the elements of the division of labor. Community social organization took that into account, and markets traditionally played their part, too.

The penetration of the market into subsistence agriculture cannot, therefore, be represented as the disruption of a self-contained circuit of food production and consumption at the household level. Such a transformation had occurred long before in the history of West African village societies. Even where the circulation of commodities was minimal, complex social organization intervened systematically in the economic affairs of households.

The notion of self-sufficiency or subsistence is thus always relative, never absolute; and it applies to units of any scale. Individuals may do a great deal for themselves, but not everything. Families or village groups may aspire to self-sufficiency, but they never wholly succeed. Nation-states may seek to withdraw from the world market, but such withdrawal must always be partial. Although self-sufficiency and commodity economy may be represented as polar opposites, they are nevertheless always combined in the organization of groups at any level. A transition from subsistence to commercial farming cannot therefore be conceived of as a leap from one kind of economy into another, but can perhaps be viewed as a quantum jump, a shift in degree along the continuum from self-sufficiency to greater economic interdependence through the expansion of the market. Nor is it particularly useful to talk of the intrusion of "money" or "the cash economy," which implies an abrupt confrontation that never took place in modern times. There *are* some uses for the subsistence – commerce dualism. We may ask, for example, whether commodity production is surplus to production for one's own basic consumption requirements. Clearly, too, reliance on commodity production much reduces the significance for member units of a locally constituted division of labor and as such may be accompanied by a process of individuation. So the issue to be addressed here is best served by a formulation that asks, What have been the consequences of an increased dependence on agricultural commodity production in rural areas that were previously restricted to a high degree of local self-sufficiency in foodstuffs?

Such a question implies consideration of the productivity of traditional agriculture. The two main determinants of agricultural productivity have been seasonality and population density. In the savannah, rainfall is concentrated in a few months of the year, leaving around six months free when there is no work to be done cultivating crops. In the forest, by contrast, some crops can be grown the whole year round and efforts do not have to be focused on one annual harvest. The population has traditionally been more concentrated in parts of the savannah than anywhere in the forest, but overall densities have been low and land has always been freely available. What has mattered more than land is membership in social groups capable of carrying out all the activities necessary to keep people safely in their chosen patch of territory. Large areas of empty land emerged during periods of warfare, as a buffer zone between hostile populations.

It would be wrong to say that labor was the scarce factor of production in traditional agriculture: In some cases it was fully utilized during a bottleneck in the agricultural cycle, and in others it was clearly underutilized, because people preferred to do something else with their time than grow food they did not need. When people's work schedules are barely differentiated from their general social routines, it does not always make sense to reduce them to classical political economy's abstract category, "labor." But, if there was a scarce factor of production in traditional agriculture, it was not land; and there were only the two factors.

Labor productivity was relatively high in all parts of West Africa in the sense that output was high per unit of labor input. This is bound to be the case when natural fertility is doing most of the work that has to be done by human beings under conditions of preindustrial intensive agriculture. Hence the preference of West Africans for large tracts of land to support a small number of people. But this productivity was much lower than in any kind of mechanized agriculture, and the amount of time devoted to production may not always have been voluntary (being limited by water supply and unevenness in the agricultural cycle). Moreover, though it makes sense for a family to acquire its food with the minimum effort necessary (and that includes the storable surpluses for bad years in the dry savannah), productivity per person was kept much lower than would be thought desirable by agents of the market or the state. And the productivity of land, by unit area, was extraordinarily low, when compared with the farms of England or the paddy fields of China. It should be remembered that the process of increasing yields from a given land area and population generally involves *reducing* the productivity of a unit of labor input. In other words people work harder to produce more and often disproportionately so.

What this discussion means is that West Africans had a form of agriculture well-suited to their environmental conditions and low population density. The yield to the amounts of energy that they expended was higher than in the preindustrial peasant agriculture of Eurasia, but the yield per man or unit of land was lower. This is because taxes and rent on property were rarely supported by West African farmers. Increased population density or an intensification of production for sale could obviously change all this. So could a form of state geared toward extraction of value from the countryside.

The issue of productivity and ''commoditization'' is synthesized when we consider the rise of a locally rooted regional capitalism. For much of the last two decades, discussions of West African export agriculture have rested on the semantic issue of whether indigenous producers are to be termed ''peasants'' or ''capitalists'' (Hill 1970; A. G. Hopkins 1973; Helleiner 1966). This is not as idle a debate as it may seem, because government policy would be seriously affected if it assumed that the bulk of production was contained in one type of organization when in reality it was in the other. But the two terms are not very precise: Just as one writer may suppose that every country dweller is a peasant, another may consider any innovative act the work of a capitalist. I shall argue that the distinction is a meaningful one, separating as it does small-scale commodity production by relatively undifferentiated units and large-scale commodity production based on the purchase of wage labor with money capital. Despite all the gradations between the two, peasant agriculture is marked by the first, and the transition to the second involves an agrarian revolution initiated by capitalist producers. The question is how these terms illuminate West African history during the last 150 years.

The key factor is productivity. The essence of productivity is the output generated by a given level of input. Labor productivity viewed in these terms is a measure of the efficiency of use of a fragment of a person's time. But ''productivity'' is also used in relation to the total amount done by a given person or population, as well as to the yield of a measured amount of land or the return on a sum of money capital. It is also, somewhat confusingly, often applied to the money income earned by a person. I shall use the term ''productivity'' only in the first sense. Thus a population may increase its output, its land yield, its rate of return on capital, and its income without significantly altering the productivity of a unit of labor time. All of these things are true for West Africa.

One hundred fifty years ago, a small population extracted a fairly satisfactory livelihood from a large land area, much of which was unoccupied. Because they were aided by nature's fertility, they did not have to spend as much time producing their basic food requirements as did more intensive farmers elsewhere in the preindustrial world. The productivity of their agricultural labor was thus relatively high and their output as a population and as a land area relatively low (because they did not support an extensive stratification system through direct transfers from agriculture). Since then many more people (through population growth) have committed much more time and most of the remaining extra land to agricultural production. Land areas are now more densely settled, and some land is fairly intensively farmed. A large part of this additional production is of export crops, not foodstuffs. Many people have increased their wealth as a result of this expansion, and most people are more prosperous. They are now doing more things and getting paid for doing them. The story is by all accounts an impressive one.

But what has happened to the efficiency of labor in all this? More people work harder on a larger land area, but is their productivity higher? It could easily be lower, in that intensification of agriculture may have led to an adoption of techniques that absorb more labor for a given level of output. Labor productivity normally declines when a low-density population with large amounts of virgin territory is pushed by state formation, population growth, and division of labor along a path of agricultural intensification. In the West African case, however, it is more likely that labor productivity has remained broadly static, as the population has spread out to occupy the land mass. Pockets of intensive cultivation would be offset by the transfer of many savannah dwellers into the emptier forest. It is, of course, difficult to compare productivity between an export crop and a food crop; organization, factor inputs, and environmental conditions often vary considerably. Output would probably have to be measured in terms of food crop values – an imperfect measure that would reflect a number of variables exogenous to productivity as such. But in the broadest possible terms, it can be said that West African export agriculture remains at the same level of labor productivity as traditional food agriculture.

The central issue is the use of machines. These have not been introduced into any branch of indigenous agriculture on a significant scale. Irrigation and oxplows do not increase the efficiency of farming labor as much as they expand the possibilities open to a given labor force in the annual cycle. Handtools remain the instruments of agricultural labor. This may be because machinery has proved too costly or difficult to use in certain environments, but the result is the same: Labor is not released for other tasks by improvements in its efficiency. It is indus-trialization and mechanization that propel the rich countries forward, and for all the general improvements in its economic condition, West Africa's stagnant productivity has left its people further behind now than 150 years ago.

This is, I think, the appropriate context for a discussion of how to characterize indigenous export agriculture. When development takes place through increased use of existing factors of production (labor and land) and no basic changes in technology and organization are introduced, the mechanism of growth is described as ''vent for surplus'' – meaning that expanded levels of market demand release factors of production that were lying idle. Several authors (e.g., Helleiner, A. G. Hopkins) consider this to be a fair description of West African export agriculture so far, and so do I.[7] There were no pressures to make increasing labor efficiency a major consideration for indigenous farmers: Accumulation of virgin land and external economies in distribution and transport were often much more important. Consequently, production, even when it was organized by a wealthy man using money capital to establish the farm, was small-scale, and labor was a combination of peasant family and wage forms. Clearly it would be misleading to characterize this as a homogeneous "peasant" economy. And much rests on what would be considered innovation in the sphere of technology and organization. The groundnut and cocoa industries were both established by new kinds of organization (although this is truer for Senegal and Ghana than for northern Nigeria), involving the use of risk capital and paid labor. Use of the phrase "capitalist farmer" in some cases is not wholly unjustified. I am restricting the term to production units where the emphasis is on generating cost reductions and increased labor efficiency through improved technology and large-scale organization of wage employees, supervised directly by an owner of capital or his representatives. In such cases, patterns of behavior predicted by the neoclassical theory of the firm are more likely to operate. Although there are some isolated examples of capitalist enterprise in both the public and the private sector of West African agriculture, the overall economic conditions are still nearer to the "vent for surplus" model than to those of an industrial market economy. A major consideration in this work will be whether there is any prospect for an agrarian revolution capable of jerking the prevailing pattern of small-scale commodity production onto a course of steadily rising productivity.

Political economy and underdevelopment

The previous section spoke of markets, technology, land, and capital. Since the 1870s, orthodox economics has found itself able to deal with these factors as if their interrelationships owed nothing to forms of state and class structure.[8] Before the marginalist revolution it was conventional to call economics "political economy," a term contrasted with the "domestic economy" required for managing large households and one that had been current since the Scottish Enlightenment. The only group to retain the expression in modern times has been the followers of Marx, and the recent expansion in its use marks a degree of Marxist penetration into orthodox social scientific circles.

In practice, the classical political economy of Mill and Marx was already a fairly self-sufficient model of advanced capitalism, in which Marx emphasized the class antagonism of capital and labor; but neither paid much attention to political organization (Mill 1909; Marx 1959). The tendency to treat economic activity as if it were autonomous from the sphere of government was thus shared by both main strands of political economy, and it was undoubtedly fostered by the apparent success of the nineteenth-century liberal state in promoting Britain's economic development.[9]

For the nations of West Africa, not even the appearance of a separation of state and economy is plausible. First, their dilemmas are more those of post-Renaissance Europe than those of Victorian England; and second, the synthesis of politics and economics was made explicit by the governments of the colonial period, and the successor states have gone even further toward combining the two in public practice. Indeed, the character of each of these states is the single most important variable in any attempt to understand the history of commercial agriculture during the last twenty years. Accordingly, the ongoing process of state formation since decolonization will be given great prominence in Chapter 4, which is the hinge of this work.

It is convenient (and diplomatic) for outside observers to treat the political status quo as given in any analysis of recent economic trends in West Africa. Alternatively, when aid officials or anthropologists notice government as a social force, they may be inclined to organize their perceptions around some such category as "the incompetent bureaucrat" or "corruption." It is in the belief that the rulers of West African states both are rational in their approach to agriculture and possibly pose the gravest obstacle to its further development that I give the subject such extended treatment.

The point is that, during the precolonial, colonial, and postcolonial phases of modern state formation in West Africa, the expansion of commodity economy has proceeded at a rate far in excess of the evolution of appropriate political and legal frameworks, leaving the organization of property, law, land, labor, and money transfers grossly inadequate to meet the pretensions of both governments and business enterprises. The result has been a growing discrepancy between the apparatus of a modern state and a dominant, decentralized agricultural sector operating at low levels of productivity. The entire tradition of modern economics (including political economy after Adam Smith) has passed this problem by, because it belongs properly to the preclassical literature addressed to the problems of preindustrial states tossed about in the seas of an emergent world market economy.

The preclassical tradition of economic thought reached its finest expression in the work of Sir James Steuart, whose *Principles of Political Oeconomy* (1767) appeared nine years before Smith's *Wealth of Nations*. Steuart, whose ideas have influenced much in my book, recognized that successful transformation of an agricultural society lay in the hands of a benevolent and effective state – a conception to which he gave the name "monarch." In this recognition he was accompanied by his Italian, French, and Spanish peers of the era from the Renaissance to the Industrial Revolution.[10] This literature provides many fertile analogies for the study of modern underdevelopment, for the good reason that the preindustrial economic structures familiar to these authors are nearer than any stage in the recent development of the industrialized West to present-day Third World conditions.

What other directions are open for the seeker of analogues to West African conditions? The literature of nineteenth-century Germany, Italy, and Russia speaks directly of transitional problems arising through confrontation with a superior exogenous capitalism. Lenin's account entitled *The Development of Capitalism in Russia* (1974) is classic, as is Chayanov's marginalist *Theory of Peasant Economy* (1966), which was designed to refute Lenin. The literature on Italy's Risorgimento is rich and complex (Gramsci 1973; Zangheri 1969). The whole theme of German history and social science from the mid-nineteenth century was the political and cultural specificity of German attempts to establish an industrial capitalist nation-state. No one gave that topic a fuller theoretical treatment than Max Weber, and it is his investigations, known as *Economy and Society* (1978), that provide the intellectual structure for much of what I have to say here about the role of the state in regional economic development. Indeed, the central proposition of this book may be said to be Weberian: namely, that successive political forms, both of state and of rural property and office, have been the determining influence restricting West Africa's development since it first came into contact with the Portuguese five hundred years ago. And, as a corollary, the pressing need now is for new political forms capable of shaping a path toward higher productivity and improvements in collective welfare.

Weber never said, nor do I uphold the idea, that political forms may be brought about by an act of will alone. On the contrary, there are definite material and social conditions prerequisite to the establishment and continuity of specific state forms. In this instance, the material basis for West African forms of state is a backward agriculture that sets limits on attempts to introduce centralized bureaucracies predicated on advanced commodity economy and the surpluses of an industrial economy. In turn, these preindustrial states restrict agricultural development in order to preserve their own material and social base, so that a vicious circle quickly ensues, trapping the peoples of West Africa in a variety of repressive, paternalistic, or militaristic regimes that live by extracting what they can from the poor population of the countryside. Within this broad uniformity, each country's form of government is the most direct indicator of its particularity.

As the previous section shows, I have broadly incorporated Marx's theory of commodity economy as my own. The Weberian element is added to make up for a lack of specificity in Marx's theory of the state. I do not intend to review here the neo-Marxist literature on underdevelopment, except to point out that I reject the notion that forces emanating from the world economic system determine the relative backwardness of West African economies.[11] The next chapter examines these issues more fully, but it may be appropriate to mention here the central role of Samir Amin in setting up this particular polemic. Amin's work has been immensely helpful in my own attempt to see West Africa through the lens of political economy. But his emphasis is always on the extraction of value from underdeveloped areas by metropolitan capitalism; he sees this exploitation as the main impediment to their development and growth (Amin 1973). It follows that West Africans should withdraw as far as possible into a self-sufficient regional economy separated from the nexus of metropolitan exploitation.[12] There is much to like in such a diagnosis and prescription. But they leave the internal social processes of economic and political mobilization much underspecified, and they aim the piercing light of analysis on external enemies, often at the cost of a realistic appraisal of local conditions and history. My study attempts in part to redress such an emphasis.

Organization of the work

Chapter 2 sketches West Africa's economic history, paying special attention to the structure of indigenous societies. The time span of the description extends beyond the limits of the modern period into the era of the Atlantic slaving economy (Curtin 1969, 1975). Discussion of the origins of the region's economic backwardness is linked to an outline of the main phases of development during the last 150 years. My source in this has been the fertile combination of historical and anthropological work that has marked West African studies during the last two decades: Without the generalizations of A. G. Hopkins (1973), Goody (1971), Suret-Canale (1971), Meillassoux (1971a), and many others, writing this chapter would have been unthinkable. As in the case of Amin's corpus, although I often depart from the interpretations and emphases of these writers, their books are the building blocks of this study. Although it is less evident, my own previous work (Hart 1978) in the shadow of the great ethnographer Meyer Fortes (1945, 1949) is the source of much in this chapter. I have called the perspective adopted here "anthropological" more in the hope that other anthropologists will extend themselves to this level of generalization than as a description of what they normally do. Nevertheless, it can be said that anthropologists have played a more than equal part in bringing West Africans to the center stage of international comparison and social theory: The British school of Fortes and Goody and the French Marxist school of Meillassoux, Rey, and Terray have set an unusually high standard of theoretical and synthetic work, which makes the region a crucible of much that has been innovative in social anthropology since World War II.

Chapter 3 introduces a large amount of substantive information on West African agriculture. The case materials are presented in narrative form loosely organized around the history and ethnography of various significant crops grown in the forest and savannah. Although the emphasis is on commercial farming in the modern period, the relationship between cash cropping and the noncommercial division of labor in the countryside is a recurrent theme. Pastoralism and rural crafts are treated as subsidiary aspects of the main problem. The sources are extremely rich, but uneven. The principal export crops of the twentieth century, such as cocoa and groundnuts, can boast of several major studies each; the same can be said of the region's pastoralists – the Fulani, for example, have attracted at least three brilliant ethnographers (Stenning 1959; Dupire 1960; Riesman 1977). The work of Hill in southern Ghana and northern Nigeria (1963*a*, *b*, 1972) has been outstanding, and Pélissier's 1966 study of the Senegalese groundnut economy is monumental. Some of the secondary export crops, such as cotton and oil palm, have not received as much attention; and food crops have only recently begun to be studied systematically, largely as a result of growing U.S. interest in West Africa during the 1970s (see B. Lewis 1980; W. O. Jones 1972; Anthony et al. 1979). The well-publicized drought in the Sahel has brought forth a voluminous literature (Comité d'Information Sahel 1975; Copans 1975*a*; Dalby and Church 1973; Dalby, Church, and Bezzaz 1977), which I have used selectively without choosing to isolate the topic in this analytical description.

Chapters 4 and 5 address the principal social forces in West African agricultural development, namely, the state, the market, and capital. Chapter 4 argues that the political forms of the state in precolonial, colonial, and postcolonial West Africa have been the dominant influence in the sphere of rural development, and that this is only to be expected when the economy is preindustrial and as backward as it is throughout the region. The source, in an abstract way, is Weber; but some support for this approach may be found in recent Marxist writings, such as those of Anderson (1974). Chapter 5 asks whether West Africa's agricultural development has been or is likely to be capitalist. This question is subsumed under the larger issue of the rise of the market economy in the region during the modern period. Several English historians have focused on the market in West Africa, McPhee (1971), Hancock (1941), and A. G. Hopkins (1973) being the most notable and comprehensive. Marxist overviews of the region's history are dominated by the work of Amin and Suret-Canale. These writers are no more political in some ways than the liberal historians (myself included), but there is a stridency in their polemics that often overpowers the analysis and description. By far the greatest single influence on the thought expressed in this chapter has been Lenin's *The Development of Capitalism in Russia* (1974), with its clear-headed refusal to romanticize either peasant life or its negation, money capital.

Chapter 6 takes the view of concerned outsiders, such as aid officials and aid-financed researchers, and looks at the impact of commercial agriculture on the welfare of West Africa's indigenous societies. Though the emphasis is social throughout, ecological and nutritional problems are touched on under the rubric "standard of living." How do we judge if rural West Africans are worse off, if the exodus from villages is a disaster, whether growing social inequality is a fact? How has rural social organization, including relations between men and women, been changed? In sum, is the commercialization of agriculture a good or bad thing? Naïve as these questions are, and impossible to answer effectively as they are, they do nevertheless shape public attitudes abroad to the plight of West Africans today.

Chapter 7, "What is to be done?" could bear the alternative label "Can anything be done?" West Africa's dilemmas appear to be nearly intransigent, at least in this generation. Nevertheless, it is our duty to confront the policy options that pertain to the region's agriculture. I argue that commercialization has not significantly raised agricultural productivity and that, until it does, West Africa's other development ambitions are so much pie in the sky. The mixture of large- and small-scale farming organization and, just as important, the political forms capable of forcing through the appropriate measures present formidable tasks of conceptualization and implementation. Modern economics is one principal obstacle to the realization of these goals, the political fragmentation of West Africa another. The tradition of classical political economy, both liberal and Marxist, provides a sound intellectual basis for thinking out these problems. I have mentioned my debt to Steuart, Mill, Marx, and Lenin. Of all modern economists the best exponent of the classical tradition and a major influence on my thought is W. A. Lewis, especially in his recent historical work (1978a, b). This book, drawing on all these predecessors, is written in the hope that the spirit of its questions and some of its answers will find their way into the great debate concerning West Africa's future.

2

West Africa's economic backwardness in anthropological perspective

Small landed property presupposes that the overwhelming majority of the population is rural, and that not social, but isolated labor predominates; and that, therefore, under such conditions wealth and development of reproduction, both of its material and spiritual prerequisites, are out of the question and therefore also the prerequisites for rational cultivation.

Karl Marx, *Capital* (1959:III, 787)

The regional setting

West Africa is the nearest tropical region to Europe, from which it is separated by the Arabic civilizations of North Africa and the Middle East. Much of its people's history depends on this fact; but for all that, the origin of the tripartite relationship between the regions bordering on the northeast Atlantic and Mediterranean seas remains shrouded in mystery. For modern Europeans, the history of West Africa goes back only five hundred years to the time when the Portuguese began to explore an African route to the east round the flanks of Islam. For Arabs it began in the eleventh century, with the temporary expansion of Almoravid conquerors beyond the Maghreb down the coast toward the Senegal River. They did not stay long: Those who have attempted to conquer West Africa never have. The Phoenicians, Greeks, and Romans left fragmented records of their encounters with the black peoples of Africa. But the West Africans themselves never developed an indigenous literate tradition, although the body of medieval African documents in Arabic is substantial. The early development of their societies is thus largely a matter for oral myth, archaeology, and the fragmented observations of travelers – the stuff from which speculative history is made.[1]

We owe this continuing gap in the accumulated record of humanity's achievements to the existence of the Saharan wastes and an inhospitable Atlantic coastline, barriers that effectively limited West Africa's earlier contacts with the outside world to the intermittent expeditions of those brave enough to risk long journeys over deserts of both land and sea. It is rather more difficult, however, to understand why social developments internal to West Africa failed to culminate in the kind of literate civilization that marked the emergence of complex society elsewhere. After the Sahara last began drying out some five thousand years ago, the precipitation of some of its inhabitants into the southern periphery did not leave West Africans with an unpromising environment to live in. The western Sudan provided extensive grass lands, some valuable mineral resources, and the great causeway of the Niger River, as well as some other major streams debouching into the Atlantic Ocean. Further south the savannah of the Sudan gives way to a dense tropical rain forest stretching as far as the coast in most places, where swamps, a heavy surf, and infrequent natural harbors offer persistent discouragement to ships. In the east the forest runs into the great jungles of the Congo basin, and the savannah opens out into a corridor stretching beyond Lake Chad to the Nile. The wet forest lands are less promising terrain for human inhabitation, and the history of settlement in West Africa reflects this fact. But the savannah interior of the Niger and Senegal river valleys spawned an indigenous culture probably as complex and ancient as any in the world.

Archaeological research into this last great unexplored center of prehistoric civilization is still in its infancy. But the Arab historians reveal to us, in their glimpses of the Sudanic empires of Ghana and Mali during the Middle Ages, a fully fledged civilization based on what appeared to be great wealth, a concentrated population, and advanced political achievements (Levitzion 1976; Mauny 1961). Two examples will make the point. The geographer Ibn Hawqal saw in 951 a bill of credit made out to a trader from Awdaghust in Ghana, the sum of which (42,000 dinars) was unheard of in the Muslim world at that time. And when Mansa Musa, the king of Mali, went on a pilgrimage to Mecca in 1324, his gifts and expenditures were so munificent that a temporary surfeit of gold in Egypt caused general price inflation there for a prolonged period (Gugler and Flanagan 1978:7–10). Indeed, before the discovery of the Americas, West Africa supplied the Mediterranean world with most of its gold; and it has been a major source of tropical products (such as ivory and gum) and slaves throughout the recorded past.

This whole area, then, was no isolated aboriginal paradise of hunters and gatherers. It was a region whose history had been linked with that of its neighbors to the north for millennia and whose societies – in common with those of its neighbors – had long been formed along the whole gamut from urbanized states to the fragmented communities usually associated with remote groups of fishermen, hill farmers, and forest dwellers. It is impossible to determine how far back we would have to go before it could be asserted that the region's rural areas consisted mainly of small groups geared toward local self-sufficiency. This point has to be made strongly, because most development models, when applied to the Third World, deny the historical dynamism and social complexity of the regions concerned.

After half a millennium of increasingly intensive commerce with Europe and the rest of the world, the West African region today has been polarized into two zones – one quite developed, one neglected and depopulated. They correspond to the ancient division of forest and savannah; but the historic relationship between the two has been reversed as the result of an overwhelming economic shift toward export by sea. The coastal zone now boasts of huge ports that funnel the minerals, timber, and agricultural products of the forest out onto world markets. Here metropolitan cities like Abidjan and Lagos administer the affairs of postcolonial governments that still depend heavily on their former masters (and on some new ones). The Sudanic interior, now deprived of the trans-Saharan trade that brought its earlier glory, serves mainly as a reservoir of cheap labor for the south. Its proud, Islamized peoples dream of the day when the historical dominance of the savannah will be reasserted over the pagan, lightly Christianized folk of the coast area.

After their recent experience of decolonization, West Africa's many peoples (each with its own distinctive language) are now living in a balkanized cluster of English- and French-speaking independent states. These are dwarfed by the growing might of the one black African power that now stands at the threshold of national greatness – Nigeria. Despite the efforts of new leaders to promote a sense of national identity, they are not *nation*-states at all. Only Upper Volta (where the Mossi people predominates) and Mali (the historic center of the Manding diaspora) can aspire to building nations on any firm ethnic foundation. The rest must struggle with the jigsaw puzzle left by a departing colonialism as the territorial boundaries of sixteen separate countries. Excluding Nigeria, which dominates the eastern part of the region, West Africa's modern states fall into two clusters (see Map 1).

One is a corridor of Francophone states stretching from the Atlantic Ocean in the west to Lake Chad in the east. Known collectively as the Sahel (meaning the "coast" of the Sahara in Arabic), they are Senegal, the Gambia – an Anglophone enclave – Mauritania, Mali, Upper Volta, and Niger. (Chad is sometimes included in this list, but I have chosen to limit the region to what was Afrique occidentale française [AOF].) All of them are poverty-stricken ex-colonies of France sharing a common predicament in the face of the encroaching desert. Senegal is a partial exception, being one of the region's more prosperous economies. To this group we should add the small ex-Portuguese dependency, Cape Verde.

The other group consists of small coastal states, usually reaching back in a narrow strip through the forest to a portion of the Sudanic savannah: Sierra Leone, Guinea, Guinea Bissau, Liberia, the Ivory Coast, Ghana, Togo, and Benin. (Here, again, I have excluded Cameroon on the grounds that it was not part of the AOF.) Of these, the Ivory Coast and Ghana alone have the social structure, population, and resources to attempt a reasonably viable modern political economy. After Nigeria, they represent (along with Senegal) the second tier of independent states left behind by the British, French, and Portuguese.

As tables 1 and 2 show, West Africa in 1977 contained 138 million people, living in a land area of some 4 million square kilometers. Population growth at a

21

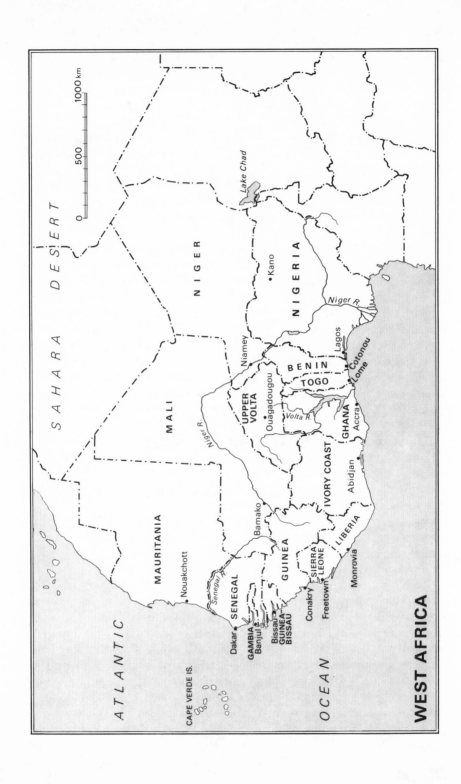

WEST AFRICA

SAHARA DESERT

ATLANTIC OCEAN

1000 km

500

Lake Chad

NIGER

NIGERIA

•Kano

Niger R.

MALI

Niger R.

Niamey

Lagos

Cotonou

BENIN

Lomé

TOGO

UPPER VOLTA

Ouagadougou

Volta R.

GHANA

Accra

MAURITANIA

Nouakchott

IVORY COAST

Abidjan

Bamako

LIBERIA

Senegal

GUINEA

SENEGAL

SIERRA LEONE

Monrovia

Dakar•

Conakry

Freetown

GAMBIA

Banjul

Bissau

GUINEA BISSAU

CAPE VERDE IS.

Economic backwardness in anthropological perspective

Table 1. West Africa: income level, urbanization, and population density

Country	GNP per cap. ($)	World rank (of 126)	Pop. (millions)	Percent urban MRE[a]	Population density per km² 1960	MRE[a]
Ivory Coast	765	65	7.5	33	11	23
Nigeria	513	76	79.0	18	56	86
Liberia	410	87	1.7	30	9	15
Senegal	377	89	5.2	24	17	27
Ghana	370	90	10.6	32	29	44
Togo	278	97	2.4	15	27	43
Mauritania	272	98	1.5	23	1	1.5
Benin	208	104	3.2	23	19	28
The Gambia	208	105	0.6	24	29	49
Guinea	199	109	5.0	16	13	20
Sierra Leone	199	110	3.2	21	31	45
Niger	194	111	4.9	10	2	4
Guinea Bissau	160	—	0.9	23	15	20
Upper Volta	139	117	5.5	7	15	20
Cape Verde	130	—	0.3	—	—	—
Mali	117	123	6.1	17	3	5
West Africa	430	—	138.0	20	—	29

[a]Most recent estimate, normally 1977.
Sources: World Bank (1977, 1980).

rate of 3 percent per annum will have boosted the aggregate by a tenth, making 150 million a conservative estimate for West Africa's population in 1980 – a sizable number, to be sure, but one that is less than 4 percent of the world total. The people are spread extremely unevenly. The three states that include large chunks of the Sahara – Mauritania, Mali, and Niger – have densities of 5 per square kilometer or less. The majority of the remainder cluster around the regional density of 29 per square kilometer. Four coastal states – Ghana, Togo, Sierra Leone, and the Gambia – have population densities nearer the average for Third World countries (41 per square kilometer). Nigeria, with 79 million people packed into 14 percent of West Africa's land mass (86 per square kilometer), is on a par with China and southern Europe at almost five times the average density for sub-Saharan Africa as a whole.

Nigeria, even before it became rich as a result of oil, was – along with the areas surrounding the Senegal and Volta rivers – one of the region's wealthiest, most densely populated countries. Its citizens now outnumber other West Africans by five to four, and the difference is likely to grow. Its gross national product accounts for seven-tenths of the regional total. Yet it is not the most developed country in the region. When West Africa was decolonized two decades ago, Ghana and Senegal were both more advanced, and following their relative decline, the Ivory Coast now has a per capita annual income some $250 higher

The political economy of West African agriculture

Table 2. Nigeria, the coast, and the Sahel compared

	Population		Land area		Gross national product		
	millions	%	thousand km^2	%	$ billions	%	$ per cap.
Nigeria	79.0	57	575	14	40.5	69	510
Eight coastal states	34.5	25	743	18	13.5	23	390
Seven Sahel states	24.1	18	2,772	68	5.0	8	210
West Africa	138.0	100	4,090	100	59.0	100	430

Sources: World Bank (1977, 1980).

than Nigeria's, which ranks seventy-sixth out of 126 countries in the world. The coastal states taken as a whole have a per capita income of only just over $100 less than Nigeria. It is the Sahelian states whose poverty is outstanding; though all but two West African countries lie in the bottom third of the international income scale, Mali, Upper Volta, and Niger are among the very poorest. Even when we consider degree of urbanization, the populations of the Ivory Coast, Ghana, and Liberia are one-third concentrated in towns and cities, whereas Nigeria is slightly below the regional average of one-fifth. Again, the three landlocked Sahelian states bring up the rear when it comes to urbanization as an index of division of labor. A rank comparison of West African states shows that, whereas there is only a weak correlation between population density and degree of urbanization, both are positively correlated with income level: It is especially true that the richer countries are more urbanized, with Nigeria the glaring exception.[2]

The fifteen non-Nigerian countries had a combined population in 1977 of less than 60 million: Their average population was thus roughly equal to that of Scotland or Norway. Their total gross national product was and is less than a tenth of Britain's, a nation with similar numbers of people and only 4 percent of the land area. It is hard to visualize what an income of a dollar a day looks like, when every man, woman, and child in the United States receives a dollar an hour around the clock ($8,750 in 1977). On this scale the citizens of Mali spend in a year what Americans spend in five days (a ratio of more than 70:1). The Reverend Jesse Jackson has supplied another figure of speech to point the contrast: If U.S. blacks transferred 1 percent of their annual income to West Africa, it would double the budgets of all fifteen governments outside Nigeria. We are talking, then, of a poverty-stricken region made up of fragmented states, some of them as prosperous as their powerful neighbor, but most of them lacking both the size and wealth to offer their citizens a plausible future.

Another index of West Africa's backwardness is life expectancy at birth, which ranges between 41 and 48 years (see Table 4, in Chapter 6). The basic similarity

24

between living conditions in Nigeria and elsewhere in the West Africa is revealed strongly by this indicator, with coastal countries such as Benin, Ghana, and Sierra Leone sharing the upper end of the range with Nigeria, and the Sahelian countries, as is to be expected, bringing up the rear. A life expectancy of 48 years is 25 years less than the average for all industrialized countries. It would be redundant to continue with the figures on infant mortality, health, housing, nutrition, and literacy that translate a gross statistic on life expectancy into a dossier of underprivilege. West Africans are increasingly part of a world system of communications that reveals to them where they stand on the scale of humanity's self-improvement. They now have their own states to act as vehicles for the realization of their aspirations. But only one West African state can be sure of its future place in the sun; the rest are caught in a stranglehold between the infinitude of popular ambition and the paucity of real resources available to draw on.

In an age of increasing centralization, it is hard to imagine that this state of affairs can remain the same for long. The recent formation of a tentative regional economic grouping known as ECOWAS (Economic Community of West African States), dominated informally by Nigeria's size and oil wealth, is one example of an emergent awareness that the region's existing political and economic structures are hopelessly inadequate to cope with the problems of backwardness and inequality that West Africans face. At the beginning of this century, control over West Africa's population of less than 40 million was shared between four foreign imperial powers. Today, despite a boom in both population and commodity production, this stands as one of the poorest and most divided regions in the world. The main forces that drive the expansion of a global division of labor do not originate here. The area's polities are, with the exception of Nigeria, small, weak, passive members of the international community. By any modern standards they are underdeveloped; and even if all the states of West Africa were politically united, they would still be economically backward relative to most of the rest of the world.

The problem of backwardness

The attempt to confront West Africa's development problems today naturally brings to the fore the question how we account for the historical process of its having become underdeveloped in the first place. It is no secret that the regional economy is abnormally geared toward foreign trade. Thus an UNCTAD (United Nations Commission on Trade and Development) report for 1969–70 pointed out that intraregional trade in West Africa constituted less than 3 percent of total trade, compared with 20 percent in Latin America, 64 percent in Western Europe, and 7 percent in Africa as a whole. It is hard to avoid striking superficial attitudes about this external orientation of the *économie de traite*; yet I have no interest in pursuing the arguments in detail at this stage. Many of us have been – and some still are – reluctant to specify the endogenous causes of West African underdevelopment, both because we defer to native opinion and because we retain a measure of colonial guilt over the creation of such skewed economies. Several writers seem to have treated West Africa as an empty container for their favorite thesis on world capitalism, whether pro (modernization theory) or con (dependency theory).[3] Numerous authors (mainly French) explain West Africa's backwardness as the inevitable result of the workings of a predatory capitalism in the region, siphoning off resources to the advantage of the advanced industrial countries. Others (mostly British and American) see western expansion as a process of diffusion – the spread of technology, the market, and civilized social institutions – that has brought real material benefits to West Africa. Both sides treat the social history of the indigenous peoples as somewhat secondary to the imposition of externally derived forces.

It is easy to see why. International clout these days comes from the volume of fixed and liquid capital a nation can draw on, the industrial skills and organization of its citizenry, the size of the home market, military might, command over technological resources, and so on. In all these respects the West African states lag far behind; and it is difficult to imagine how they will overcome poverty without taking fairly rapid strides in the direction indicated by the history of the advanced nations.

To say this is to pass no value judgment on West African cultures. West Africans may often seem more humane, more sensible, more attractive than most members of the industrial societies. Their various ways of life may be highly adapted to the conditions they found in the region. But however admirable we may find some features of West Africa's customary societies, we should not forget that they are still dominated by a harsh material environment to a degree that is unacceptable to modern populations. In an age when some nations enjoy great prosperity – and the individual health and collective security that usually goes with it – most West Africans are very poor, they die young, and their states are the unwilling pawns of greater powers.

If the region's condition is to be improved substantially, we must not ignore the historical role of geography in West African development. In addition to the social organization of global economy over the last few centuries, there are some more enduring features of West Africans' history to take into account, namely, their struggle to overcome the natural limitations on their growth posed by the environment. West Africa is very hot and frequently humid; it is particularly wet in the coastal forest zone and extremely dry in the interior. Endemic diseases of a fairly intransigent character abound, and sometimes whole communities are radically impaired by the high level of parasites on the bodies of most active adults. Before this century, mortality rates were extremely high. West Africa's coastline and rivers are not conducive to navigation and cheap waterborne transport. There are very few significant land elevations, but overland transport is slow and difficult. The soils are light and the forest dense. Neither the plow nor irrigation works were traditionally employed to intensify production. With one or two major exceptions in the savannah, attempts at political centralization were limited by the sparse density of a low-productivity population; the same demographic constraints obviously restricted division of labor and market development. Social organization placed a premium on human labor, performed either by kinsmen or by slaves, and with the exception of some pockets of savannah agriculture, economy rested on efficient use of that labor through extensive farming of agricultural land.

These conditions must have been roughly the same for several millennia. They were not produced by involvement in the world capitalist economy. Whatever distortions or improvements may have occurred as the result of such involvement, the underlying conditions remained: a sparse population, disease ridden and poor, farming at low levels of productivity, limited by transport facilities, organized in weak polities, and exposed to the vagaries of climate. We will see in the following chapters whether 150 years of agricultural commodity production have laid down the potential for escape from these restrictive material and social conditions. An evaluation of the part played by recent historical developments in sustaining West Africa's economic backwardness is an underlying theme of the later sections of this chapter.

Historical periodization

What I call the "modern" period in West Africa's economic and political history is the time since the region first became significantly involved in agricultural production of raw materials for the markets of industrializing nations. The logic of West African development has ever since been dominated by that relationship. Dating this transition is always arbitrary, and I have chosen round numbers for the sake of mnemonic simplification, if nothing else. It is reasonable to speak of the last 150 years as a single period, because it was in the 1830s that production of vegetable oils for export began in earnest. We should remember, however, that some parts of the region were not directly involved in the process of global industrialization until the beginning of this century.

The period 1830 to the present has seen three main phases, marked by the pattern of political relations between West African peoples and outsiders. The first is the nineteenth century, a period of crisis for the region that began with the dismantling of the Atlantic slave trade and ended with the formal incorporation of West Africa into colonial empires, a process that was completed only at the turn of the century. This phase (1830–1900) may be characterized as one of growing European imperialism and internal disorder (Fieldhouse 1973; A. G. Hopkins 1973; chap. 4). The period of direct colonial rule was relatively short (1900–60). The Portuguese dependencies had to wait for emancipation from colonial rule, but by the early years of the 1960s the present political map of West Africa had been effectively drawn. The last two decades, then (1960–80), constitute the third modern phase, that of the successor states struggling to find an independent existence in a world political economy that has advanced considerably since West Africans first began growing groundnuts for export. (A preliminary account of the main features of the modern period of West African development is given in the last three sections of this chapter.)

What does "traditional" mean in the West African context? To the extent that we need such a concept (and we probably do, for shorthand's sake, when talking of indigenous social forms), it refers to the characteristic features of the societies that evolved in the period prior to global industrialization. These societies were not in any sense primordial, because West African history has been dynamic and international for many centuries. It may be useful to distinguish between the period of the Atlantic slave trade (1500–1830, very roughly) and that which went before (pre-1500, the medieval phase of West African history, corresponding with its Islamic and European equivalents). Here the dividing line is the arrival of the Portuguese in the late fifteenth century, opening up West Africa to an Atlantic trade that came to be dominated by the transport of slaves to the New World. Before that period most international influences (trade, war, religion) came across the Sahara and were felt mainly in the savannah. But at that time coastal forts sprang up, and contending European powers fought for control of the region's trade. It should be pointed out that, although this new foreign presence had profound effects on the shape and direction of West African commerce, the Europeans were in no position to dominate the indigenous polities; they adopted a mercantilist posture that rested more on good will than on force. It took the growing technological and economic discrepancies produced by the Industrial Revolution to give the Europeans a chance to envisage incorporation of West Africa under their formal rule. Before the nineteenth century they lived on the edge of a narrow coastal strip relying entirely on independent inland powers and merchant classes for their supply of slaves.

The following sections give an abstract account of the kinds of societies that we think of as traditional in the West African context. This account is based on the limited historical information available for the period prior to the nineteenth-century crisis and on ethnographic information from more recent times extrapolated back into the pre-modern period. It will be evident that such sources must be suspect, especially if they permit us to retain a static picture of West African societies. The important point is that the immediate precolonial period was one of revolutionary change, as West Africa adjusted to the onslaught of the forces of industrialization. Before 1830, the forces for social evolution were more endogenous than external, despite the obvious significance of the Atlantic slave trade.

The historical periodization adopted in this book may be summarized in this way:

A. Traditional period
  1. Medieval era (pre-1500)
  2. European mercantilism/Atlantic slave trade (1500–1830)

Economic backwardness in anthropological perspective

B. Modern period
  1. The nineteenth-century crisis (1830–1900)
  2. Colonialism (1900–60)
  3. The successor states (1960–80)

A geographical typology of traditional West African societies

In order to make some sense of the variety of social forms typical of the West African region during the heyday of the Atlantic slave trade, we should turn to historical geography before venturing to offer more abstract social scientific analyses.[4] The contrast between forest and savannah is so basic that it cannot be overstressed. The great belt of tropical rain forest was a backward and inhospitable area in comparison to the savannah, which faced north to the Arab Mediterranean and Middle East, whence it had long come under the proselytizing influence of Islam. The marked ecological differences between forest and savannah encouraged the development of a regional division of labor, quite independently of the stimulus arising from foreign trade with the Maghreb. There were very few domesticated animals in the forest, and trees were sparse on the savannah: These facts alone were the basis for a long-standing exchange of the products of pastoralism and arboriculture between the two major subregions. That the products of mining and manufacturing were likewise unevenly distributed over the West African region gave rise to further internal differentiation in production and trade. This underlying geographical source of variation in the societies and cultures of West Africa has never been eliminated: The principal axis of stratification is and always has been a line from dry north to wet south, from the Sahara to the Gulf of Guinea; and the forest, except where it is penetrated by the great inland rivers, stands as a substantial barrier between these outermost limits of the region's ecology.

From the sixteenth century onwards, Europeans on the coast exerted an increasing pull on West Africa's political economy, drawing population and trade farther south in an inexorable movement that gave the region its Janus-faced posture, attracted by two opposite poles – the Sahara and the Atlantic, the worlds of Islam and Christianity. By the nineteenth century, it was possible to discern five separate zones stretching along the north–south axis, each with its own distinctive social organization: the desert margins, the savannah, the transition from savannah to forest, the rain forest, and the seacoast.

On the edge or "coast" (Sahel) of the Sahara, Arab traders and Berber nomads mixed with the indigenous population at the northernmost outposts of black Africa. Great cities grew up here as long ago as Europe's Dark Ages.[5] Timbuktoo and Gao flourished at the point where the "inland sea" of the Niger bend reaches up into the desert margins. Merchant capital gained its greatest freedom in these independent entrepôts, which also boasted the holiest mosques and the most notable scholars. Here, too, are the Sudanic frontiers of West Africa, where

The political economy of West African agriculture

Kanem Bornu and Lake Chad guard the routes to the Nile. It is a crossroads: Many groups now living much farther south trace their origins to this area, and its resident peoples are often racially mixed. The southern fringe of the Sahara is a mysterious place, with the secrets of West Africa's first civilizations buried below the sandy surface of its desert wastes. Today, bands of nomadic Tuareg warriors struggle to retain a way of life established long ago when they exacted tribute from merchants crossing the desert and raided sedentary agriculturalists of the savannah for slaves and food (Baier 1980; Swift 1977). Life is harsh here, and social organization reflects the exigencies of power more starkly than is normal in West African polities farther south.

The second zone shades into the first, according to the fluctuating historical shifts of ethnic boundaries, brought about by changing weather patterns and the cumulative effects of mankind's presence in the area. Here lay the advanced medieval civilization of West Africa's savannah interior, linked to the first zone by close ties of political economy and culture, and defined by the river valleys in which its most centralized polities grew up. The open terrain – making for greater ease of communication (including armed surveillance) – and a dry climate suited to the storage of grain surpluses, when combined with exposure to Mediterranean and Red Sea influences, favored the development of the region's most ancient states, a process that culminated in the extensive empires of Mali and Songhay (Ajayi and Crowder 1976). The social division of labor was as advanced here as in many parts of India, without perhaps attaining the same degree of refinement. Urbanization produced a stark gulf between the populations of town and countryside, as an Islamized city-dwelling elite characteristically assumed superiority over a subject peasantry from which it was often divided by ethnic criteria. Occupational divisions reached castelike proportions. Pastoral nomads maintained a sharp separation between themselves and sedentary agriculturalists. Peasants who found their way into mercenary armies and merchant entourages were usually forced to change their religious affiliation and ethnic identity. A multitude of craft professions were widely practiced by hereditary, endogamous castes who formed artisan guilds in the towns and kept their distance from the peasants in the villages (Nadel 1942). The preoccupation of the ruling classes was with taxes and slavery. The variety of levies on all kinds of economic activity was often remarkable. Slavery was omnipresent and in some places food was exclusively produced by slaves. Slaves were also often to be found in prominent positions as administrators and soldiers.[6] Islam generated an educated elite of lawyers, priests, and teachers whose literacy in Arabic was shared by the merchant class.

This complex system of social stratification permitted several significant variations, which require clarification by further research. The relationship between the professional/commercial classes and the ruling aristocracies is not always clear, for example, nor is the financial basis of the links between town and countryside, resting as it does on a combination of taxation, rent, and slave

30

estates. The important point is that many of West Africa's great modern nations sprang up from this savannah history – peoples like the Mande, Wolof, Hausa, Mossi, and Fulani. Here was the home base for Hausa and Dioula trading networks that still thrive today. The history of the savannah interior is not dead history, even though the conditions of its greatness have long been on the wane.

Next, as we move south, comes the third zone, a middle belt straddling the ecological divide between forest and savannah, an interstitial zone in several ways. Being farthest removed from both northern and southern centers of state formation, this area contained large pockets of acephalous peoples, societies that managed to avoid incorporation into larger states, if not involvement in slaving (often as the unwilling victims of marauding armies). They were aided in their resistance by the existence here of whatever passes for high ground in the West African context – the Jos Plateau and the Fouta Djallon, for example – as well as a terrain of orchard bushland frequently broken by hills and nonnavigable streams. Entrepôts and petty kingdoms rose and fell in a subregion marked by chronic political instability and continuous population movements, and one frequent result was dense concentrations of refugees in areas sometimes self-consciously maintained by neighboring states as reservoirs for slave raiding. The area is best known for the stateless peoples whose highly corporate social structures, based on segmentary lineage organization and animist religion, are closely documented in classical ethnographies – the Tallensi, the Tiv, the Dogon, and so on.[7] These ancient peoples are fighting cultivators who have refused rulers and whose society, although poor, is self-consciously organized on an egalitarian basis to maintain its freedom when geography offers a relatively secure refuge. Like their counterparts in remote hill regions elsewhere in the world, they have long been valued as recruits into the armies of more effete civilizations.

Passing through the transitional middle belt toward the Atlantic coast we come to the fourth zone, the tropical rain forest. The agricultural peoples of the forest came here from the coast and savannah long ago; they usually had a tradition of chiefship and often were governed through political associations such as secret societies. In some areas (such as Iboland), these peoples kept their distinctive acephalous, but hierarchical, organization until modern times. The most striking consequence of the Atlantic trade, however, was the rise of powerful indigenous states out of the struggles to control slaving and commerce in the forest zone (Forde and Kaberry 1969). This process of political centralization culminated in some large kingdoms, usually situated some distance inland away from the divisive presence and military/naval installations of the Europeans. Owing to their ability to command access to the coast from the interior during a period of intensified slavery and rising African consumption of European manufactures, these new states – Ashanti, Dahomey, Oyo – began to shift the balance of power in West Africa away from the Islamized savannah.

The forest kingdoms encouraged settlements of Muslim merchants, organized huge armies, and built palace bureaucracies on a grand scale.[8] Slaves were employed in a variety of productive tasks, notably in gold mining (which was often dangerous) and as skilled craftsmen in the centers of government. But, for all this, society still retained a markedly "tribal" character, certainly more so than the medieval states to the north. Corporate lineage organization often linked rulers to a mass peasantry led by their own elders and chiefs, although sometimes an aristocratic military elite was ethnically separated from the peoples whom it had conquered and absorbed. Religion remained animist and acquired a deserved reputation for ritual cruelty to noncitizens. Most important, the social division of labor was less advanced than in the savannah, and this difference was reflected in a minimal sociocultural gap between the towns (which were glorified armed camps) and the countryside. These young pagan states constituted the main threat to European dominance on the coast.

The fifth, coastal zone consisted of an almost unbroken series of port towns huddled around the beleaguered European fortresses that were built during the period of the Atlantic slave trade. They were devoted principally to the transshipment of slaves and European manufactures. Occasionally Africans were able to form independent federations of urbanized coastal settlements – it would be too grand to call them "leagues of free city states" – as in parts of the Niger Delta (see Dike 1956; G. I. Jones 1963) and in the savannah region around the estuary of the Volta River. But the guns of the European ships and forts, allied with their purchasing power for local goods and services and monopolies over valued imports, gave the Christian white men a great deal of political and cultural influence on the coast. They did not seek to rule there, being content to operate through the mediation of local chiefs whom they were sometimes pleased to call "kings" and "princes." Africans on the coast during this period became a cosmopolitan, mixed-blood elite, living an urban life, frequently converting to Christianity, and enjoying some access to Western education. They turned their backs on the old West Africa of a savannah interior, which most of them had never seen, and committed themselves to forging a new social order oriented toward the North Atlantic trading communities of America and Europe.

These, then, are the five roughly horizontal strata that made up the West African region during the period that immediately preceded the modern era. For all the variety of cultures, local-level organization shared some common features; and all parts of the region were linked by an overland commerce conducted mainly by Muslim merchants operating out of the interior. Violence and warfare were endemic; weaker peoples yielded their land to the strong and sought refuge elsewhere. Slave raiding was intensified by the growing demand on the coast. But these actions were carried out exclusively by peoples indigenous to West Africa: Although they may have allowed Europeans a foothold on the coast and Arabs a privileged status as guests in the north, West Africans did not yet have to suffer conquest by foreigners, and they still controlled the societies they had built up over centuries of even more pronounced isolation from the outside world.

Indigenous state formation and commerce

What part did the indigenous states play in the promotion or restriction of commerce?[9] It is obvious that there was an intimate connection between commerce and state formation. The key to the organization of trade at the regional level is to be found in the highly stratified areas where warrior aristocracies, merchants, and slaves were concentrated in the largest numbers. After this has been said, however, there are many detailed questions about the long-run effects of trade on West Africa's political structures that remain largely unanswered. For example, it is not clear how the savannah states of the interior fared economically while the power of the forest kingdoms waxed on the fruits of the slave trade. Did their economies decline, stagnate, or grow during the period 1500–1830, and with what consequences for relations between rulers and ruled? Certainly Kano, the center of a Hausa–Fulani emirate in what is now northern Nigeria, was the biggest city in West Africa at the beginning of the nineteenth century, with a flourishing textiles industry and long, wide boulevards.[10] At the other extreme, the existence of volatile decentralized coalitions of small African towns at some of the most active centers of European commerce on the coast should lead us to be wary of making facile connections between long-distance trade and the formation of states.

The most prominent feature of West African trade was the control exercised over the internal commercial economy by an ethnic diaspora of Hausa and Dioula/Mande merchants (A. Cohen 1971). In the absence of a universal state law underwriting contracts, these merchants took on themselves the responsibility for maintaining a customary order in transactions that often depended on long-term credit. Itinerant stranger communities such as these have often grown up in preindustrial economies to meet the commercial needs of societies whose rulers' main concern is with the conduct of warfare and administration.[11] There were many routes between north and south, so that the rulers of petty and not-so-petty states on the way could not afford to tax the merchants too highly in case they moved elsewhere (Terray 1974). Indeed, the benefits of a resident commercial community, ready to buy slaves and the products of slave labor, as well as to sell prestigious imported goods, were great enough to persuade these rulers to welcome the merchants with favorable trading conditions. Some of the forest superpowers, such as Ashanti and Dahomey, commanded enough territory at the beginning of the nineteenth century to establish state monopolies in certain branches of trade, but this was rare. In general, the Muslim merchant caravans carried their own protection through a territorial patchwork of fragmented states and stateless peoples. As a result, they were privileged and not unduly taxed visitors to the centers of state power and the honored guests of local big men in the more remote areas.

But the crux of the matter is not the division of trading profits between capitalist profits and tax revenues: It is, of course, always the organization of production for sale. How far did West Africa's ruling classes themselves go in establishing control over commercial production? Was merchant capital content to buy goods from others, or did it play a part in organizing production? We can make only tentative suggestions on these pivotal matters, because historians have in general not seen fit to pose the problem in this way.

West Africa's rulers could not rely on tribute for the commodities with which to purchase European firearms, cloth, spirits, and manufactured utensils; for tribute from the peasantry was invariably in the form of foodstuffs or unskilled labor services, which could be and were used to maintain standing armies, nonproductive bureaucracies, and public rituals. But the rulers *were* in a position to supply slaves, as long as they could expand by military conquest. War captives far outweighed internal recruits to slavery from debt bondage, imprisonment, and the like (Meillassoux 1971a; Miers and Kopytoff 1977). Because the indigenous states did not have the repressive means to tolerate heavy strains on their own internal structures, they always had to turn outward for slaves toward the conquest of similar polities or, less expensively, to the stateless zones of refugees whose pursuit of collective freedom coincided with the states' need for a ready supply of noncitizens as slaves.

There is evidence that some ruling aristocracies put the slaves to work in mines, rather than selling them directly. But monopolies in the metals trade were easier to achieve than monopolies over the products of arboriculture and animal husbandry (e.g., kolanuts and hides), which remained largely in the hands of the free peasantry and the merchants who bought from them. In these branches of production, estates based on forced labor cannot compete effectively in the market with free peasant producers unless they are backed up by strong central governments of a kind that did not exist in West Africa. Manufactures were produced by palace specialists in the forest, by casted guilds in the north, and by peasant part-time workers everywhere. With the exception of the indigenous cloth and iron industries, long-distance trade was generally in raw materials, not manufactures, which were made up at or near their place of final consumption. When the ruling class was able to control manufacturing production, therefore, it was invariably as consumers rather than as commodity producers.

It is not surprising that military aristocracies, faced with a shortage of alternative sources of commodities, turned for their basic revenues to slave raiding or conquest and the sale of slaves to merchants, rather than to the organization of commercial production itself. Slaves had the additional advantage, in a land beset with transport difficulties, of being the only commodity capable both of walking to the point of sale and of conveying some other valuable commodity along the way (animals fared rather badly in the forest). The transition to management of rural estates based on slave labor or servile commodity production, which marked the evolution of ruling aristocracies in most parts of Eurasia, did not occur before the late nineteenth century in the forest zone. The social and geographical conditions just did not exist to keep a bonded labor force producing substantial surpluses for a landlord class: Even slaves had to be made pseudo-kinsmen after the first generation, because only newly uprooted foreigners could be kept in check. The picture in the older established savannah states to the north was nearer to the Eurasian model. A more advanced division of labor offered greater opportunities for some societies to follow the course of medieval civilization elsewhere: routinized government revenues from money taxes, a more important role for finance capital, various forms of commodity and noncommodity production by magnates' estates and slave villages, and so on. It is because of this greater interpenetration of the state and commerce in the north that indigenous merchants were at home there and strangers in the south.

The pressure toward local self-sufficiency

Enough has been said so far to dispel any lingering images of the rural inhabitants of West African traditional societies as isolated, homogeneous peoples living in a peaceful matrix of subsistence agriculture. But although some coastal and savannah populations could never be thought of in these terms, most of the rest of the region's rural areas have long been occupied by people living in small villages surrounded by their kinsmen and devoting much of their labor to food agriculture. What, then, about the countryside, where agriculture, animal husbandry, and domestic crafts were often united in family work teams? Here groups of kinsfolk were attached to the land through membership both in lineages and in a variety of animist cults that together gave them rights of territorial occupation, a common means of self-defense, and a degree of security from spiritual dangers. How did this underlying framework of West African social order relate to the more-or-less commercial political economy generated by the rise of states linked to foreign trade in slaves? More specifically, what inhibited the commercialization and intensification of production in rural areas occupied by free peasantries? This question goes to the heart of the pressure toward local self-sufficiency in West African agriculture. To answer it, I will construct a composite ideal type of a traditional people living mainly from agriculture within the framework of an underdeveloped division of labor.[12]

The members of acephalous societies belonged to corporate descent groups whose needs commanded the bulk of their labor in subsistence food farming and public defense. Land was inherited within unilineal descent groups or acquired with the cooperation of members of similarly constituted groups. Production, distribution, and consumption were all largely contained within clusters of households organized as lineages under the ritual leadership of old men selected by their position in a genealogy. The dominant principles of economic organization were reciprocity (sharing between equals) and redistribution (pooling by a central authority, such as lineage head or chief);[13] but this did not prevent individuals in a fragile social order from seeking to acquire wealth in their own right. Relations with other groups usually involved marriage (the circulation of women in exchange for prestigious bridewealth items like cattle) and alliances based on an ideology of common descent or shared occupation of a territory.

Authority relations hinged on stratification of the male population by age and kinship: Both politics and production rested on socially and psychologically complex relations of both solidarity and antagonism between lineage elders and their eventual replacements, the young men (Meillassoux 1975*a*; Dupré and Rey 1978). Women's functions were mainly reproduction of children for the descent group and performance of a large number of productive, necessary roles around the home, including food farming and processing. Whether these descent groups were structured patrilineally or matrilineally seems to have depended on whether the men were away fighting much of the time and on the differences between savannah and forest agriculture (Murdock 1959). Women were dependent pawns in a male-dominated social structure, with no rights to travel beyond the confines of the local settlement, except when visiting relatives with the permission of the men (fathers, brothers, husbands) who controlled their lives. The well-known figure of the West African "mammy," living from trade independently of men, was not a traditional feature of these rural societies away from the creolized coast.

Population could be fairly dense in places, but was generally scattered and sparse (as low as 1–5 persons per square kilometer). The abundance of land meant that mobility was very easy, both for individuals, who knew that they would always be welcomed as recruits into neighboring farm groups, and for villages, whose regime of shifting cultivation could result in a substantial territorial drift through time. The sanction of political withdrawal was thus always available to members of a descent group who felt themselves abused or exploited. In the savannah zone, landed property was of some corporate significance because it was often based on prior occupation of the best farming sites and on the investment of generations of skilled labor. In the forest zone, the system of long-fallow rotation over a cycle of fifteen years and more removed much of the value of landed property as such, but enhanced the value of holding a large unoccupied territory in reserve. Hence the priority given to collective identities derived from political rights to hold offices belonging to corporate descent groups.

In both areas, communal solidarities were founded on a mixture of territorial and political–ritual considerations. And everywhere a family setting up its homestead away from established settlements faced an extremely unattractive assortment of dangers – from pests, disease, predators of all kinds, and the risk of economic failure. The accumulated wisdom built up by a defined population occupying the same territory for generations gave authority automatically to those who embodied the community's traditions, the older members. The prevalent pattern was thus one of rural communities built around the reproduction of a stable population and the production of its subsistence needs, with hierarchy restricted to the prerogatives of age and position in a kinship system.

Members of such communities could not organize production on the basis of markets because there was no established division of labor requiring a continuous flow of commodities between production units. In these circumstances, specialized producers who depended on the market would be left with surpluses of some goods and shortfalls of others, including necessities. Hence community members first guaranteed that their own subsistence needs would be met and then perhaps produced for the market. As free owners in a relatively abundant agricultural environment, they did not alienate land or labor by selling it to the highest bidder, because they could not be certain that the local market would deliver them what they need when they need it and at a reasonable price (A. G. Hopkins 1973:chap. 2). It takes only a few examples of failure by groups or individuals who have overcommitted themselves to dependence on the market for the community to come to value its traditional norms of self-sufficiency very highly indeed. Lessons concerning the dangers of schemes for quick wealth are built into the customary perceptions of many West Africans, who though far from incapable of grasping economic opportunities as they arise, would be loath to abandon social mechanisms with the proven ability to ensure their long-run security.

There have long been limits, then, on accumulation through production of foodstuffs for the market. The prevailing division of labor established weak and intermittent levels of demand. No one knew when the next harvest would come or how poor it could be, so customary attitudes of resistance to the sale of foods had a sound basis in economic logic. In addition, storage and transport facilities for bulk foodstuffs were extremely difficult, especially in the region's wetter zones. For these reasons, local markets in West Africa were opportunities to exchange small surpluses of staples; to increase the variety of foodstuffs in the diet through purchase of garden produce and hunters' catches; to acquire the minute quantities of salt, cloth, and similar imported luxuries that consumers could afford; to buy handicrafts, utensils, and the like (sometimes produced by part-time specialists); to drink millet beer or palm wine; and above all to meet people, especially members of the opposite sex.[14] These markets were dominated by women and young men from the immediate locality. They provided the less-privileged adult sections of the community with a meager means of supplementing their earnings, but they could never be a source of accumulation on a scale sufficient to threaten the position of the older married men who ran the majority of the community's households and public affairs.

The one major exception to this rule, in those savannah societies where agriculture and animal husbandry were joined together, was accumulation through trade in livestock. Fowls, goats, sheep, and cattle offered an ascending scale of assets for potential accumulation through natural increase and astute trading by ambitious young men who were unwilling to wait their turn to join the village gerontocracy. Livestock management thus constituted the most common medium of individual enrichment in such areas. But elsewhere the social structure removed even this threat to the corporate order of the agrarian lineage by making animal husbandry the exclusive prerogative of ethnically separate pastoralists. The livestock market loophole was in any case peripheral to the organization of social production in traditional West African villages.

But the rural population was also part of a regional trading network run by long-distance merchants of alien origin who had to traverse the territory as a routine feature of journeys between entrepôts located elsewhere. If control over the circulation of women was crucial to the authority of elders, so too was control over the highly valued trade goods that often constituted the only items which could legitimately be exchanged for women – cloth, iron bars, and the like. The merchants who brought such goods had to buy food and catering services on their travels, and they might need some local protection. Strategically placed influential men could offer such services, and, as the "landlord" intermediaries with wealthy foreigners, could thereby control access to a major source of power and relative affluence. Some might expand production through selective participation in the interlocal market network, converting family growth (via polygamy and the acquisition of domestic slaves) into a spiral of differential accumulation that might tend to break down the egalitarian facade of corporate village society. No doubt slavery and commerce did combine in some cases to permit the aristocratization of lineage society. But commercial expansion in these societies was checked by a number of factors: First, there were inherent restrictions on demand for rural products in the regional trading system; second, competition from the heads of related kin groups would reduce the likelihood of significant accumulation by a few individuals; and third, accumulators of family labor had to co-opt the women and young men who supplied the bulk of it.

Besides, it was not in the interests of the elders to allow the commercial division of labor to develop beyond the point where they could easily restrain the mass of young men and women from entry into the market. Such a development could well undermine the very social framework that gave them their privileges in the first place (hence, during colonial times, the elders' widespread resistance to releasing young men for wage labor or cash cropping). There can be no doubt, therefore, that the rural social order constituted in itself a powerful blockage restricting the development of the market as long as its institutions remained relatively undisturbed by outside pressure.

It was, of course, always open to individuals who found their lot oppressive to escape from the restrictions of village society. Employment as a mercenary or in a merchant caravan was available. But travel without the protection of kinsmen was always risky and best left to professional outsiders. The pagan peoples of forest and savannah have long been deeply suspicious of each other, and they were happy to leave long journeys into foreign parts to men protected by the "medicines" of Islam. This insularity, too, was a powerful force acting to promote local self-sufficiency.

West African village societies were thus the product of regional and local forces acting simultaneously both to integrate them into a growing network of commerce, slavery, warfare, and state formation and to sustain them within an inward-looking lineage order of agrarian self-sufficiency. The overall material background of sparse population and difficult terrain ensured that areas remote from the major entrepôts and capitals were little touched by commodity production.

A note on kinship and slavery

The dominant forms of labor in West Africa's traditional economies were kinship and slavery. The one is a model of community and consensus in our lexicon, the other the epitome of domination and coercion. In practice they had much in common. Some would say that African slavery (particularly domestic slavery) was a benevolent institution, in that slaves were often treated like kinsmen; but it could equally be said that kinsmen, especially junior males and women, were often treated like slaves.[15] The point is that social organization based on kinship does not conform to the ideal of warm family love that for many modern Americans is the standard. It can be consensual, *if* weaker members of the domestic group can walk out; and it can be a form of domination, in varying degree. Nor is slavery its antithesis, but rather a natural outgrowth of the expansion and development of kinship organization.

Much of one's attitude to the modern breakdown of traditional social forms depends on how one views rural family life – as a free voluntary association of equals bound together by ties of blood and affinity, or as an unequal structure of domination in which overlord, chief, and slave master are merely extensions of the role of patriarchal household head. The position adopted here is that, just as any concrete kinship relationship may modulate between love and exploitation, so too whole kinship structures may vary, according to circumstance, in the degree to which it would be appropriate to view them as consensual or coercive. Of particular interest is the effect of an expanded use of slaves on the organization of relations between kinsmen, especially on the difficult father–son relationship or more generally on elder–junior male relations. In one case, it has been suggested that slavery bound kinsmen together, so that its abolition contributed greatly to the breakdown of family ties (Pollet and Winter 1978). In another, sons were almost substitutable for slaves and vice versa, so that their collective social power was reduced and the relations between elders and juniors might be said to verge on class exploitation.[16] The matter is complex, for recruitment of kinsmen and slaves was based on diametrically opposed principles. If we can sort out the main ways in which these two institutions were variously combined, we will have gone far toward understanding the rural societies on which agricultural commercialization made its impact.

It is particularly important to stress that traditional villages based on kinship were not necessarily models of social equality. The main task of kinship was to organize reproduction and coordinate production. In its essence, reproduction is a sequential link between the generations; no society on earth represents the parent–child relationship as *equal*. Inequality is the distinctive feature of West African kinship: Even brothers are differentiated in rank by age. Descent is the great divider, as well as, under conditions of segmentary opposition, a unifier. Relations between men and women are ambivalent, to say the least. Social life organized through kinship, then, is fundamentally disunited, and it is in response to this disunity that participants stress the opposite in their ideological pronouncements, emphasizing the idea of community and pretending that kinship ties express only solidarity. We, who retain in our language and sentiments the ideology without the substance of a society organized through kinship, project our own romantic nostalgia onto the faction-ridden and anxiety-prone family life of African villages. Then, in the name of this fictitious utopia, we declaim against developments that shift the focus of social life away from that narrow-minded sphere, or invent nonexistent social forces of external oppression to explain why West Africans, like countless millions elsewhere, yearly vote with their feet on the relative attractions of town and country life.

The question of slavery and kinship in traditional West African societies is thus not merely a historical conundrum: It is a test of the character of rural social life, a way of judging the institutions whose continuity some would make a prominent objective of public policy now.

The origins of the modern era

As we have seen, it would be mistaken to imagine that the economic and political explosion of the nineteenth century jerked a stable or homogenous "tribal" society into unwilling confrontation with the forces of European expansion. The groundwork for West Africa's response to an intensification of its involvement in the global commercial economy had been laid in centuries of complex social evolution. Those unstratified peasantries that had managed to stay free (the so-called acephalous societies) were joined in a dynamic and shifting region-wide relationship with the old states of the savannah interior and the booming kingdoms of the forest near the Atlantic coast. As the nineteenth century dawned, the threat of a clash between these latter states and the European-dominated settlements of the coastal strip loomed very large indeed, especially when Britain turned its navy against the slave trade.

What had been the effects of West Africa's involvement in the emergent global economy of 1500–1830? It is widely recognized that the growth of world trade in this period gave some countries in Europe the opportunity to break through, by the end of it, to industrial capitalist development. This was the period that Marx (1959) characterized as "the primitive accumulation of capital" by means of that combination of trading, piracy, looting, and financial chicanery that has earned itself the label "mercantilism." Obviously West Africa fell progressively behind the economies of trading partners whose political systems were more attuned to the needs of a rising capitalist class. It is not so obvious, however, that the

40

region's commercial development and prosperity were adversely affected by the Atlantic trade, no matter how heinous we may now find the export and import of human beings for sale.

The Atlantic slave trade began soon after the Portuguese explorations of the late fifteenth century; it ended officially with the shift to "legitimate" trade in the early nineteenth century, but it continued in strength until the late nineteenth century. An estimated 10 million slaves were exported by sea during the entire slaving period (Curtin 1969; A. G. Hopkins 1973:89–92), and this figure does not include the continuation of a trans-Saharan slave trade on a smaller scale. The internal demand for slaves was also very high. Slave raiding was thus the staple item in the political economy of West Africa's ruling classes. As such, it cannot have contributed a great deal to the peaceful development of agriculture, industry, and trade; rather, the division of labor was probably retarded by intensified resort to slavery. Other exports to Europe, apart from gold and ivory, were materials (e.g., gums) useful to various manufacturing trades like printing and dyeing. The Nigerian leather trade with Morocco is centuries old. West Africans imported from Europe textiles, metals, metal products, guns, alcohol, and trinkets.

The lucrative exchange of slaves for manufactures appears to have been instigated by the Europeans to their advantage. They certainly made some money, though not as much as they hoped and often at considerable cost to their own lives. If there was a net drain of value from West Africa during the period of the Atlantic slave trade, it was not because the Europeans were able to enforce "unfair" prices on the natives, because there was a rough balance of political forces on the coast between the two sides and a reasonable degree of competition in the market. Rather, West Africans lost out because the productivity of Europe's labor force was constantly rising, a trend exacerbated beyond all previous experience by the Industrial Revolution; this meant that the terms of trade had to deteriorate in favor of Europe as long as West African productivity stagnated.[17] This growing productivity gap, then, is the mechanism that pushed West Africa further behind Europe than it had been in the Middle Ages, while at the same time generating economic growth in the region, especially near the coast. The fact that Europeans accumulated capital at West Africans' expense, as they surely did, does not mean that the latter were made absolutely worse off by the process.

West Africa entered the era of the Atlantic slave trade with several handicaps, most notably the restrictions on the growth of its population posed by environment and epidemiology. Its social structures reinforced an underdeveloped division of labor by giving power to military aristocracies and lineage elders. The slave trade made both of these factors worse: Warfare and slave raiding were intensified and millions of people were lost to the region through export and premature death. Nevertheless, the mercantile economy was also given a boost, and new centralized kingdoms were able to institute a palace division of labor from which production might be developed. But, even as some West Africans may have prospered from expanded international trade – and it did expand enough to shift the whole emphasis of the regional economy from north to south – this growth was not allied with any systematic improvements in productivity. As a result, a region that entered the nineteenth century still on rough terms of equality with Europeans ended it as the victim of wholesale conquest.

The nineteenth-century crisis

It was only in the nineteenth century that West Africans were put on the defensive by European expansion, as the effects of industrialization began to make themselves felt. The region's position as the nearest tropical area to Europe was at this point fully exploited for the first time: Previously, the West Indies, Ceylon, and the East Indies were more important. Beginning in the 1830s, but especially from the 1850s on, West Africa became a major source of vegetable oils, from oil palm stands in the coastal forest and from groundnuts in the coastal savannah. The explosion of European demand was occasioned principally by the consumption needs of the new urban industrial population – for candles, soap, and later margarine. The invention of vulcanization in 1880 created a wild rubber boom, which was short-lived, but which served to indicate how far West Africans had been drawn into the global economy as agricultural producers (or, more accurately, as tree-crop collectors). The growth of this "legitimate" trade took place against the backdrop of an abolition movement that became more effective as the century progressed. At first unilaterally banned by Britain, slavery and those whose livelihoods depended on it were pushed more and more into the background in order to make way for the supply of industrial raw materials. This is the core of the "nineteenth-century crisis" (A. G. Hopkins 1973:chap. 4; McPhee 1971).

Despite foreign experiments in plantation production, economic control over the new export crops remained in the hands of West Africans. In some cases, slaves who could no longer be sold were put to work producing vegetable oils (Coquery-Vidrovitch 1971*a*). Elsewhere the loss of revenue was not so easily overcome by the ruling aristocracies; and everywhere the old political order was threatened by rising new classes of merchants and farmers. The status quo was further placed in jeopardy by Europe's growing technological mastery, which now shifted the balance of power decisively in its favor. Some forest states like Ashanti grew strong enough to challenge Europe's coastal enclaves. But by the late nineteenth century, military technology had improved sufficiently to make it feasible for the Europeans to fight land wars against such powers. The decision to colonize the area beyond Dakar, Lagos, and the forts was taken piecemeal; but the colonial carving up of West Africa (which may be dated to 1883) was completed in a matter of two decades, the last two of the century. France had the lion's share of land, Britain the bulk of the people and trade. Portugal and Germany occupied minor slivers of territory. The reasons for this upheaval in West Africa's affairs belong to the history of Western imperialism and colonialism, and they are much debated. Even though a good case can be made highlighting economic considerations within the region itself, the origins of West African colonization belong in the wider struggle for global domination waged by the industrial powers of Europe at the end of the last century (Munroe 1976; A. G. Hopkins 1973; Fieldhouse 1973). Then, as now, West Africa was a sideshow.

The crisis was manifested in the interior by an *increase* in warfare and slave raiding. (There was probably considerable depopulation, owing to military and economic disruptions.) The nineteenth century saw a continuing series of political upheavals. The most effective challenge to the old political order was posed by Islam, in the shape of populist marabouts not unlike the Ayatollah Khomeini.[18] There were several *jihads* (religious wars) leading to the establishment of new states. A few military freebooters (such as Samory; see Person 1970–1) were able to set up temporary states before being eliminated by European conquerors. The accelerated shift of commerce to the south (reinforced by rapid improvements in maritime transport, such as the steamship) gave new opportunities to the Muslim merchant class and further reduced the significance of the trans-Sahara connection. On the coast itself, "merchant princes" arose to fill some of the gaps left by a rapidly crumbling indigenous political order.

This encapsulated version of nineteenth-century history is intended to draw attention to the fact that the period immediately prior to colonization (the "precolonial" period) does not deserve to be sanctified with the label "traditional society." Far from being the stable embodiment of indigenous social forms, it was a time of great conflict (both with Europeans and internally), population mobility, and social change. In this respect West Africa went through the sort of upheavals that all the world's regions experienced in the nineteenth century. The force behind these economic, political, and religious movements was the cataclysmic impact of global industrialization, which now added to local forces the logic of production processes initiated elsewhere.

Colonialism

"Progress . . . was assured with the advent of the three R's in the nineties – Rule of British, Railway construction and Ross's medical achievements." (McPhee 1971:xi). The explicit function of colonialism was to impose a system of direct political rule on a West African region that had been extremely fragmented. It might be supposed that this political structure would be designed to facilitate the extraction of economic values from the colonies. This was not entirely the case. The British were interested principally in trade, and their actions were subordinated to that end. The French, however, saw Afrique occidentale française as part of Greater France; they were far more interested than the British in territorial sovereignty and political control for its own sake. This difference of emphasis was reflected in attitudes toward public finance. The British colonies were expected to be self-financing, and this was a stricture that severely limited military expenditures, for example. The French authorities, on the other hand, had use of a conscript army paid for by the mother country. The gap between the two metropolitan powers was not absolute, but it grew larger as the British policy of economic liberalism was reinforced by an exodus from the French territories to the Gold Coast and Nigeria, where export-crop booms were fed by this source of labor. Colonial policy was much more repressive in AOF, where coercion of labor and tribute served only to depress indigenous commercial initiative.[19] The economies of territories like the Ivory Coast were thus retarded by colonialism, whereas nearby British colonies enjoyed early economic growth through expansion of agricultural production for export. Much that has occurred since World War II needs to be understood in terms of this fundamental difference between the two colonialisms. However, as each decade since decolonization passes, the colonial heritage becomes weakened, and older divisions, such as that between forest and savannah, reassert themselves.

The colonial period (in general, 1900–60, although in the areas surrounding Dakar, Freetown, and Lagos, colonies had existed much earlier) saw a rapid expansion of forest agriculture, with production still in indigenous hands.[20] After oil palm and rubber, new crops took hold – cocoa, coffee, fruits, and similar products aimed at the consumer markets of the industrialized countries. Groundnuts and cotton were the export staples of the savannah, with northern Nigeria joining the Senegambia as a major groundnut-producing area. Much of this export trade was controlled by British and French merchant houses, supplemented sometimes by Levantine businessmen known as "Syrians." The *économie de traite* was based on a more-or-less direct exchange of export crop income for imported manufactures – cloth, liquor, and light consumer goods (see Suret-Canale 1971). The tendency of this trade to be monopolized by a few European firms was only partially offset by occasional outbreaks of competition.[21] These firms were a major political force in the colonies, especially after mining, which had offered such bright prospects in the beginning, turned out to be an insignificant industry in West Africa. The predominantly mercantile emphasis of colonialism in this region was reflected in policies preserving the control exercised by indigenous populations over the land and in fairly liberal labor laws (compared with those in mining and plantation colonies elsewhere in Africa) (McPhee 1971:229). The failure of European capital to penetrate West African production had important consequences for the legacy of public institutions that the British and French left behind two decades ago.

Probably the most important contribution made by colonialism to West Africa's economic development was its improvement of the transport infrastructure. A great deal of foreign capital flooded into the region at the beginning of this century to fund projects that often turned out to be excessively optimistic. But regardless of the immediate returns to the original investors, these ports, railways, docks, bridges, and roads brought a veritable transport revolution, which vastly enhanced the commercial economy. Internal market linkages, as well as the import–export sector, were expanded: The kola and livestock trades, for example, took on new life once distribution costs had been cut so dramatically.

The administrative revolution of colonialism also had powerful effects on local economies. Peace and taxation were associated with greater population mobility, with the rise of new political elites, and with a much-increased commitment to commodity production. The colonial rulers stimulated urban growth; the construction industry was a major and often overlooked vehicle of indigenous enterprise during this period. But colonial fiscal policies were conservative; so there was a low limit to public expenditures, and the centers of government (mostly on the coast) did not grow particularly large.[22] Despite this restriction on the divergence between town and countryside, the colonial era did see a widening of the gap between the coastal forest and the savannah, with the latter becoming (often as a direct result of public policy) a progressively neglected reservoir of labor for the export-crop zones of the forest (Amin 1971, 1974*a*).

Intraregional inequalities of this kind reflected a growing dependence of the West African colonies on a world economy to which their access was controlled by the dominant metropolitan powers. The marked cycle of booms and slumps, which had been a characteristic feature of nineteenth-century trade, was continued and intensified under colonialism; the period 1930–45 constituted an unremitting depression that had traumatic effects on West African production and commerce. It is worth remembering that one-sixth of the colonial period was taken up by two world wars in which West African economies were skewed even more than normally to serve the interests of the metropolitan countries.

After the last world war centralized trading mechanisms (marketing boards or stablization funds) were devised that enabled the colonial governments to skim off a large surplus from export-crop sales, used in the case of Britain to help pay war debts (Bauer 1954; Fitch and Oppenheimer 1966). This step was an important forerunner of state controls over the economy introduced later by the successor governments. The late colonial period saw a continued dependence on agricultural exports, although there was a limited metal-ores boom in the 1950s from which Liberia and Mauritania, in particular, were able to benefit. The external orientation of the colonial economies was reflected in their failure to supply the basic consumption needs of the population drawn into the export enclaves and the towns. In consequence, large amounts of foodstuffs (rice from Burma, sugar, tea, etc.) were routinely imported. Some countries, notably Nigeria and the Gold Coast, had flourishing internal market economies by the end of the colonial era (Hawkins 1958; Anthony et al. 1979); others had experienced export growth without any dynamic linkages to production and investment in the home economy. It is important to emphasize these variations, especially in view of a common tendency to regard colonialism as a unitary expression of central capitalist interests that had uniform effects on West Africa's local economies.

World War II was a watershed. Before it, most people thought of the European imperial presence in West Africa as almost eternal; after it, the emancipation of indigenous peoples from formal rule by their erstwhile conquerors seemed only a matter of time. The British, especially, knew that they could not stay on in West Africa against the will of the people: Cumulative pressures during the 1950s, especially in the Gold Coast and Guinea, ensured that both the main colonial powers had to yield to African political leaders much sooner than some had thought likely. The West African region was very quickly converted into a balkanized cluster of states who won their independence more or less without a fight. The main story of this book is that of their attempts to win control over the processes of economic development (still mainly agricultural) on which their nationhood is predicated.

The successor states

The main feature of the last two decades has been the emergence of the state as an economic and political force on an unprecedented scale.[23] Power is shared by three classes: the holders of political office and the political parties that brought West African territories to independence; the military and police, whose coups have displaced the first category in numerous instances; and an administrative bureaucracy that carries on the traditions of the colonial state. These ruling classes are supported or lightly checked by civil interests that are basically very weak: chiefs, unions, and a miniscule indigenous business class. More important is the rulers' continuing dependence on the ex-colonial powers, on the United States and the USSR, and on international agencies such as the International Monetary Fund (IMF) and the World Bank. For this reason, some have called the successor states ''neo-colonial,''[24] a term indicating the subservience of West African polities to external economic interests, such as those of the multinational corporations that control the region's nonagricultural extractive industries. Certainly the international donor agencies play a significant part in regulating the pattern of West African development. And France still maintains monetary control over most of its former colonies.

But to portray the successor states as colonialism under new management is to miss the point about what has been going on over the last twenty years. Each government has embarked on ambitious programs aimed at raising living standards and extending its own control over the territory it inherited, no matter how irrationally the boundaries may have been drawn. These programs have led the new states into patterns and levels of expenditure of which the colonial regimes never dreamed. The colonial trading economy has been threatened – even dismantled in some places. What has taken its place is an overcentralized political system, with the state as principal entrepreneur in an economy that is still based on a dispersed population of small agricultural-commodity producers. The structure of international trade is still more or less the same – agrarian exports for imported manufactures – and the productive agents are largely the same as in colonial times; but the internal economy is now dominated by a political apparatus that is beginning to weigh ever more heavily on the decentralized agricultural base. The role of the international agencies appears to be to rescue the successor regimes from the contradictions of their development policies or to nudge them toward strategies more compatible with their material resources.

The liberation of the state from colonial fiscal restraint has seen massive increases in public expenditure on infrastructure and social services (see Table 3, in Chapter 4). Construction has been favored more than transport: Where the colonial regimes built roads and bridges, their successors raise multistory buildings and fill them with government officials. The greatest achievement of the new ruling classes has been their commitment to educational and health objectives on behalf of the people who once voted them into power. Colonial governments cynically restricted their educational expenditures to the needs of a small civil service; modern governments must open the chance for self-improvement to all. But education is very expensive, and social services absorb most of government revenue after interest on debts has been deducted from the annual budget. Government expenditure has been financed by intensification of the rate of agricultural exploitation (using monopsonistic trading controls inherited from the colonial era); by external borrowing and inflation of the public debt through internal monetary measures; by investments in agriculture, industry, and trading; and by any other means that come to hand.

Direct taxation is an inadequate financial base because the bulk of the citizen body is employed in a decentralized agrarian economy. Excise duties do not grow as fast as population and revenue needs. So the successor states have added the roles of banker, industrialist, and landlord to the merchant functions they inherited from their predecessors. But this rickety structure of preindustrial socialized economy is falling apart, especially since the energy and commodities crisis of 1973–74. The reasons are many: Imported energy costs and global inflation in general may be damaging to New York, but they can bring West African economies to the point of collapse; aid is not as easy to come by as it was in the Cold War days of big-power rivalry during the 1960s, and it comes with closer scrutiny of internal economic management; ecological deterioration has hit the Sahel states especially; administrative incompetence is normal; world recession looms as a particular threat to a region that owns no strategic resources beyond Nigeria's oil and Niger's uranium; staple exports are stagnant; import consumption is profligate; and home industries have been weakly developed. Above all, there has been a universal failure to find an economic strategy compatible with the scale of public finances on which West African states now base their claim for legitimacy. In the absence of such a strategy, a form of state must emerge that is compatible with a backward preindustrial economy operated in the main by a population of depressed smallholder farmers. Such a future was not what the leaders of the anticolonial struggle had in mind.

The aggrandizement of the postcolonial state to its present position of dominance in the West African economies has had the effect of accelerating the drift of population out of the countryside.[25] Each capital city is like a latter-day Naples, with the headquarters of government surrounded by a mob of people living directly or indirectly off the concentration of public expenditures there. Income is thus drawn out of export agriculture and spent disproportionately in the towns. Consequently, urban populations have mushroomed, reaching a third of the total in some countries. If we remember that no agrarian region sustained an urban population larger than a tenth of its own size before 1800 (Cipolla 1978), some idea of the scale of the economic conjuring trick involved here will be evident. Local food agriculture is of course insufficient to supply the urban population, and food imports have grown rapidly. Any potential stimulus to the internal market for foodstuffs has been further depressed by government price controls, food subsidies, and aid transfers (e.g., PL480 shipments from the United States). But the main obstacle to the commercialization of food production is the low productivity of food farmers.

In this climate of gathering crisis and economic uncertainty, attempts have been made to stimulate local food production. In view of its low bulk and high nutritional value, it is no surprise that many of these attempts have focused on rice.[26] There can be little doubt that before long West Africans will subsist principally on rice, supplemented by locally grown cereals and root crops. The question is, How much of that rice will be imported? Rice cultivation lends itself to irrigation, and the new states are very interested in large-scale projects controlled by their own agents. These projects are usually less efficient than smallholder schemes, but governments are more concerned with stable revenues than with abstract measures of total economic yield. The idea of an agrarian state deriving its income from irrigated peasant rice production has not yet been embraced openly as a development strategy in West Africa. Could "oriental despotism" take root in the region?[27]

The answer to that question depends heavily on what has been happening to the rural population in the last two decades. Has the work force been sufficiently prepared by famine, impoverishment, and proletarianization to constitute a reliable, hardworking, paddy-field peasantry? My assessment is that it has not. Agricultural intensification means getting people to work harder, and that undertaking usually requires coercion. The compulsion would have to be especially severe in the forest areas, where labor-efficient techniques of production yield up the population's food need with comparatively little effort (hence the popularity of cassava, or manioc, which, despite its nutritional deficiencies requires almost no labor input). Even in the dry savannah it has been calculated that, whereas Asians spend an average of three thousand hours per year each growing their food, West Africans are able to generate a richer diet from one thousand hours of work.[28]

There is no doubt that the last twenty years have seen a great deal of development beyond the monolithic *économie de traite* of the colonial period. For one thing, the appearance of homogeneity that colonial rule gave the region is beginning to wear thin, as the idiosyncracies of the various political economies stamp the several states with unique histories and as some of the fundamentals of West African geography reassert themselves against the distortions of colonialism. Nigeria appears to be moving, via a phase of civil war and military rule, toward achieving the true status of a modern nation-state; yet despite its relative wealth and large, concentrated population, it still faces many obstacles to the task of constructing a coherent social order. The rest of the successor states are, to a greater or lesser degree, in disarray. The major exception is the Ivory Coast, which has taken over Ghana's role as the main growth point of the region outside Nigeria. The descent of Ghana from its position of continental leadership to today's mixture of bankruptcy and civil disorder is a tragic commentary on the contradictions facing these new states. It is possible, but not likely at this time, that a movement toward greater regional unity under Nigeria's leadership (nineteenth-century German unification under Prussian hegemony offers an inexact comparison) will enable West Africans to win a measure of political and economic emancipation from their present state of inept dependency on forces originating outside their region. Otherwise, the most powerful force for partial integration of some of the region's more vulnerable countries is the attention now given to a number of Francophone states (especially in the Sahel) by the United States, especially since the famine of the early 1970s. American wealth is vying with French traditions of metropolitan control for informal influence in the region; and when the alternative appears to be ruination, many of the smaller states may well find this attention attractive.

It should not be thought, from the emphasis adopted in the foregoing, that the economic structures of colonialism are still basically unchanged, with the exception of greater government intervention. As we shall see, this latest phase in the development of West African agrarian economies has introduced many potentialities for new departures. Capital-intensive enterprises, in both the private and the public sectors, now flourish in limited areas. There is much more money about these days, and the internal commercial economy has expanded by leaps and bounds since World War II. The expenditures of the new states have been a major stimulus to this expansion. Many organizational innovations have been introduced, not always successfully. It may even be that demographic trends and 150 years of commodity production in export agriculture have led in some areas to situations in which land is a scarce factor of production and labor more dependent on wage employment, so that agrarian capitalism may flourish. Unprecedented numbers of people are leaving the land.

Many view the prospect of such developments unfavorably, seeing them as destructive of old social forms and of valuable rural lifeways. Others are worried about the political dangers of unruly urban populations without a secure stake in the countryside. Whatever one's opinion on these matters, it is clear that new solutions will have to be found to the problems of state formation and economic development that have plagued the West African region ever since it began the long process of involvement in the international trading economy. A break-through to higher productivity levels in agriculture and a reconsideration of the role of the state seem to be minimal conditions for avoidance of imminent economic collapse. The 1980s will be a time of great instability and uncertainty. What is needed above all is a capacity to take the long view of current policy dilemmas.

Conclusions

We have seen that in medieval times parts of West Africa were as advanced as the Islamic Mediterranean and Near East, a civilization that was itself a match for those of Europe and the Far East. During the period of the Atlantic slave trade, West Africa became underdeveloped in comparison to the Europe of its trading partners. This was the time also when maritime transport drew population and commerce toward the coast, undermining the supremacy of the Islamic interior. The underdevelopment of traditional economies has a multiple causality. The region suffers from some long-standing ecological and epidemiological handi-caps. The enhanced prominence of slavery after the arrival of the Portuguese reinforced unprogressive elements in West African social structures and disrupted the growth of population and production. Above all, economic backwardness was the result of a growing discrepancy between labor productivity in Europe and West Africa during the period of mercantilist expansion. This inequality was pushed to unheard-of extremes as a result of industrialization. The relative purchasing power of West African exports deteriorated drastically, and the income gap between the two regions expanded to the levels that we see today.

The Europeans were emboldened to colonize West Africa by their technologi-cal superiority, but they soon abandoned the idea. The effect of this foreign imposition was undoubtedly to lock the region's economies even more securely into an international trading orientation that gave many benefits to expatriate merchant houses, but also left ownership of the means of production in indige-nous hands. After decolonization, new anonymous powers (the World Bank, IMF, etc.) arose to supervise relations between West Africa's nation-states and the international economic order. The continuous aggrandizement of the state over the last 150 years has largely done away with the political order of the Atlantic slave-trade era, so that new problems and possibilities have arisen with respect to organizing economies that are still mainly agricultural. With the exception of Nigeria, the future of West Africa has probably never looked so hopeless as now, when rocketing fuel prices further exacerbate the contradictions of each country's political economy.

Neither international nor local conditions can be identified as the single primary cause of West Africa's cumulative impoverishment relative to the more advanced sectors of human society: Both have been locked into a single nexus of historical development for half a millennium; but neither is sufficient to account for today's picture. I believe that global industrialization has subsumed West African development under the logic of its own expansion, but the story of how West African societies and material conditions have contributed to that history also deserves to be told.

Instead of asking why West Africa has failed to become an industrial capitalist society, it might be more fruitful to ask why conditions in one country produced a revolution with immense consequences for the rest of a world that was making no effort to escape from the agrarian economy of the postneolithic era. The answers to such a question lie in Britain's agricultural division of labor, in its nascent industries, in its towns, and in its laws. Moreover, any country or region that has successfully emulated Britain has had to revolutionize the conditions of agricultural production, within whose matrix the bulk of all preindustrial populations is contained. So whatever the influence of international economic arrangements (and they are not always benign), West Africa's states must revolutionize their agricultural sectors if they wish to escape from permanent backwardness and poverty. No single factor is more important.

3

The organization of agricultural production

The population of a country in which commodity economy is poorly developed (or not developed at all) is almost exclusively agricultural. This, however, must not be understood as meaning that the population is engaged solely in agriculture: it only means that the population, while engaged in agriculture, itself processes the products of agriculture, and that exchange and the division of labor are almost non-existent.

V. I. Lenin, *The Development of Capitalism in Russia* (1974:40)

The traditional organization of farming

Any discussion of modern developments in West African agriculture should begin and end with the rural division of labor that constitutes the social context of productive strategies. This chapter begins with a brief recapitulation of traditional economic structure in areas marked either by a complex structure of commodity production or by a simple division of labor. After a detailed examination of forest and savannah agriculture in the modern period and a more cursory look at the use of livestock, the chapter concludes with an assessment of the effects of these developments on the rural division of labor as a whole. As we have seen, traditional agriculture was carried out within the framework of a wider division of labor, which was developed to a high degree in some places, notably in the savannah civilizations around the Niger and Senegal rivers. The division of labor was less developed in the intermediate belt and in the forest away from the coast. Nowhere was it more complex than in Hausaland (northern Nigeria), which contained about a sixth of West Africa's population in precolonial times.[1]

In the advanced societies of the Sudanic zone before the colonial era, agriculture was not the greatest task of all sectors of the population. Many lived in or near towns and cities where they earned their livelihoods principally from manufacturing and services. In places, farming was performed only by slaves or serfs tied to a ruling class whose main business was warfare, slave raiding, and politics. This class derived additional income from taxes on an extraordinary variety of products and activities, which they levied on free men and women who lived in villages partially committed to agriculture. In the rural areas closest to the main centers, farmers were individuated, lacking membership in stable corporate groups and living in production units organized around joint families of agnates. Elsewhere, corporate villages sometimes farmed a common field in order to produce revenues for the state. The range of production strategies was thus rather wide. It was normal in this part of the savannah for an ethnic division of labor to exist between pastoralists and the bulk of agriculturalists. The former were usually called Fulani,[2] and they were a major part of the political upheavals that reorganized the region at the beginning of the nineteenth century. Separation between the two groups meant that animals were not used in mixed farming, although intensive manuring was normal in the close-settled zone around Kano and the Voltaic area, for example. Craft specialization reached the point of guilds aimed at urban markets: In the countryside casted specialists were usually endogamous, and they also farmed for themselves, because demand was not high enough to guarantee them a living from crafts alone. Merchants were generally specialized, but in the central areas everyone was in some degree a merchant.

The pervasiveness of commodity economy was variable in the Sudanic zone; transport was so bad that, unless the population was densely settled over a wide area, thirty miles would be sufficient to close off a village's access to high-volume markets. Production of food for the market was thus an option restricted to peoples living near urban centers or to the population of Hausaland in general. Production of agricultural raw materials for industry (especially cotton for textiles) was well developed in suitable areas. Commercialism was accompanied by a significant emphasis on private property and by the replacement of lineages with cognatic kin groups in which patrilineal descent played a residual part. Nevertheless, agricultural productivity remained low, although the technology used may have been more labor intensive than that employed elsewhere in West Africa. The basic tool remained the hoe: There was no use made of the plow or irrigation. Animal traction was more or less absent, except for the use of donkeys for transport in some area. Yet even with these limitations on agricultural growth, an extraordinarily varied economy grew up. Here is M. G. Smith's description of the traditional sexual division of labor in the Hausa province of Zaria during the early 1950s:

Men rule, farm, dye, build, work metals, skin, tan and work leather, slay and handle cattle and small livestock, sew all sewn clothes, make musical instruments and music, trade, keep bees, weave mats, may be Mallams (teacher–priests), wash clothes, weave narrow cloth on the men's loom, go on long-distance trading expeditions, make pots, do carpentry – native and European – are the doctors and magicians, the barbers, employed farm laborers, brokers and taxpayers. They also fish, hunt and do all the family marketing, keep goats, sheep, chickens, ducks, turkeys and pigeons, and took part in war.

Women cook for their families, process and sell cooked food (snacks) on their own behalf, sweep and clean the compounds, are solely responsible for delivery and safe care of children, draw wood and water, are custodians of the cult of Bori (spirit possession), tease and spin cotton, weave cloth on the women's broadlooms, thresh, grind and pound corn and food and are, before marriage and when they are old, traders in the markets and from house to house. Women do one another's hair, may (but usually do not) farm, and help with the groundnut, cowpea, cotton and pepper harvests. Very occasionally women become mallams or professional musicians or magicians. In new towns, where prostitutes are numerous, women sometimes work at the dye-pits. Women may not inherit land, nor houses where there are related male heirs, and under Maliki law daughters receive half of the inheritance of sons, but usually inherit the personal possessions of their mothers. Women are expected to provide themselves with luxuries and snacks as they require and on the marriage of daughters, women of the paternal and maternal kin provide most of the dowry.

Both men and women make pots and fire, care for chickens, goats and sheep, do hairdressing for their respective sexes, attend the Koranic schools, trade and are required to perform the obligatory duties of Islam. [1955:60]

It should be noted that this list does not include guild or caste specialists such as blacksmiths, jewelers, and the like.[3] Even so, it should serve as a caution to anyone who would subsume traditional agriculture under some such label as "peasant farmers." The Islamic Sudan was and is a sophisticated economy built around a high degree of specialization, of which no element was so deep as the division of labor between the sexes.

In the more remote parts of the savannah and forest, sex, age, and kinship were the sole determinants of the division of labor. The main tasks of small groups formed on the basis of common descent were reproduction, food production, and warfare (defense of territory, women, and movable property); the ideology of kinship relations and divisions according to sex and age generally sufficed to organize these activities. The most important job was to ensure the continuity of the group through a long-term process of recruitment by birth and marriage. Acquisition of wives by a group of men large enough to be demographically viable demanded organization at a level higher than the domestic group. Descent-group hierarchies thus gave power and authority to older men over their juniors. Agriculture was the next most important task. Of all productive activities it occupied the longest time in the year, involved the coordination of the most complex operations, and, at some critical phases, required the cooperation of the largest number of people. In addition, food was the basic source of energy in an economy where clothing and shelter were conveniences rather than necessities and the main use for fuel was cooking. So agriculture dominated production, and other activities were made to fit in with its annual cycle. The other important collective activities – and these united the largest groups – were the common occupation of a territory, defense of it, and ritual regulation of human relations with nature within it. Each of these categories was closely connected to warfare and politics, which in this area were often "tribal"; that is, they consisted of self-help by equally armed groups organized, if at all, by low-level chiefs. But these public activities were essential to the ordinary tasks of production and reproduction and ensured the adherence of small groups to the larger entities that commanded their allegiance.

Because of the general abundance of land and low population density, agricultural production techniques minimized labor inputs and drew to the greatest extent possible on the self-renewing capacities of nature (Cleave 1974; Dumont 1966*a*). Shifting cultivation or bush fallow rotation was thus a highly rational combination of the available factors of production.[4] In the forest, only the clearing of farms involved heavy labor, and the bulk of cultivation was undertaken by women, using simple hand tools such as the hoe. In the savannah, heavy agricultural tasks requiring pooled and disciplined male labor were more normal, and it is possible to see in this distinction the reason for the correlation between forest or savannah and matrilineal or patrilineal descent. At any rate, men and women usually shared farming equally in the decentralized savannah zone. Coordination of production schedules by elders was matched by their control over the management of joint herds and of food crop distribution. Child labor was frequently used for tasks such as supervision of cattle. (The separation of agriculturalists and pastoralists became less common farther south in the transitional zone between savannah and forest.)

Technology was generally underdeveloped in remote areas: Animals were used rarely for traction, and none but the simplest tools were to be found. Crafts were less specialized than in the areas with a more complex division of labor; certainly there was no element of hereditary occupational specialization. Consumer wants were less varied and labor consequently less divided; local markets were small scale, intermittent, and mainly agricultural, with few manufactured items appearing for sale. The dry season, more marked in the savannah, was a slack period during which craft production, construction, trade, and ritual activities – some involving extensive cooperation, others more individuated – were carried on. Every farmer had a specialized source of dry-season income. There was thus plenty of room for individual enterprise within a framework dominated by collective agriculture. Individuals could usually cultivate spare plots in time left over from group farming on commonly held lands; and just as the product of pooled labor was shared, so too personal labor generated private property. Individual accumulation was possible, but made difficult by the emphasis on cooperative social relations. Agriculture dominated the division of labor when it was relatively simple, and commodity relations were weakly developed.[5]

All of this says nothing of the concrete tasks of which agriculture is composed. Although an aluminum smelter may be established according to the same abstract principles more or less anywhere in the world, farming must always be adapted to local environmental conditions. This is particularly the case where the division of labor is weakly developed and social life is closely interwoven with a common set of material activities. And local conditions may be extremely varied. Thus the need to economize on labor in scaring off pests (say monkeys) could be the key determinant of a collective field-rotation pattern, or a weeding bottleneck the main reason for maintaining a given pattern of labor sharing. The hard clay soils of bottomlands in the savannah require strenuous young male labor, whereas some root crops of the forest can be harvested by a child. Water drainage and exposure to flooding may be the reason why a certain people stay in the hills and avoid lowlands, with marked consequences for their pattern of settlement; and so on.

There is enormous variability of climate and environment in West Africa, leading to a very wide range of local adaptations. A great variety of crops and animals are combined in the region's traditional agriculture, many of them in the farming practices of single peoples. Before monocrop specialization for export became normal, West Africans used to employ a highly differentiated set of production strategies, especially in the savannah, where unpredictable rainfall was the main influence on planting patterns. All of these considerations consti- tute the accumulated wisdom of peoples living on their own land for generations. They are liable to be lost from sight when development programs are formulated for large, generalized areas; and they are certainly so lost when a book such as this dwells on the abstract properties of a regional agriculture torn out of its many contexts. Yet any development practice (as opposed to development theory) must find ways of incorporating the material and social matrix of traditional agricul- tural forms into its plans.

Forest crops

West Africa's forest zone is an arm of the great tropical rain forest of the Congo basin, stretching along the coast as far as Guinea Bissau, with one major break between Accra and Dahomey, where the savannah (which gets to be rather lush in places) penetrates to the ocean. It is a narrow strip, varying between 100 and 300 miles in depth. Large amounts of the region's export crops are grown in the coastal forest: Its staple industries – oil palm, cocoa, rubber, timber, and numer- ous other tree crops – have been and continue to be the basis for a prosperity that often stands in stark contrast to the poverty of the inland savannah. The indige- nous population of the forest supported substantial kingdoms in the eighteenth and nineteenth centuries, and the forest is now host to a swarm of settlers and short-term migrants, largely of savannah origin. The cultivation of forest crops for export began near overseas transport centers on the coast, and the frontier has moved steadily inland since, as virgin areas became gradually absorbed into the new "plantation" economy. The oldest centers of forest cash-crop production are Nigeria, Benin, Togo, Ghana, and Sierra Leone; more recently, the Ivory Coast has enjoyed a tree-crop export boom. Now, for the first time, there is in some areas little usable forest left. Production has begun to stagnate, even decline, in parts of the tree-cropping belt. It would be wrong to speak of an economic crisis in forest agriculture, but the efficacy of existing methods of cultivation must be increasingly subject to critical scrutiny.

The organization of agricultural production

Oil palm

The palm tree is a valuable resource in West Africa. Its nuts yield an oil useful for cooking, soap making, and numerous other tasks. The kernels can be crushed to a variety of ends. The trunk may be tapped for palm wine. The fronds are a source of fiber for roofing, matting, and similar purposes. So nutritious and useful is the oil palm that it played a major part in supporting from early times one of the densest populations of tropical Africa, namely, that of southern Nigeria. In addition, the palm tree's products have long been exported from the forest zone, particularly from eastern to northern Nigeria, where the Niger River provided a transport medium linking the forest and savannah.

But it was Europe's Industrial Revolution, and Britain's in particular, that transformed West Africa's palm production. The demand for cheap vegetable oils to be used in industrial manufacturing and consumed by the growing urban working class was initially met almost entirely by West African supplies. By 1830 Britain was importing ten thousand tons of palm oil from the region annually, and that figure increased geometrically throughout the nineteenth century (McPhee 1971; A. G. Hopkins 1973). At first the oil was used principally for making stearic candles. Later it became a major component of margarine. When kernels came also to be exported, the crushed fibers were used in making cattle cake. In the twentieth century West African palm exports came directly into competition with the products of the planations of Southern Asia (especially Malaysia and Sumatra), as well as with the United States' extraordinary capacity to grow soya beans and various oil-bearing seeds. Since World War II, the growing sophistication of manufacturing processes – both of vegetable oils and of their synthetic substitutes – has put palm products in an even more vulnerable position. Nonetheless, agencies such as the World Bank spent considerable energy a decade ago ensuring that virtually every tropical forest region would be committed to palm oil production in some degree. West Africa has come, then, in the last 150 years, from the position of monopoly supplier of palm oil to that of an overcommitted competitor in one of the most open and unreliable sectors of world trade.

Like most other West African agricultural products, the oil palm has been cultivated largely by the indigenous population. Unilever, the great British/Dutch firm founded by W. H. Lever, sought unsuccessfully several times during the colonial period to establish large-scale plantations in the region; such plantations were forced to establish themselves instead in places like the Congo, where vast natural forests of oil palms lay waiting and where the authorities were less solicitous of local labor and land-tenure practices. Recently, the military government of Ghana at last gave Unilever a major oil palm concession; and elsewhere in West Africa large-scale modern processing plants have been introduced as the focus for extensive estates sponsored by governments and international agencies.

57

But the predominant pattern of production has been for local people to collect palm products from the trees using methods consistent with customary practice. Although foreign-owned estates prefer to plant dwarf trees in regular rows as means of rationalizing the labor of harvesting, West African methods have been more haphazard. At first, rather than risk climbing the taller, free-growing palms, they merely cut them down for their nuts. This somewhat destructive approach to the problem of collection did not last long. More generally, the palms were allowed to grow in groves, often mixed with other trees, and their fruit was harvested by young men under the supervision of elders, who controlled the sale of the crop. However, because the other products of the palm (especially palm wine) continued to be valued for local consumption, cultivation of the trees was not exclusively geared toward maximizing the yield from those parts suitable for export. Productivity has thus been extremely variable and generally low; and product quality has not always been high. Throughout the colonial period it was confidently asserted that West Africa would be eliminated from world competition if it did not make a wholesale switch toward the rationalized plantation methods that had been adopted so successfully elsewhere. Yet the region continues to export a good quantity of palm oil and kernels, apparently without any substantial change in its production methods.[6]

It is difficult to avoid the conclusion, however, that the early largesse offered by abundant forest lands to a relatively small population has long ago run out. Continued oil palm production on a significant scale requires systematic replanting, improvement, and rehabilitation. A major scheme in eastern Nigeria has been implemented with the hope of rehabilitating some of the oldest oil palm areas; results have been mixed.[7] There is some evidence that old arrangements for organizing labor in the oil palm areas no longer work. In the nineteenth century, especially in Togo and Dahomey, native aristocrats and merchants who could no longer find a market for slaves in the Atlantic trade put large numbers of them to use collecting palm products. Obviously this mode of operation went out of fashion when the region was colonized. Since then it appears that production has been contained largely within the framework of village organization. There are few histories and ethnographies of oil palm production comparable to those which illuminate the cocoa industry. It would be a good thing if there were more: Togo and eastern Nigeria would seem to be suitable starting points.

Rubber

After the early explosion of oil palm production for export, there was a brief boom in rubber. West Africa, long an exporter of gums to Europe and North Africa, ceased such exports in the latter part of the nineteenth century, owing to competition with Egypt and the discovery of chemical substitutes. Invention of the vulcanization process in 1880 triggered a worldwide scramble for rubber, and for two or three decades leading up to World War I, it became one of the hottest items of trade all along the coastal forest belt.[8] The source was wild rubber trees, and they were tapped with no thought for conservation. Frequently the tappers had no previous experience of cultivating tree crops. The Baulé of the Ivory Coast were principally traffickers in slaves, and for them the rubber trade emerged temporarily as an alternative source of revenue to be derived from their slaves: Like the "Brazilians" of Togo and Dahomey (a creolized merchant class who had been heavily involved in illegal slaving), they put the slaves to work collecting the tree produce, in this case tapping rubber (Weiskel 1979). This was almost purely a mode of extraction from the forest; even less than in the case of the oil palm was there any hint of arboriculture. The boom quickly died out, but it had important consequences for the development of crops with a longer-term future, especially cocoa. The destruction of parts of the forest that was often entailed in reckless oil palm and rubber collection made it easier to plant cocoa; and trading profits accumulated in these branches of forest agriculture were essential to the financing of cocoa farms in the early days of the industry.

Just about the only significant locus of modern rubber production in West Africa is also the region's most glaring exception to the rule that large foreign plantations have not taken root. In 1926 the Firestone company of tire manufacturers received, in return for bailing out a bankrupt Liberian government, a lease on a million acres for ninety-nine years at very low rent, and much of this land was subsequently put to cultivation of rubber trees (Liebenow 1969; Clapham 1976). Later B. F. Goodrich opened up a smaller, but still substantial, rubber plantation. As mortgager of a corrupt and weak Liberian government, Firestone has long been a state within the state – one, moreover, that has won extremely favorable terms for the conduct of its enterprise. In particular, it has been able to rely on the government's support to ensure a steady supply of unorganized labor at low rates of pay. The political economy of the whole operation barely squares with modern African aspirations (or even with the norms of French or British colonial practice). Just after World War II, rubber accounted for 90 percent of Liberia's exports; but partial diversification of the economy, owing to an iron ore boom in the 1950s, and the growing pressure of national and international opinion have led to a modification of what used to be West Africa's most nakedly exploitive arrangement in the sphere of agricultural production.

Cocoa

The one commodity in which the West African region exercises world dominance is cocoa. The rise of this tree crop, beginning in the late nineteenth century, is an exciting story, and it has deservedly drawn a good deal of attention from social scientists and historians. It was introduced to the Gold Coast and southern Nigeria in the 1880s, and so rapid was the growth of cocoa exports in subsequent decades that the British abandoned any lingering thoughts of relying on expatriate plantation and mining interests. Instead, they sat back to draw revenues at the ports from taxation first of the indigenous population's purchases of imported manufactures and later of their burgeoning agricultural exports.

Ghana quickly became the world leader in cocoa, reaching this position before World War I. It accounted for two-fifths of total world production at the time of its independence in 1957. By then its forest population of some 4 million was supported at the highest living standard in black Africa by an economy whose engine was essentially a monocrop farming regime. In the last two decades, however, the Ivory Coast in particular and also Cameroon have increased their share of the market, whereas Ghana's share and even output have become half what they were "when cocoa was king." The region's main competitors are Latin American countries such as Brazil and Ecuador, and Papua New Guinea is a new nation with some potential for growing cocoa. Despite the relatively small number of producer countries involved, the recent attempts of cocoa exporters to form a cartel for the purpose of maintaining or raising prices have been marked with only limited success and recurrent failure. In general, world market price fluctuations have been massive, exacerbated by the elastic demand for a product that is after all only a consumer luxury good and by extremely uncertain conditions of production, the annual variations of which (rainfall, crop disease, availability of production factors, etc.) are made the subject of speculative prognoses by Western brokers and journalists.[9] Export-crop marketing boards and stabilization funds, introduced after World War II by colonial governments, ostensibly to maintain producer prices at secure levels, have ensured the transfer of the problem of uncertain income, in the postcolonial period, to the state itself (Bauer 1954). Ghana's bumper crop in the mid-1960s was rewarded, owing to its large share of the world market, by a slump in the price sharp enough to reduce the country's earnings dramatically. The fall of Nkrumah's government was intimately linked to this event (Fitch and Oppenheimer 1966).

The political economy of cocoa at the national level has been addressed by a number of scholars in recent years (Beckman 1976; Kotey, Okali, and Rourke 1974). But the most interesting questions relate to the organization of this unique African industry on the ground. The ethnographic researches of Polly Hill for the Gold Coast, Marguerite Dupire and others for the Ivory Coast, and Sara Berry for southwest Nigeria offer a mine of original information from which many other secondary accounts have been extracted.[10] Debates about details of social organization are by now fairly refined. Yet it could not be said that our knowledge and interpretations of the cocoa case are a closed book. The general summary that follows is not intended to be contentious, although some may find it so.[11]

The initiative in growing cocoa was from the beginning African, and it has remained so till today. European planters made several attempts to establish enterprises in emulation of the successes enjoyed by indigenous farmers, but with the exception of a few plantations in the Ivory Coast, they failed. The rise of the cocoa industry was never a case of subsistence agricultural producers turning some idle labor to use in growing cash crops for export. The bulk of early farmers were migrants, moving into virgin territory in order to plant a tree crop that would take several years to mature. They relied to some extent on family labor and no doubt grew their own food; but after some time much of the labor required during the farm-establishment phase came to be hired on a daily or seasonal basis in the market. Sometimes these farmers formed companies for the purpose of acquiring, clearing, and distributing land, before splitting up into individual enterprises.[12] Sometimes they were supported by kin from their home lineage who may have seen the enterprise as an extension of family property. One thing is sure: Getting into the cocoa business required money capital (mainly at first for buying land) and the flexibility to create new forms of social organization. Many of the people who were quick to enter cocoa farming were able to draw on profits made in the oil palm and rubber booms, even on slaving profits; others were traders or came from merchant families; and yet others had secure employment in professional occupations (Berry 1975; Adegboye and Abidogun 1973). After the initial development of the cocoa industry, it became normal for land to be bought on the installment plan, an arrangement that further removed the necessity of tying up scarce liquid capital in fixed assets.

At first the people who controlled access to forest lands were themselves content to draw some revenue from selling or leasing land to the immigrants (the precise legal standing of these contracts being debatable). But later they, too, became heavily involved in this lucrative industry: Indigenous chiefs and their families became prominent cocoa farmers. The forest population was swollen by migrants from the savannah, seeking employment on both a seasonal and a year-round basis (cocoa complements the savannah farming cycle in its pattern of peak labor demand). The problem of relations between citizens and strangers, particularly with respect to land rights, has since become especially severe in the cocoa areas; but the matter is too complex and particular to discuss at any length here.

From the very beginning, farmers sought more than one holding of land, and as the cocoa frontier moved further inland, successful farmers began to multiply their holdings, leaving established farms to the care of others while they moved on elsewhere to set up new ones. Not all cocoa profits were reinvested in new farms: It was not uncommon for cocoa farmers to reside in towns where they invested money in transport, housing, services, and trade or supported large families and groups of followers in the name of maintaining or pursuing occupancy of high political office. But those entrepreneurs who were serious about cocoa found their efforts absorbed by the establishment of new holdings – that part of the farm cycle which requires the greatest degree of managerial control and ingenuity. It was also the phase in which most labor was hired on a cash basis, being supplied casually by local inhabitants who had regular access to their own food supplies or by savannah migrants who might not have had such access.

The fact that many farm owners were overextended – either doing other things in towns or supervising the establishment of new farms (or from time to time both) – meant that established farms were left increasingly to the care of others. Resident farmers turned to a variety of sources for additional labor. One expedient was to employ kinsmen, but this practice often led to an unwanted blurring of notions of proprietorship. So a common alternative was to hire someone, usually a migrant from the north, on a basis known as *abusa* or *abusan*. This person was responsible for maintaining the farm in good condition and harvesting the crop. He could grow his own food and would also receive one-third of the cash crop. Crop-sharing time was one occasion on which farm owners could reliably be found at their farms. The holder of an *abusa* contract is still normally referred to in English as "caretaker" and is also frequently called a "laborer." Yet it is clear that as often as not he works under minimal supervision as a sharecropping tenant. One possible explanation for refusal to call him a tenant is that the farm owners themselves have ambiguous tenurial rights, which are politically sensitive in the local arena (Robertson 1979). By calling their tenants laborers, they avoid any connotation of a sublease that might conflict with customary land rights, even when the owner may believe that he bought his farm outright. It should be noted that *abusa* contracts are themselves considered heritable – a situation that is far from any conventional idea of wage labor.

In any case, this system has allowed a massive expansion of cocoa growing: It has led to a great influx of migrant laborers, some of whom have been able to graduate from short-term laboring to sharecropping and eventually farm ownership in their own right. Not all cocoa farmers are able to sustain the accumulative spiral described here; many remain at the level of smallholder family farms. But the bulk of cocoa exported is grown by a small percentage of the farmers, major landholders whose holdings may be scattered through a dozen lots or more. These entrepreneurs are rarely specialized in cocoa growing alone; they often reside away from the farms; and much of their income is derived from rent paid by tenants whose work is largely unsupervised. Given the conditions of farming in the forest interior, labor must be allowed to grow its own food. This situation, when combined with the absence of any major technological discontinuity between export-crop and food farming, prevents the establishment of truly capitalist production units, organized through the operation of advanced equipment by reliably supervised wage laborers.[13]

Cocoa farming in West Africa is still an industry contained within the matrix of indigenous family life. The development cycle of domestic groups combines with the life cycle of cocoa trees to generate a constant flux, a rhythm of growth and decay. A common pattern is for the older trees to be passed on to the care of younger family members (who may or may not take on formal *abusa* contracts with the principal owner), while new farms remain the direct concern of older, more prosperous members of the family. The point is that yield/work ratios decline as the trees age and reach zero at the time of replanting. To this natural dynamic may be added the periodic crises of crop disease and the cumulatively depressing effects of state intervention. The oldest centers of cocoa growing are only now, almost a century later, having to face the prospect of rehabilitating neglected farms. The West African rain forest is still occupied unevenly, and areas like Ghana and southern Nigeria have long been sustained by the alternative between moving on and preserving what has already been established. In the process it has been discovered that cocoa will not grow everywhere and that prime sites need to be improved and rehabilitated. There is not much usable land left unoccupied now.

If the same entrepreneurial drive that generated the cocoa industry in the first place is to be tapped for this next phase of rehabilitation and modernization, state controls and revenue extraction will obviously have to be relaxed. One major reason why the productive organization of the cocoa industry has remained so determinedly small scale and noncapitalist is that the state has skimmed off much of the wealth that it has produced, through monopsonistic marketing arrangements, thereby reducing incentives to reinvest in farm maintenance and improvement. Shortsightedness has not been a failing of the farmers alone (Bauer 1954; Beckman 1976, Fitch and Oppenheimer 1966).

Other export crops of the forest zone

Coffee has not been grown as successfully as cocoa in West Africa, for reasons that are historical as well as ecological, but coffee was a substantial part of the Ivory Coast's post–World War II export boom (Amin 1967). Fruits, such as pineapple and bananas, have been grown for export, especially in ex-French colonies like Guinea and the Ivory Coast. In both cases expatriate planting companies have been dominant, perhaps because of the importance of quality control in producing fruits for the world market. It should be noted that *Cannabis sativa* (known locally as "Indian hemp") grows well in West Africa and has found its way in significant quantities to Europe. Legalization of marijuana might open up a major legitimate market for the region; as things stand, West Africa is not yet Europe's Colombia.

The principal export crop of the forest zone before colonization was the kolanut, highly valued as a stimulant in the savannah and desert areas of the north. The kola trade is still fairly traditional in its marketing arrangements (A. Cohen 1966). Because it is not exported outside West Africa in large quantities, kola has been neglected by students of forest production. It could, however, be an important staple crop. It is collected from free-standing trees and therefore its production has usually been decentralized, traditionally being left to women and young men (Terray 1969). But control of kola distribution was an important part of the political economy of precolonial forest kingdoms, and it is a major source of merchant wealth today.

Timber is not a tree crop in the narrow sense of the word, but systematic harvesting of the tropical forest for its hardwoods is an extremely important part of the economy and ecology of this area, especially as this harvesting impinges on the lives of the indigenous people and on their agricultural practices. Timber is the forest's one wholly capital-intensive, foreign-owned industry (excluding the mines that are located in forest areas).[14] Vast concessions have been granted to international firms at various times, with the result that countries like Ghana, the Ivory Coast, and Liberia now derive substantial foreign-exchange earnings from timber exports. The firms are usually significant local employers; their huge trucks pound the narrow roads of remote areas; and their political impact is not negligible. In some cases indigenous populations have felt that their land reserves for shifting cultivation have been seriously encroached upon; and this has led to some difficulties with the state. But it should be said that these large, highly capitalized firms are capable, should they be given appropriate incentives, of managing the valuable timber resources of the forest over a long period (through extensive replanting, more effective haulage and milling equipment than is presently used, etc.) in ways that are not normally open to indigenous cultivators.

Food crops

The principal foodstuffs grown in the forest zone are root crops such as yams and cassava and tree crops such as plantain. As subsistence staples, these are high in bulk and low in nutritional value relative to the grains grown elsewhere in the region. But they have the considerable advantage that they can be grown and harvested in flexible quantities throughout the year at the cost of low inputs of human labor. Because food rots easily in the topical rain forest, its storage in the ground until it is needed makes a great deal of sense. Given the general abundance of land, this has meant that food production has received a relatively low emphasis in the forest: Much agricultural work there was traditionally the domain of women (Boserup 1970). The task of provisioning families has often been a light one; certainly the extensive farming techniques of a low-density forest population left much labor available for other tasks. Warfare and slave raiding absorbed the energies of many of the men during the immediate precolonial period. Some of these energies were later diverted into export-crop production, whereas women food farmers still had the time to develop the home marketing system. When large numbers of strangers came into the forest zone, as both planters and laborers, it was essential to their survival that they be easily able to grow their own food with a short time lag. The resulting mixture of subsistence and commercial farming may help to account for the fact that there never developed in the forest a rural proletariat dependent entirely on wages for its livelihood.

Forest commercial agriculture thus did not stimulate a market for basic food-stuffs, although rising incomes from export crops certainly accelerated the demand for imported foods like sugar, rice, tea, and sardines. Rapid urbanization in the coastal forest belt since the last world war has, however, generated a demand for locally grown foodstuffs, and many town dwellers have the food tastes of their home areas in the forest. The most labor-efficient crop is cassava, or manioc, and its flour (known sometimes as *gari*) is consumed in vast quantities by the city populations. This may have negative nutritional consequences. More promising is the rise of maize as a staple crop of the forest zone. Over the last few decades, commercial maize production in areas of secondary forest growth has become a major source of urban food supply, one that is from time to time threatened by the dumping of American corn under aid arrangements, but that nevertheless flourishes in the hinterlands of the major cities and beyond. Programs that began in the colonial period have been remarkably successful in raising yields through the introduction of new varieties of maize over the years. Yams and plantains are transported great distances, despite their bulk, to compete with home-grown and imported cereals in the urban food markets. Fruits and vegetables are also sold in bulk from the forest areas, not merely from market gardens in the suburbs, but through wholesale trading links reaching far into the villages of the countryside. Oranges, bananas, lemons, pineapples, peppers, tomatoes, onions, okra, eggplant – all these are big business. And of course there is palm wine and its distilled derivative, local gin, a major industry in much of the forest belt near large cities.

The forest should not, then, be thought of only as an export-crop producer: Its capacity to yield a variety of commercial foodstuffs has already been proven. Years of declining or stagnant real incomes from growing cocoa or oil palm have led to an increasing willingness to explore local food-growing possibilities. In areas where the task of clearing the ground has already been partially carried out, the idea of extensive maize production for urban markets has already begun to be realized. Elsewhere, scattered through the forest belt, attempts have been made to grow sugar, jute, and various industrial raw materials. Given the existing distribution of population and transport networks, it makes sense to explore the opportunities for commercial diversification that exist in the forest.

Savannah crops

The tropical forest does not end abruptly, nor does it reach the entire coastline of West Africa. As one moves north, the transition is protracted and gradual, so that cropping regimes may overlap considerably between the two main ecological zones. And for a large part of the coast north of Casamance and east of Accra, the savannah penetrates as far as the sea. There is, moreover, a long coastal strip between Casamance and the Ivory Coast in which rice is grown, often in swamps but also on cleared higher land: This "rice-growing belt" will be included in the present discussion. Nevertheless, the West African savannah generally means a landlocked dry place, whose often densely settled peoples make a precarious living from intensive cultivation of cereals during a short wet season. Even more distinctively, the savannah is a place where livestock may be raised and used as a source of food, manure, and traction. Water is the scarcest resource, especially as one approaches the fringes of the Sahara; hence the importance of rivers and, during this century, of irrigation works. Recently that part of the savannah zone known as the Sahel (a term that ought to include the northern parts of many of the coastal states if it refers to exposure to desiccation) has suffered from well-publicized ecological deterioration and attendant famine. It is widely touted that reckless agronomy induced by commercialization was partly responsible for the disastrous effects of this climatic shift. As a result, the savannah has had more than its fair share of attention during the past decade.[15]

Groundnuts

Groundnuts (or peanuts) stand to the savannah economy as oil palm once did to the forest. The difference is that groundnuts still dominate the exports of the Senegambia and northern Nigeria and to a lesser extent those of countries like Mali. Only Senegal – owing to its proximity to the French port Dakar – was heavily involved in the sale of groundnuts as a source of vegetable oil before the twentieth century. The other areas had to wait for colonial expansion and the railways. By the mid-1960s, when Paul Pélissier wrote his classic study, *Les paysans du Sénégal* (1966; see also Copans et al. 1972; Amin 1971), the country's commercial groundnut economy covered about half the cultivated surface; supplied at least three quarters of rural money incomes; contributed 23 percent of GNP and about 80 percent of exports; and, through oil-processing plants, constituted 42 percent of total industry. Here is a country made classically homogenous by its incorporation into the global economy as a supplier of raw materials. Instead of having generated a diverse home market, articulating several specialized economic zones, the whole national economy has become just one compartment of the world market. When Senegal's receipts from groundnuts declined after France withdrew preferential trading arrangements in the 1960s, the multiplier effect of the loss on the national economy was overwhelming. Yet before we begin to decry this gross example of a people's exploitation by metropolitan capitalism, it is worth keeping in mind that Senegal's population of 5 million has one of the highest per capita incomes in West Africa. And this is despite an average real growth rate (1960–76) of *minus* 0.4 percent compared with Nigeria's rate of 3.5 percent over the same period (World Bank 1977). The colonial groundnut economy made Senegal rich, by West African standards, before it came to haunt the postcolonial state.

The groundnut succeeded for two main reasons: It could be farmed using old techniques and equipment, and it did not require a peasant tradition or any special aptitude on the part of the grower. This last quality made it a suitable employment for the nonfarming elites whom the French deposed. The Senegambia was an area so attuned to the needs of the Atlantic slave trade that some large ethnic groups, of whom the Wolof were the most conspicuous, had been able to dispense with peasant farming more or less altogether (Curtin 1975). The traditional hierarchies of slaves, soldiers, chiefs, and hunters were undermined in the nineteenth century by an early French policy of colonization, by the abolition of slavery, and by loss of feudal taxes. Once they became sedentary, these peoples chose groundnuts as a source of money to shore up their shattered prestige and then set freed slaves to work growing them (Klein 1977). The population, which had been concentrated for defense purposes, could at this point spread out over the land. Before long this movement became part of a general process of Islamization that placed Muslim groups such as the Mourides at the forefront of commercial development (Cruise O'Brien 1971; Behrman 1967). Converts to this version of Islam worked under the direction of religious leaders and contributed a good share of their product to the common ends of the group, which were as much political as religious. As other groups became involved in the groundnut economy, commercialization often was synonymous, in Senegal's fluid agglomeration of "tribes," with Islamization, Mouridization, and Wolofization. Despite the emergence of the postcolonial state as an active agent in the rural economy (through cooperatives), these long-established interests still constitute a powerful force maintaining the social structure in a mold cast many decades ago.

The wastefulness of land use under the modern groundnut regime has been well documented (Pélissier 1966; Dumont 1972). The nonfarming groundnut growers could hardly be expected to know how to conserve the soil, nor could the *navetanes*, seasonal workers who were given land to cultivate during their "time off" from farming their employers' land; even groups with a reputation for good conservation techniques in their own traditional agriculture maximized the immediate return on their labor (at the expense of the land's long-term fertility) when they migrated to the groundnut belt. The litany of complaints by French authors includes the irrational use of cattle by peasants inured to their own religious traditions, specialization that reduced flexibility, slow and painful response to technical innovations, and so on. The colonial regime encouraged a trading policy that saw large sections of the indigenous population becoming heavily indebted owing to manipulation of the farmers' vulnerability and commercial malpractices (Suret-Canale 1971; Coquery-Vidrovitch 1975). Decolonization has rearranged some of the actors and redistributed some of the benefits, but the pattern of an indebted peasantry tied to a stagnant export industry is by now well fixed. Senegal's failure to branch away from dependence on groundnuts may be attributed to the very strength of the crop's initial success in the country, a success produced by the massive social changes that accompanied the transition from slavery to global industrialization in the nineteenth century.

The other major groundnut success took place in Hausaland just before World War I, when the railway was extended to Kano (Hogendorn 1970, 1978). The railway had been expected to bring cotton to the coast, but it was swamped with groundnuts, and the supply has continued at high levels ever since. What is interesting here is that colonial policy had nothing directly to do with the boom, nor did the British merchant houses have a direct effect. Rather, Hausa merchants, living in the major cities as dealers in cattle, kola, and local market items (A. Cohen 1965, 1966; cf. Hill 1966), had a preexisting network of agents spread throughout the villages, men who could buy up crops as futures against the promise of trading credit. Thus they could offer a special cloth as a lure to commit peasants in their favor. This was normal practice and the networks were of long standing, because the villagers had been part of the region's commodity economy for centuries. The merchants divined the suitability of groundnuts for their area and were sure that they could offer a good price. They were right. Despite continuing efforts by the colonial and postcolonial regimes to socialize the groundnuts trade on lines followed virtually everywhere else, the Hausa merchants – whose hierarchy is now reduced at the top to a mere handful – have kept their grasp on the trade. Very recently, an attempt by a would-be government monopsony to oust the merchants was thwarted by means of massive cash loans from a foreign bank that then found their way, via a horde of village agents, into the pockets of groundnut producers before they could be signed up by the government. This is one of the few cases where indigenous merchant capital has survived the onslaught of the twentieth century; and it is no accident that these merchants are part of an ethnic group with great political and military power in the Nigerian state.

Finally, some mention should be made of the many savannah peasantries that have taken up groundnuts, perhaps less wholeheartedly, outside the Senegambia and northern Nigeria. In Mali, for example, Bambara peasants have integrated groundnuts into their traditional millet regime with varied results. Some are specialized in groundnuts, whereas others grow millet surpluses for sale, thereby enhancing local exchange. Elsewhere cotton is the speciality. This gives Mali a flexibility that Senegal, for instance, does not possess. A recent study of the Ségou area (J. V. D. Lewis 1979*a*) shows that division of labor along these lines may penetrate as far as the village level. Thus some villages are made up of recently settled populations; they concentrate on commercial production of groundnuts, and their social structures are individuated and unstable. Other villages are longer established and maintain conservative institutions built on the retention of collective male labor for millet farming; commerce is restricted, despite the relatively high returns to groundnut sales, because these villagers feel that the long-term survival of their lineages depends on keeping the young men attached to traditional food farming. By this criterion, therefore, the groundnut is a symbol of individuation and social fragmentation, as well as, in some places, an agent of soil erosion and desertification. I suspect that the groundnut industry has had a bad press of late; a more balanced picture may emerge soon.

Cotton and industrial raw materials

Many parts of the savannah traditionally wove cloth spun from cotton. Kano was a major textiles center at the beginning of the nineteenth century, being surrounded by village-based industries much as Manchester was surrounded by the mill towns. Strips of cloth were easily portable and served as a form of currency in some areas. Here, then, is the one industrial raw material that was already produced in large quantities by savannah agriculture before the modern era; but that production was embedded in a complex division of labor, from which it could not easily be extracted as an export-oriented industry. Both the major colonial powers were excited about West Africa's prospects as an alternative to such cotton suppliers as the southern United States, India, Egypt, and, later, the Sudan.[16] Both allowed home-based textile interest groups to play a major role in the promotion and even subsidy of West African cotton growing. When the railway was built to link Kano and the Niger River, Englishmen could hardly wait for the deluge of cotton to arrive at their shores. Winston Churchill forecast that Kano would be the Mecca of Lancashire. Instead, Hausa farmers made such a killing from groundnuts that they bought more cloth, made locally of course, and diverted cotton from the export to the home market through the rise in demand.

In a nutshell, this has been the story of cotton in West Africa all along. The reasons are several. First, the price is low because of world competition and monopsonistic trading conditions. Second, unlike groundnuts, cotton cannot be eaten if the market is saturated (and gluts were a normal feature of the early colonial trade). Third, cotton involves more work and fits in less well with the savannah food-producing cycle. Fourth, cotton is less pleasant to handle. Fifth, there was already a textiles industry that fixed cotton production in a mold from which it was less likely to expand as an export crop. Sixth, the diseases that afflict cotton have not been successfully overcome in this part of the world. The combination of these considerations has meant that cotton, as the savannah's second major export staple, has never really emerged as a significant earner of foreign exchange for the West African region.

Cotton growing has been associated with some of the region's largest irrigation projects and in particular with the Office du Niger in Mali, a colonial scheme of considerable pretensions that never really worked as it was supposed to, but that survives today as a central element in the Malian government's plans for agriculture.[17] The office drew on migrant workers from Upper Volta (mostly Mossi) for a large part of its labor force, and there was a fair amount of conflict involved in that aspect of the operation (Hammond 1959). Moreover, the administration of the scheme was top-heavy with expatriates who often knew more about armies than farming. The inadequacies of the office have been well documented in a number of places (De Wilde 1967; Dumont 1966*a*). The fact remains that, even if the expense has been great, the nation of Mali now has a major capital resource with which to pursue an intensification strategy for the production of cotton and other crops. One success story involving intensive smallholder production of cotton using oxplows, rather than irrigation, is told for Gombe emirate in northern Nigeria (Tiffen 1975). Here a large number of farmers have been able to enrich themselves by adopting intermediate technology in the shape of oxen and iron plowshares, whereas there had previously been no tradition of either. It would seem that there is no drawback to cotton production in West Africa, as long as marketing conditions are favorable and farmers are not overburdened with administrative charges. Production of cotton for the regional home market ought to be a major source of income for the savannah in the years ahead.

Much of the savannah is too far from overseas and local markets to have been drawn into a wide range of staple exports of raw materials for manufacturing industries. Traditionally, tree products such as shea butter and kapok were exchanged, over relatively short distances, with the forest zone; and it is possible that improved transport and larger markets near at hand could stimulate a diversified commercial agriculture in the savannah. The most obvious industrial crop is tobacco, which is already grown both on large estates controlled by cigarette manufacturers and as a supplementary cash crop by peasant smallholders. Fibers, such as jute, can be grown under savannah conditions. Again, the main obstacle may be not production but externalities such as transport costs and the size of the market. Much more research is needed into the potential for production of industrial raw materials in the savannah areas.

Food crops

The traditional food staples of the savannah have been millets and sorghums, hardy cereals of which many varieties are indigenous to West Africa. In the transitional zone between forest and savannah, root crops (especially yams) are sometimes the major food crop. Much depends on aridity: The more humid southern edge of the savannah favors storage of food in the ground; but farther north cereals may safely be stored in granaries for years. Rice, discussed later in this section, has only recently been introduced into the savannah on a major scale. Maize grows under savannah conditions, and wheat has long been produced there. In addition to groundnuts, which are a food crop as well as a source of oil for export and home use, savannah farmers raise a number of legumes, often in intercropping patterns that are thought to fix the nitrates in the soil and thereby preserve its fertility. Although the savannah areas have to import all their fruits from the forest, they grow a great variety of vegetables – onions, tomatoes, peppers, okra, and others – often in quantities sufficient to justify sending them long distances to urban markets. When one adds the protein sources available in small livestock and fowls, it can be seen that the savannah subsistence regime offers a varied and nutritious diet, provided that food is available in sufficient amounts.

Unlike the forest dwellers, savannah farmers cannot afford to treat subsistence food production as a secondary consideration. They generally attend to their food needs first and to commodities afterward. Because food farming is crammed into a short and unpredictable wet season, they look to the rest of the year for income-generating activities. Often these activities involve migration to the south or pursuit of a craft specialism or trade. Where water supplies have been made available for dry-season irrigation (and there are thousands of small dams in the savannah), extremely high yields of tobacco, rice, tomatoes, and peppers can be won from small garden plots (Netting, Cleveland, and Stier 1978; Nukunya 1975). There are markets for millet, sorghum, and the like, and many farmers sell part of their subsistence crop as the year wears on, especially in the infamous "hungry season," when next year's crop is being prepared and no new food is yet ready for harvesting. But there has not evolved a regional market in these traditional foodstuffs, comparable to that in forest products. Partly this is because of distance from centers of demand (with Hausaland the permanent exception to this rule); partly it is because savannah cereals are still embedded in a logic of self-sufficient collective farming that is not easily adapted to the needs of large-scale commerce. Suffice it to say that the most innovative cereal crop, rice, is rapidly becoming in places the savannah's main food export.

Here, then, one is most likely to encounter the proposition that increased peasant cash-crop production means a reduction in food output and therefore a need for importing foodstuffs. The lack of subsistence flexibility in savannah agriculture, compared with the forest (where production schedules are shorter and more reliable), is a principal reason for the area's vulnerability to famine: A switch to nonconsumable cash crops, a sudden drop in the price (or a rise in food and energy prices, which amounts to the same thing), and before long starving northerners are lining up for food aid and medicines. It may be that decolonization encouraged many northerners to believe that the state would always assist them if the market mechanism failed. If so, their experiences in the last decade may have given them a powerful stimulus to retreat into a greater reliance on subsistence agriculture. Even then, they can hardly win, because without the benefit of modern markets, death from famine was probably higher in precolonial days than it is today. For large parts of the savannah, therefore, commercialization of agriculture is tied up with the chronic food problems afflicting the area. Part of the answer would seem to be to raise the productivity of farmers growing both export crops and foodstuffs for sale in the market; and that is where rice comes in.

As West Africa turned toward export agriculture, and as state-fed urbanization grew, the region began to import more and more food. Some of it was luxury foodstuffs (now necessities) like sugar, sardines, and tea. But the most important item has long been rice, usually bought from Burma, Thailand, and Indochina at a price lower than that at which comparable staples could be produced for the market at home. West Africa, a region of small farmers who, if they can do anything, ought to be able to produce food, is a food-deficit area. Import-substituting commercialization of food agriculture is the highest development priority facing West Africa now. And it can only be based on improved efficiency in agriculture, so that a more productive and possibly smaller rural labor force can profitably feed both itself and the burgeoning nonagricultural population at a cost compatible with world market prices. Without this improvement no other development initiative can succeed.

The growing food crisis has already stimulated various responses from West Africa's governments and producers. Food marketing has been improved; irrigation projects have been introduced with the sole aim of growing foodstuffs; import quotas have been placed on certain foods. A great deal of groundwork has been done, and a great deal of experimentation, both with crops and with social organization; so the region is not starting from scratch in this matter. It seems increasingly obvious that a major focus of this initiative is going to be on rice. There are a number of reasons. First, it is the cereal being imported already as the principal staple of urban diets. Second, farmers have been able to increase rice production substantially over the last two decades. Third, there is a large coastal belt – from the western Ivory Coast to Casamance – where rice is both indigenous and widely grown. Fourth, rice lends itself to irrigation and can therefore be grown in river valleys and inundated areas of the savannah during the dry season. Fifth, it has already proved amenable to mechanization in some areas. Sixth, it is the most nutritious cereal for bulk and therefore the most suitable for commercial distribution over long distances. With these advantages and several more, it seems likely that rice will be the central focus in any attempt to reduce West Africa's food deficit.[18]

Rice is grown in West Africa both as a dry, rain-fed crop on upland soils and as a swamp crop in bottomlands and artificially irrigated areas.[19] Extension teams from several countries, especially Taiwan, have sought to graft Asian methods of transplanting onto existing West African practices, which were usually much less labor intensive and produced lower yields for a given acreage. Not surprisingly, results were often disappointing; but some productivity gains were made on small-scale projects enjoying a high level of expert supervision. Larger schemes, usually involving government control, have introduced to the savannah the possibility of double-cropping; clearly this method increases the food production of peasants, but it may take their labor away from equally remunerative and necessary tasks, such as craft production or trade. There is evidence that smaller independent schemes (''perimeters'') in Senegal were so successful in augmenting incomes that the peasants had to struggle to avoid being taken over by a government anxious to monopolize the industry (Adams 1977*a*, *b*). The abuses normal in irrigation projects all over the world are present here, too (Wade 1975).

The organization of agricultural production

Excessive centralization of managerial control; corruption and patronage; over-charges for production inputs and subsequent indebtedness; unreliability of the water supply; neglect of ditches, ground leveling, and field maintenance; unfair advantages to richer farmers – all these charges and more have been made against government-controlled projects everywhere in the region. The result is that irrigation-fed rice agriculture has made extremely uncertain gains in the productivity of food farmers, often at tremendous cost to all concerned.

More promising developments include a remarkable commercial rice boom in northern Ghana.[20] It would be misleading to call this a case of free enterprise, because many of the participants were government officials and soldiers who used their positions to secure huge loans from publicly owned and foreign banks. But in a very short period during the early 1970s, these farmers introduced mecha-nized methods and wage labor to bottomland rice agriculture with impressive results. Leasing tracts of up to several thousand acres from local tribal authorities in an underpopulated savannah area, they bought fertilizer and machines, hired skilled and unskilled labor, and grew a great deal of rice. Within two years, Ghana, which had been importing vast quantities of rice annually, was able to export a small surplus. The story does not have a happy ending, however; for the country's chronic political instability and an associated collapse of the marketing mechanism meant that the rice boom suffered a relapse and became embroiled in a mess of smuggling, infighting, and corruption, with inevitable consequences for recorded output. But the lesson of this case is that, given both capital and a high level of effective demand, efficient methods can be introduced into rice agriculture with spectacular results. What is needed is a large number of similar social experiments, involving public and private agents, wet and dry land, and peasant and mechanized methods, all aimed at producing an agrarian revolution capable of meeting West Africa's commercial food needs.

Livestock

There are about 30 million head of cattle in West Africa today; small livestock are abundant in the savannah areas; and poultry and eggs are a significant industry near the major cities. Livestock production in the broadest sense is thus no minor aspect of the West African economies. But I have chosen to give the subject minor treatment for several reasons. First, the topic of this book is strictly commercial agriculture, and a narrow intepretation might limit that term to the cultivation of plants. Second, the livestock industry is mostly separated from agriculture, being organized by nomadic pastoralists of the dry savannah interior. And finally, a number of specialist studies focusing on Sahelian pastoralism have emerged of late (see, e.g., Shapiro 1979). So I will limit my discussion here to brief notes on a topic that has been treated much more thoroughly elsewhere.

The separation of agriculturalists and pastoralists is a historical process of specialization for which several possible explanations exist. But in West Africa there is a marked climatic shift from wet forest areas, where endemic trypanoso-miasis (carried by the tsetse fly) precludes livestock raising, to the edges of the Sahara, where animals survive more effectively than domesticated plants. There is an intermediate zone between these extremes, on the southern edge of which farmers combine livestock raising with grain cultivation (in an area with residual tsetse infestation), and in the northern parts of which sedentary agriculturalists live symbiotically with nomadic herders. This latter division of labor is the normal situation under which West Africa's livestock are kept. Allowing for these gradations, therefore, we may speak of a coastal/forest zone without animals and a savannah zone with specialist herders of animals. This regional division has long been the basis for a north–south trade of animals and animal by-products (mostly skins and hides) for tree crops such as kola and oil palm products. Even today the butchers of the south rely on Sahelian pastoralists for the bulk of their meat. This trade is strongly Islamic in its organization and goes back for centuries.

The cultural and social organization of livestock raising differs markedly between the pastoralists and those few agriculturalists who also keep cattle. For both, despite their ethnic distinctiveness, cattle are a form of stored wealth, to be used especially in acquiring wives for patrilineal descent groups. But for the pastoralists cattle are also the main source of food (milk, blood, meat), and their movements determine the whole rhythm of group life; whereas the farmers use cattle mainly for manure, do not rely on them for food, and do not allow herd management to intrude greatly into the farming cycle. An intermediate case is that in which sedentary agriculturalists acquire cattle as wealth objects but prefer to leave them with professional herders, rather than mix their own farming practices. It is also not uncommon for pastoralists to exchange milk and manure for grains and other agricultural products. The two groups have long interacted peacefully in most areas; the complementarity of their production schedules is a strong inducement to symbiotic co-existence. But conflicts do arise. Pastoralists have historically been able to organize themselves as an effective politico-military force; and more recently, in clashes over rights to water, sedentary agriculturalists have been able to exclude nomadic herders from water holes dug for the latter's benefit (Nicolas, Doumesche, and Mouche 1968). The ongoing saga of relation-ships between specialists in animals and specialists in plants will be a salient feature of West African development for a long time to come.

Although large animals have been present in the West African savannah for millennia, the region never made much use of them for traction – either for the oxplow (knowledge of which clearly antedated the modern era) or for the cart. Horses, donkeys, and possibly oxen were employed in transporting people and goods; but the main source of labor, in transport as in agriculture, was human. Why was the plow not a traditional feature of West African farming, especially in the densely settled savannah areas?[21] The answers to the question may be suggestive when applied to modern difficulties encountered in the intensification of agriculture. One answer may lie in the separation of herding and cultivation: If there were good ecological reasons for that division, oxen might be expensive or impossible to maintain on the farm. Another might be that the demand for labor in the farm cycle as a whole was not alleviated by quick ground preparation at the beginning. West African topsoils, often not deep, could easily be damaged by plowing, where the hoe would conserve them. Or, perhaps quite simply, there was no need to intensify agricultural production in the absence of an effective demand for more commodities. And most plausible of all, hoe agriculture may actually have involved less work for similar yields, or at least for yields not enough smaller to justify the cost of maintaining a plow and oxen. It must be considered, in addition, that a plow is not just an instrument, like a radio or a bicycle, but part of a complex form of social organization, involving craft specialists and animal control, which is not easily introduced into an established pattern of production. Variations in the success of recent efforts to diffuse the plow throughout the West African savannah depend, as we will see shortly, on the degree to which large animals were already incorporated into village economy.

These considerations did not deter colonial agronomists from entering vigor-ously into the search for ways of introducing "mixed farming" – herding and cultivation – to West African agriculture.[22] Preoccupied with improving yields from a limited land area and anxious to transform indigenous farmers into model European peasants, they were convinced that the answer lay in an integration of cattle raising and crop production. (Experiments in green manuring were carried out for tsetse-infested areas; but West Africans appear not to have relished forking edible crops back into the ground while they were still uncertain of their own food supply [Faulkner and Mackie 1933].) The idea of mixed farming is to grow fodder for cattle whose manure is concentrated and whose traction power is used for plowing and transport within a scientifically designed crop-rotation system. It is an approach tailored to an agriculture built around land scarcity and intensive peasant labor, neither of which conditions existed in West Africa; for these and other reasons, mixed farming has not been a great success there, either in the colonial era or since.

Delgado's 1979 work in Upper Volta shows why cultivators may avoid mixed farming even when research station results are very positive. (In this case oxplowing was shown experimentally to reduce labor needs and raise yields; see also Sleeper 1978) The most important point is that agriculture and pastoralism were here traditionally separated. Cultivators found the introduction of cattle both time-consuming and socially very difficult. They were concerned about liability for crop damage in the absence of defined cattle pathways; they did not have the time to supervise the cattle; they resented having to feed them; and they were forced to build fences to protect their own crops. Labor released by plowing at one bottleneck meant an even worse bottleneck at later phases of the crop cycle, such as weeding and harvesting. All of these difficulties provide compelling evidence why mixed farming would be likely to fail in this part of Upper Volta.

But the oxplow has been successfully introduced in several parts of the West African savannah, such as northeast Ghana and Gombe in northern Nigeria. Perhaps a crucial variable is whether cattle were traditionally integrated into agriculture. Where they were, most of the objections no longer hold: Children are socialized to look after cattle; the problem of dealing with crop damage is obviated by established pathways and modes of conflict resolution; no new construction has to take place. Above all, the farmers are used to handling and, literally, living with cattle. The matter of whether plows are laborsaving devices then becomes an empirical question. There are some clay bottomlands under water in the dry season that can be turned over only by plows. In areas where the method has taken root, bullock plow teams are hired out by specialist operators; and even if the land area under cultivation is limited by labor shortages later in the crop cycle, it still pays to have twenty days hoeing done in one day by a plow team, if the price is acceptable and if the farmer has something better to do than bend his back in the sun all day. There is, of course, the problem of long-term soil damage by plowing; but that can be resolved only by extensive research.

The main competitor with the oxplow is, of course, the tractor. West Africa has imported many tractors, and they have not always been used wisely. Nor have they always been the best tractors: Ghana once received tractors that had been designed for snow plowing and could not operate in temperatures above seventy degrees Fahrenheit! The energy crisis highlights even further the region's vulnerability if it were to become dependent on petroleum-based agriculture. For this reason, some have advocated greater use of the oxplow as an intermediate step, preferable to mechanized agriculture as such.[23] But as the preceding discussion suggests, there may be very few places in West Africa where mixed farming can be successfully developed on the basis of a prior tradition of integration between animal husbandry and agriculture. And tractors require no more skills to maintain them than do cattle, possibly fewer. Obstacles to plowing in general, such as uneven or partially cleared ground and unconsolidated plots, apply just as much to oxen as to tractors. There is no need for West Africans to move through a European peasant phase: It is clear that most of them would rather have nothing to do directly with beasts of burden, and it would be wrong to suppose that they have any particular aptitude or need for the oxplow.

Sheep, goats, and, more recently, pigs have been a prominent feature of savannah agriculture. They can be seen today wandering around the less-regulated housing areas of the region's cities. Domestic animals like dogs are sometimes raised for meat, but not in significant numbers. Horses are expensive to keep and have low resistance to disease; they are tokens of a faded savannah aristocracy. Donkeys have recently been making a comeback against replacement by trucks.[24] Chickens, guinea fowls, ducks, and other poultry are a major feature of West African diets; and eggs are a rapidly growing peri-urban industry. There is not much to be said about the organization of these parts of the livestock industry, because they are mostly contained within small-scale production units whose main task is something else. I believe that pig-raising has a big future in West Africa, especially as an adjunct to peasant farming. Much of the savannah is Muslim, but those parts which are not – and their population is considerable – are well suited to pig farming, as recent developments in a number of areas testify. Small livestock and fowls are the most democratic branches of agriculture, because they allow each individual the hope of some small accumulation by his or her own efforts. For this reason and because they often provide a cheaper source of meat protein than beef, it would be a good idea to divert some of the attention going toward the cattle industry in the direction of these minor branches of animal husbandry.

Not all that is useful in an animal is meat; and the by-products constitute a varied proportion of the value contained in any animal. The by-products of cattle, for example, account for 30 percent of the value in Western capitalist economies, whereas pig by-products are only 10 percent.[25] Leather and hides have long been a staple export of the West African savannah. Much of the leather that we knew as "Morocco" was sent to the Maghreb from northern Nigeria, and the trans-Saharan leather trade continues to this day. I am not aware of the extent to which animal by-products are used for making soap, fats, glues, and so on in West Africa, either traditionally or in modern factories. Certainly it would be a gross mistake to neglect this valuable source of industrial raw materials.

Planning for the livestock industry is thus very much a regional affair, because its whole raison d'être lies in the articulation of dry north and wet south within a single social division of labor. Since the 1972–3 drought, Sahelian suppliers to the coastal cities have lost part of the West African market to major world meat producers such as Argentina. This has led to considerable criticism of herding and marketing practices in the indigenous livestock industry; but recent studies have emphasized the rationality of producer responses and the prospects for growth within the existing framework (Shapiro 1979a). No doubt some would like to see the savannah emptied of its low-productivity farmers and bankrupt pastoralists, so that it could be occupied by a vast corporate ranching enterprise that would transform West Africa into the next Argentina. Be that as it may, indigenous herders will be controlling the livestock supply during the 1980s.

The rural division of labor as a whole

In touching on various aspects of the livestock industry, I have raised what is perhaps the central issue in any discussion of Third World agriculture, namely, the multiplicity of occupations and tasks within which farming is normally embedded. Obviously a study of commercial agriculture cannot spend a great deal of time discussing nonagricultural employment, but it is necessary to introduce a few considerations that might otherwise be forgotten, to the detriment of our overall comprehension.

It is a common fault of analytical reasoning to reduce complexities to a single component. This is especially true of economics, whose mathematical logic cannot deal with all the variables that enter into the everyday lives of West African farmers. Thus all of their work is summarized as "agriculture," perhaps the most important single branch. And agriculture is reduced to the production of important crops. These crops are reduced to some quantitative measure of their economic value. And that measure is used in calculations of the "marginal productivity of labor" in rural areas. There is nothing wrong with this process of analytical abstraction, as long as the methodological limitations are honestly recognized. But it is dangerous if it leads policy makers to suppose that farming is practically separable from all the other tasks that West Africans routinely perform or that they have some reliable indicator of "income" or "welfare." The point is that, in advanced market economies, enterprises are structurally differentiated according to their specialized commitment to produce a limited range of commodities. Labor is specialized in the same way, and money wages are used to acquire the bulk of commodities that consumers do not produce themselves. West African villagers, on the other hand, farm for only a limited time in the year; and they do a great many other things, both during the farming season and, especially, after it. They build and repair their own houses; they prepare food and fetch water, fuel, and other domestic supplies; they spin, weave, and sew clothing; they keep animals, slaughter them, and tan their hides; they make tools, pots, baskets, furniture, and ornaments; they generate remedies for their ills; they run their own systems of conflict resolution and work hard to keep a variety of spiritual agents appeased. The list of tasks given at the beginning of this chapter as the sexual division of labor among the Hausa is more varied than most, but it is not a bad guide to the range of work commonly united within single West African villages.

Of course, not everyone does everything. First and foremost, men and women combine so that married couples carry on most of the tasks that fall within the sphere of household economy. Combinations of relatives or neighbors will help each other in farming, construction, and other heavy jobs. Children will be drawn in to take care of crops, animals, and smaller children. The range of artisan crafts may be taken up by all individuals of a given sex or by all members of a given village or, more commonly, by individuals according to their skill and taste. As we have seen, in the Sudanic zone casted workers are frequently encountered in such occupations as blacksmith, carpenter, and weaver. The more developed the division of labor, the more likely it is that specialists will dominate manufacturing and service occupations. But in general, West African villagers live in a matrix of diffuse activities all linked together. They import and export commodities to some degree, and they are internally differentiated by property, kinship, and occupational emphasis; but they are never so specialized that it would be possible to identify production units in which all the major branches of the economy are not in some way inextricably linked.

The interesting question is how far commercialization of agriculture has affected the traditional integration of the rural division of labor. This is hard to answer, partly because so little systematic research has been brought to bear on the matter, partly because of the tremendous variety of particular rural economies; but a rough sketch is possible. I will look briefly at primary activities, such as farming, animal husbandry, and fishing; distribution, including storage, marketing, and transport of primary commodities; manufacturing and processing industries; and the tertiary services sector.

We have already seen that attempts to integrate livestock raising and farming have not been very successful where they were traditionally separated; there is not much evidence, however, that commercialization has accentuated any tendency to divide these two great branches of rural economy. Market expansion has encouraged a degree of regional specialization according to comparative advantage in types of crop, small livestock, or poultry. This means that diversity may have been reduced, and rural areas have begun to exchange primary products with each other (Lawson 1971*b*). The products of hunting and fishing are of variable significance. Ivory is still exported from the more remote forest areas, as are monkey skins and other fast-diminishing staples of the hunter's trade. Fisheries are a topic beyond the scope of this book. The overall tendency, then, has been toward a reduction in the diversity of primary activities within particular rural areas, along with a vast expansion of commodity circulation in the region as a whole.

Distribution has obviously increased its significance as part of this commercialization of the farming economy. The chains linking producer and consumer permit a large number of wholesale and retail intermediaries. The system of storage, marketing, and transportation is, however, extremely open and competitive in those commodities aimed at domestic markets. Export cash crops are, as we have seen, subject to monopsonistic controls imposed by the government. Although specialized merchants occupy most of the stages between rural production and urban consumption, farmers always have the option (which they often take up during the dry season) of bypassing several links in the chain by taking their goods directly to an urban market (Hart 1970). Most farmers are thus practiced traders on their own account. In some cases the traditional sexual division of labor, which made women responsible for local marketing, has been extended to include wholesale participation in long-distance trade involving village products. In many areas, members of ethnic groups specialized in trading (Lebanese, Yoruba, Dioula) have now come to reside in villages or small towns with a view to purchasing farm products. And the appointees of government marketing boards and cooperatives are also now a permanent feature of rural life. There can be little doubt, therefore, that commercialization of agriculture has both widened the scope for farmers' participation in the marketing of their products and increased their dependency in distribution on specialized agents often far removed from the village setting.

The most contentious area involves the effects of commerce on village industries. In many respects consumption patterns have been changed, so that imported commodities have replaced traditional artifacts, or new tastes have ousted old needs. It is by no means the case that plastic buckets and cheap cotton cloth have eliminated indigenous pottery or textiles. Indeed, some local industries have expanded under the stimulus of improved transport and markets.[26] Obviously, handcrafted goods are now often luxuries where once they were necessities, but rising prosperity has democratized demand for even the most aristocratic of artifacts. The main point is that easily movable goods are now produced for regional markets or imported via regional centers. Some manufacturing and processing still takes place near the final place of consumption, that is, the village – preparation of food and drink, corn milling, blacksmithing, heavy carpentry, construction and finishing of houses. Other industries remain rural, even though their markets are mostly urban – basketry, traditional weaving and tailoring, distilling of alcohol, palm oil soap manufacture, pottery, hand carving of art objects, and the like. They remain in the village because the raw materials are near at hand or because the costs of production are lower than in cities and craft production can easily be combined with other household tasks. The traditional manufacturing sector thus retains considerable vitality in West Africa, but it is far less restricted to the local demand structure than it once was, and it is subject to competitive pressures emanating from the world market. It has two great strengths: Its transport costs are low, and its overhead costs are absorbed by subsistence farming and numerous related activities. Its weakness is the persistently low productivity of labor, a weakness that is only partly offset by local preferences for homemade goods over machine-made imports. Certainly the sphere of manufactures has shown here its historical reputation for bringing the greatest degree of specialization and differentiation to peasant economy, but it is not yet separated from that economy.

The services sector of village life has changed beyond recognition in the modern era. Diviners, mallams, and spirit-possession cults remain and guarantee specialists a useful supplementary income. But today the needs of villagers embrace schools, health services, roads, clean water supplies, radios, motor transport, agricultural extension services, law courts, and a host of tangible and intangible by-products of modern civilization. If villagers are unlucky, these needs are not always met; but in any case consumption requirements of this kind cannot possibly be met within the limits of village economy. So, quite apart from producing commodity exports, West African villagers are now heavily committed to patterns of expenditure that go beyond anything known to the traditional division of labor. Not only must the funds and materials essential to modern social services be imported, but so too must the personnel, whose skills are not generated by traditional methods of socialization. Accordingly, villages are likely to have outsiders living in them as teachers, mechanics, clerks, and orderlies. This tendency toward occupational differentiation is accentuated where villages lie within easy commuting distance of a town – and there are now many areas of West Africa where the majority of villages are so situated. This means that village residents may work elsewhere, and in these cases the inevitable nexus of rural life and farming is decisively broken. Improved transport, expansion of markets, and urbanization in the countryside are eroding the isolation and homogeneity of village economy, and the rural division of labor is evolving toward a higher degree of complexity and specialization; but nonetheless, the nexus that binds many peasants into a household economy linking agriculture to numerous other tasks in an integrated annual cycle is still the predominant reality in rural West Africa. It should not, however, be assumed to exist before it has been empirically verified, because change is both rapid and uneven.

After a long period in which developers focused only on a few agricultural export crops, the last decade has seen an emergent interest in programs that address the central fact of rural economies, namely, the integration of such farming activities into a fairly localized, self-reproducing division of labor. There have been a few studies of rural industries, notably those conducted by Michigan State University researchers in Sierra Leone and Upper Volta (Byerlee et al. 1977). Into this neglected field has been inserted the concept of ''integrated rural development.'' The basic idea of this approach is that, instead of concentrating agricultural production into a few export crops and allowing the population to pile up in one or two metropolitan cities, an attempt should be made to stimulate intersectoral linkages at some fairly local level of the economy, such as a district of villages possibly serviced by a small town. It is hoped that these island economies will combine at a higher level of the urban hierarchy; but the emphasis is on building dynamic growth in the national economy from the bottom up rather than from the top (usually a single center of government) down. Obviously, this approach involves some decentralization of administrative and economic functions. In addition to cash-crop production, integrated programs might promote a training scheme for blacksmiths (to service plow agriculture), a campaign against water-borne disease, a road improvement scheme to facilitate marketing of crops, and so on. This invariably involves closer coordination of administrative services supplied by different government departments. Ostensibly, some of the bottlenecks and confusions caused by concentration on a single objective to the exclusion of all others would be avoided; but it is one thing to envisage a rounded approach to development – with all the backward and forward linkages considered – and quite another to bring the idea home as a working package. Nevertheless, as a supplement to existing perspectives on development, integrated rural development is a major contribution; and if it draws attention toward rural urbanization, off-farm employment, and the rural division of labor, some progress will have been made.

I will discuss the policy options introduced by the idea of integrated rural development in Chapter 7. I have read no accounts of its application to West Africa, but I understand that the World Bank favors such an approach, at least as a partial solution to the region's development dilemmas. It may be mentioned in passing that the regional fund of the European Economic Community recently began allocating large sums to similar ends in outlying areas such as Scotland. And the main emphasis of my recommendations on regional development and urbanization for the Papua New Guinea Development Strategies Mission was consistent with an integrated rural development approach (World Bank 1973).

4

The state in agricultural development

Under the domination of a patrimonial regime only certain kinds of capitalism are able to develop: capitalist trading; capitalist tax farming, lease and sale of offices; capitalist provision of supplies for the state and the financing of wars; under certain circumstances, capitalist plantations and other colonial enterprises.

Max Weber, *Economy and Society* (1978: I, 240)

The revenue crisis in West Africa

The development of agriculture in West Africa is illuminated greatly if we consider the principal local actors to be the rulers of preindustrial states. The economies of these states are backward, rural, undercapitalized, and decentralized. The problem faced by all modern regimes – precolonial, colonial, and postcolonial – has been how to extract from a largely agricultural population a reliable income sufficient to support the regime's expenditure needs. In this matter the successor states are somewhat at a disadvantage, because their standing in the world depends on levels and kinds of spending that were unthinkable twenty years ago, and they are not able to take some of the shortcuts in revenue collection that were available to their predecessors. Much has been made of outside pressure emanating from the centers of world capitalism; but I would like to consider here the internal pressures and options that have pushed all the successor states to base their strategies for independent government on control of agriculture in one form or another.

Although the revenue problem is significant enough in itself, it is subordinate to the sheer necessity of establishing and maintaining a viable system of rule. Westerners have long forgotten (if they ever knew) the drawn-out process whereby their own inchoate systems of government coalesced into the nation-states whose framework made modern capitalism possible (Anderson 1974). Colonialism, while preserving some elements of indigenous political organization and destroying others, did not establish in West Africa more than the rudimentary elements of a modern state; the balkanized successor regimes, which were given their freedom without much of a struggle (Guinea Bissau excepted), thus did not take

83

over an established apparatus geared to the needs of independent nationhood. Often lacking a coherent vision of the relationship between political goals and economic realities, these regimes have subsequently staggered from one crisis to the next. Above all, preoccupation with shoring up the state by any available economic means has dominated development policy in the last two decades. The needs of commercial agriculture, in particular, have been subordinated to those of state formation. Much that would be incomprehensible when judged by abstract standards of economic efficiency or public welfare seems rational when seen in terms of the institutional and material requirements of a fledgeling state. Nor should this priority be automatically condemned as an example of corrupt self-interest on the part of undemocratic ruling elites. For without viable states in West Africa, little can be achieved in the way of securing the self-determination and material advancement of the region's peoples.

All discussions of the state in modern West Africa must begin with the colonial period. Colonialism was the temporary imposition by foreign powers of a system of formal rule. As such it differed from the informal hegemony exercised by these same powers both before and since. It has been argued that this initiative was taken in order to advance the control exercised by Britain, France, and the others over international commodity flows (A. G. Hopkins 1973), and there can be little doubt that the colonial regimes did see their task as the supervision of a new economic order linking West Africa with the metropolitan countries. But it can also be argued, especially in the case of the AOF, that colonial government was primarily concerned with maintaining its own rule as such, rather than with promoting any specifically economic purpose (see, e.g., Amin 1971).

The establishment of colonial rule did pose revenue problems, as did the extravagant transport infrastructure plans that were floated at the beginning of this century. These expenses were met by donation or coercion of largely unpaid labor services from Africans and by capital generated from local firms operating in the colony. On the whole, colonial budgets settled down to a very unambitious level (especially when the depression set in) and remained broadly in line with revenues from government taxation of the import–export sector (see Kaye 1972). If there had been any thought of paying for colonialism out of the profits of expatriate businesses, the weakness of the mining companies and failures of plantation initiatives soon put an end to it. After World War II, controls over the indigenous export trade became elaborated as marketing boards or stabilization funds, state mercantile monopsonies that accumulated large reserves, used in Britain's case to pay off part of the war debt (Bauer 1954).

French ambitions in the sphere of government, when allied to a generally weaker revenue basis in the indigenous market economy (which, except in Senegal, was more poorly developed than the rich coastal and riverine economies selectively occupied by the British), led their colonial regimes into rather harsh forms of surplus extraction: heavy tribute, corvée labor, and the like (Suret-Canale 1971). This drove many Africans to take themselves and their goods into neighboring British territories where prices were higher and conditions more lenient. The British felt confirmed in the wisdom of their "hands-off" policies, and the gap between the economies of the two West Africas was thereby accentuated.

In neither case was the politico-legal structure of colonial government dominated by a class of foreign capitalist producers. Merchants and administrators were the dominant forces in policy formulation. Thus attempts by mining companies to legislate for land alienation and repressive labor laws in the Gold Coast, for example, were effectively resisted by a coalition that included many local citizens (R. Thomas 1973). For, throughout West Africa, there were substantial indigenous political interests left more or less undisturbed by colonial conquest – the Fulani ruling class in northern Nigeria, much of Ashanti, the Mourides of Senegal, and so on.

West Africa's relative good fortune in arriving at the colonization stage later than some parts of the Caribbean and south Asia, for example, may also have contributed to the indigenous population's ability to retain control over its land. British administrators in particular were mindful of the "lesson of the West Indies":

There exist in the tropical world today many industries and many territories which once supported a flourishing planter aristocracy and an army of laborers. Today many of the planters are bankrupt and many of the laborers are unemployed. And there is no living society which can reabsorb and heal the classes which have suffered economic hurt. A plantation system is not a society; it is an economic agglomeration created for the pursuit of profit. It substitutes itself for those primitive societies which in sickness and health maintain their local members. What happens when profit fails? [Hancock 1941:199]

This sentiment, expressed after a decade of global misery at the beginning of World War II, gives retrospective justification for the refusal of early colonial governments to expose West Africans to "the soapboilers of the world" (an obvious reference to W. H. Lever and his search for oil palm plantations). Whatever the reason, one cannot quarrel with McPhee's description of the result: "West African land policy . . . has as its goal apparently the confirmation of the natives in their possession of the land, the *erection* of a virtual system of peasant proprietorship and conversely the exclusion of foreign capitalist planters" (1971:196; emphasis added).

This meant that the political economy of colonialism in West Africa was a preindustrial combination of small indigenous producers (supplemented by labor migrants from the savannah interior) and large foreign trading firms with a tendency toward monopoly. Perhaps, if we define the state as a public power held against the people, it could be said that it was more in evidence in the AOF, where force was routinely deployed as a sanction by government.[1] As an administrative apparatus, to be staffed eventually by natives, the colonial state advanced further in the British territories. But the point to be emphasized here is that in neither case were the institutions of government developed to serve the needs of an advanced sector of foreign capitalist production, such as existed in Kenya or Zambia, for example. Decolonization left the successor regimes with a problem that is still poorly understood – namely, how to build modern nation-states when the bulk of production remains in the hands of small farmers.

When they succeeded to power, the new governments and their advisers paid attention to politics and ideology – democratic mobilization of the people through parties and bureaucratic administration by an elite cadre of graduates from institutions of higher education (see, e.g., Foster and Zolberg 1971). But the results were disastrous, because expenditure rapidly outstripped government income in the absence of any successful strategy for national production. At first the budgetary gap was made good by taking colonial trading monopsonies to new extremes (milking more out the marketing boards), although this increased transfer of earnings from rural export-crop producers to the state always carried the danger of killing the goose that laid the golden eggs. A further way in which temporary budget deficits were covered was through foreign aid – the whole gamut from expensive suppliers' credits to long-term, low-interest loans from the competing superpowers. These monies were often misspent, and before long debt servicing came to absorb a massive share of each annual budget.

By the mid-1960s things were beginning to go sadly wrong for many countries. Senegal had to absorb a drastic reduction in groundnut prices that had previously been supported by France, and Ghana had already entered a prolonged slump from which it has not yet recovered. All over West Africa, corruption and high living had become normal for the ruling class; pretentions to democracy had been almost universally abandoned; the military was coming to power in one country after another. Benevolent patriarchs (''despots'' to their enemies) presided over economic booms in the Ivory Coast and Liberia. Nigeria began to tear itself apart. The Sahelian states tottered on the brink of drought and famine. About this time, those states such as Mali and Ghana which had acquired an independent monetary system discovered the option of expanding the internal public debt and financing expenditure through inflation. In order to do this they had to close their economies from the world as best they could: Countries that remained tied to the franc, the pound, or the dollar enjoyed no such freedom. Consequently, when Ghana reached treble-digit inflation in the 1970s, it was an island of economic instability surrounded by franc-zone countries offering hard currency to Ghanaians willing to reverse the pattern of international flows that characterized the colonial period.

If West Africa was in trouble during the 1960s when the world economy was booming, the last decade has, with one or two exceptions, proved to be even worse. The main exception, of course, is Nigeria, with its oil wealth and a large national economy now recovering strongly from the effects of civil war and military rule. The rest have been damaged almost beyond repair by the energy price inflation since 1973, and stagnation in the world trading economy has offered little scope for the traditional commodity exports. Insolvency is thus a chronic feature of present-day West African political economy. The poorest countries have been awarded the pauper's relief of a cancellation of international debts. But teams of experts from the IMF and World Bank now offer drastic remedies for development, in place of the lenient aid programs that were available in the euphoric days soon after independence.

The alternatives facing the new states are starkly limited. They may finance themselves through domestic inflation and external indebtedness. Otherwise, they must either tax those of their citizens who make money or set about making it themselves. Taxation of salaried incomes is easy enough, but the yield is inadequate, because the number of salary earners is absolutely small, many of them are government employees to start with, and collection methods are inefficient. Direct taxation of nonsalaried incomes, that is, of earnings made outside the bureaucratized corporate zone of public and private sector employment, is impossible: The hordes of petty producers and small traders who dominate West African economies numerically are left to go free. Taxation of capital is often restricted under the terms by which new foreign enterprises are established, and capital-intensive enterprises are in any case few and far between.

Revenues from oil and valuable minerals are the exception to this rule, but very few West African nations derive substantial benefits from such sources. Duties and sales taxes are a significant source of revenue. As we have seen, these are the most reliable when levied on commodities that cross the borders controlled by the state; taxation of internal trade is much more difficult; and as the commercial economy advances, the home market increases in relative significance, leaving the state with a proportionately lower yield from cash transactions. (Soldiers and police, flagging down lorries on the region's highways, make a levy from the internal trade, but it is doubtful whether much of this finds its way into the coffers of the state.) Evasion of duties is, of course, universal. Marketing monopsonies for export produce can generate massive smuggling rates, especially if the government becomes too greedy. Indeed, weak control over their boundaries is a chronic problem for West African states, as we will see later in this chapter.

Embezzlement at the top, black markets, smuggling, and tax evasion – all of these reflect the weakness of the state apparatus and reduce effective government revenues. Public funds dwindle while high-ranking officials squirrel away fortunes. The revenue structure is certainly corrupt and ineffective. But the base is inherently inadequate. An expanded state with modern needs has to be financed by the bulk of its own people, who are in this case low-productivity agrarian workers only partially committed to the market economy. The military absorbs vast sums of foreign exchange on hardware that can realistically be deployed only on its own people (or on itself). Needs for health, education, and urban infrastructure grow along with the population. Debts pile up in memory of past wastefulness. Cuts in expenditure after the postindependence spree are inevitable, and the rural areas will obviously be forced to bear the brunt of these. But these reductions can never be enough. How can a modern state support itself under these conditions? It cannot raid its own peasants and make them into slaves, as did West Africa's precolonial rulers. And brutality, of the kind that its colonial predecessors routinely indulged in, now attracts the full glare of international publicity.

One possibility is for the state to enter production as an entrepreneur in its own right, or at the very least to enter production in such a way as to ensure that a reliable surplus of commodities and/or money flows into its own treasury. This, I would suggest, is the appropriate framework within which to judge recent West African approaches to agriculture.

The state as agrarian entrepreneur

The West African states have extended their roles in varying degrees to include those of merchant monopsonist, merchant monopolist, banker, and rentier landlord. But the temptation to enter production directly as an entrepreneur is overwhelming. The first step is to grab as much as possible of profitable mining and similar extractive industries on the state's territory. Many West African governments have tried this, with some limited success. Nigeria, Sierra Leone, Liberia, Niger, and Mauritania are among those countries which derive significant revenues from shares or royalties in extractive enterprises. The next step is to seek to be an industrialist, usually through importing machinery and personnel from an established foreign firm. These businesses fail more often than not and usually constitute a most unreliable source of government revenue. In any case, the passion for industrialization of the 1950s and 1960s has now subsided.[2] That leaves only one remaining option: state penetration into agricultural production. In fact, given the agrarian bias of the economy, this is the only viable option facing West Africa's neophyte states. It is the most obvious one, because it has been encountered in much the same form by every preindustrial state in history.

The prime need is for large, capital-intensive projects that substantially raise the productivity of a labor force effectively controlled by the state apparatus. Nothing can beat a big irrigation scheme from this point of view. The requirements for capital planning, water control, and managerial supervision make government central to such schemes. Irrigated rice is excellent now that the home market is in food deficit. The fields can be worked by a variety of combinations of independent tenant and hired labor. The main point is that output per man must be relatively high, and a liquid surplus should be made available to the government. In practice, it has been found that output is frequently low on West African irrigation projects – owing to bad management, poor labor commitment, and technical deficiencies (Lele 1975; Dumont 1966a). And costs frequently outrun the yield because of excessive reliance on top-heavy administration, costly machinery, expensive buildings, and the like. It is largely a problem of discipline on both sides:[3] The managers have too easy a life, and the workers have the option of leaving if they do not like the job. These observations suggest that the social and material conditions that would compel a laborer to work like an Asian peasant, up to his knees in paddy water on behalf of some remote authority, do not yet exist in West Africa. There is not much precedent here for oriental despotism based on an irrigation bureaucracy, but that does not stop many governments from trying.

Given, then, that large projects of this kind invariably fail to be as efficient as smallholder production schemes under the control of peasants, we might ask why governments persist in allocating scarce development funds to such ends. The answer is that they are not primarily concerned with technical efficiency and gross economic output: They want revenue for the public exchequer and the opportunities for personal enrichment that go with it. Even when a large-scale project yields less than smaller-scale options, if that yield is a reliable source of state income, it may be counted as a plus. Even if there is no net revenue at all, the scheme is a rural manifestation of the state's active presence; it keeps a loyal cadre of followers employed; and it always holds out the prospect of greater efficiency in the future. The time scale is especially important: Large white elephants like the Office du Niger inner-delta-irrigation scheme took on a new perspective when they offered a secure basis for agriculture during the Sahelian drought. This explanation at least is superior to the condescending suggestion that African politicians prefer large-scale projects because they are more "prestigious."

Irrigation is one instance in which the government controls the basic conditions of production and seeks to derive economic benefit from such control. Another case in which the state controls the conditions of production and much else is land colonization or resettlement schemes.[4] The almost universal failure of such projects in Africa has been much documented and analyzed in the literature (De Wilde 1967; Frankel 1938). Again, despite protestations that these schemes are designed in pursuit of general welfare goals, they are meant to supply the government with revenue, after it has satisfied its creditors. At the very least, they expand the organization of the state. Failure is inevitable because the schemes cannot satisfy the needs of a labor force ripped out of its subsistence environment at a cost commensurate with the expected rake-off from production. So people leave, productivity remains low, and another project miscarries.

The third alternative is for the government to act as an agrarian capitalist, setting up state farms. The problem here is that wage labor behaves like the salaried employees of government elsewhere.[5] Anyone who has seen a rural road gang in action will appreciate how ruinous to farm output such an approach to work might be. The bureaucratic echelons have generally been inept, and state farms, too, have not succeeded in West Africa. Collaboration between foreign corporations and West African governments to establish large-scale agricultural estates (e.g., an operation producing sugar for a local mill) have not been frequent, but the prospects for success may be greater.

If the government cannot derive substantial revenues from direct control over

89

the basic conditions of production, the next best thing is to organize farmers in such a way that they must pass over a portion of their product to the government. These initiatives are normally called "cooperatives," but West Africans know what they are: a source of employment for government workers, a nexus of indebtedness to rival the Lebanese storekeeper, a means of transferring part of their labor to the state, a monopoly distributor who sells dear and buys cheap, a political payoff to the government's supporters, and a general agent of the state in the local community of farmers. Independently successful attempts at coopera-tion, like the small irrigation projects of the Senegal River Delta (Adams 1977*a*, *b*) will be incorporated, if at all possible, into the state's machinery. The issue of state-sponsored cooperatives is dealt with more fully in the next section.

The question of sales receipts, rents, and taxes levied directly from the land is touched on in the next section. The general problem, one that Max Weber (1978) recognized as characteristic of the political economy of preindustrial societies (see also Bendix 1960), is this: When a state's revenues must come from the land because most of the people live and produce there, it is extremely difficult to maintain centralized political control. Feudalism, or decentralized government, arises out of the central bureaucracy's failure to overcome shortages of liquid funds and transport/communications difficulties in a rural economy geared toward local self-sufficiency. To some extent, modern means of communication and transport may counteract this tendency in West Africa. But it remains the case that supervising a dispersed hierarchy of government (especially a taxation bureaucracy) and acting effectively to promote commodity production in the countryside are gigantic problems for the new states. Leakage of revenue is both inevitable and substantial. Under these circumstances it is understandable that many West African governments have invested in large, visible, concentrated projects in agriculture. No doubt they will continue to do so.

The important point is that modern states (even more than their precursors in history) depend on *liquid* revenues for the execution of their functions; that is, they need cash and commodities. In any West African country the state is the principal entrepreneur promoting the growth of commodity economy, because without more things of value in circulation, it cannot survive. Separation of the state and the market economy may have been a well-publicized feature of nineteenth-century capitalist polities, but such a separation is far from having yet appeared in West Africa.

Institutions of state control in the countryside

It follows from the analysis just presented that much of the state's activities in the countryside should be considered less as efforts aimed at economic improvement of agriculture than as embryonic institutions of government control in areas where there is often little historical precedent for state organization. In this section I examine these new institutions under five loose headings.

The state in agricultural development

Land law and the chiefs

One of the major tasks of modern government in West Africa has been to reorganize customary law concerning land tenure so that land may be bought and sold, may stand as collateral for bank loans, and may offer security for anyone investing significant capital sums in its improvement. The state has also needed to requisition land for its own development purposes and from time to time has considered deriving revenues in the form of taxes and rents assessed directly on the land and its occupants. It is a truism that West African societies were not traditionally organized within fixed territorial boundaries: Corporate groups and political hierarchies linked people to foci of collective adhesion that had a very indefinite spatial referent. (An exception would be crowded populations living in territories defined by earth shrines [Fortes 1945; Rattray 1932].) Buffer zones between groups left large tracts of empty land. Any attempt to draw up fixed boundaries and titles under these circumstances was bound to run into difficulties, and the early colonial authorities, in making such attempts, did just that.

In the coastal/forest areas their attempts to acquire all unoccupied lands for the state were strongly resisted and eventually dropped. Thereafter they discovered that the colonial "mandate" included preservation of indigenous rights of occupation and property. In some of the savannah areas, where densely populated states were already established, colonization took a different tack. In northern Nigeria, for example, Frederick Lugard was able to apply principles learned in India, claiming for the state all rights over the land as conqueror of the previous rulers; and this was apparently accepted. But when his successor tried to nationalize the land, he found that even in Hausaland such a task would be virtually impossible, for it involved registration of exclusive title to surveyed land. The bureaucratic and technical dimensions of this task were enormous, not to mention the disputes likely to arise from the process.[6]

Over the years various regimes have asserted the state's eminent domain over the land; and they have usually been able to requisition land without making substantial payment to the occupiers. But implementation of controls over land tenure has been slow, uneven, and laborious. One example that comes close to the model of Asiatic despotism is the system of land transactions that has emerged in Liberia. Here anyone wishing to acquire land from another must go through several layers of government before having the deal confirmed or denied by the president himself, who is the only arbiter in land sales (Liebenow 1969). More generally, however, a confusing and conflict-ridden situation has been loosely organized through the erection of a dual system of "traditional" chiefs and law courts.

A hierarchy of native chiefs, capable of commanding the allegiance of people on the ground, was essential to the orderly expansion of both colonial rule and export agriculture. The construction of this hierarchy sometimes rested on an existing political basis, but as often as not it was an invention (Rattray 1932).

91

Once it was in place, however, the state reinforced all actions of the chiefs as legitimate expressions of traditional custom. Few postcolonial goverments have seen fit to do without this prop to their rule, and by now the innovations of seventy years ago have taken on the aura of permanence. The chiefs were responsible for allocating rights of land use to newcomers. These rights could be inherited, but continued occupation of the land did not rest on any firm legal title, and the chiefs were not always reliable. Disputes over land abounded. Indeed, export agriculture generated so great a degree of litigiousness that the main beneficiaries of development were often said to be lawyers, not farmers (see, e.g., Hancock 1941; McPhee 1971). All these law cases did little to clarify the confusion of West African land tenure, which remains stranded somewhere between the ''gentile constitution'' (L. H. Morgan's 1877 term for the law of lineage-based societies) and fee simple. The point is that it takes more than a government fiat to establish modern property law in a West African country; a long-drawn-out process of increased population density, commodity production, political consolidation, legal innovation, and bureaucratic administration is a historical prerequisite for successful achievement of such a system of law. Nor can ''traditional'' institutions offer an unequivocal guide to indigenous land-tenure practices, because so much of these are a product of colonial innovations drawing on imperial experiences elsewhere. Land reform is not a significant issue in West Africa, but reform of the land law is; it will take some doing.

Chiefs have also been essential to the supply of labor for government administration, public works, and expatriate businesses. They persuaded or coerced their subjects to make roads, built huts, man irrigation schemes, and work on mines or plantations. The power of their sanction lay in their ability to make life difficult for dissidents in the only place they knew as home. The recruitment of workers to Firestone's plantations in Liberia offers a stark example of the use of chiefs in this way, as does recruitment to the Office du Niger irrigation scheme (Clower et al. 1966; Hammond 1959). Today the chiefs may still be found supplying gangs of young men to work on the farms of prominent officials and smoothing access of capitalist farmers to local land and labor supplies. As long as the state is ill formed and property relations are as yet in a no-man's-land between customary and contract law, a network of chiefs will remain central to the expansion of commercial agriculture. This is not just a colonial issue: It is a matter of the relationship between an underdeveloped state and economic transformation.

Marketing monopsonies

The entry of the state into agriculture as a merchant with monopsonistic powers has been treated at some length in the West African literature, notably by Bauer (1954). Today it is a universal feature of distribution in the new states, one, moreover, that enhances the government's interest in promoting export crops at the expense of foodstuffs, because they derive such a high proportion of their income from the enterprise (and from control over the import of foodstuffs?). The original idea was to stabilize the incomes of farmers by withholding a portion of the world price at times of boom and using the resulting fund to support prices during a slump. Farmers' incomes have become stabilized all right, permanently at a level well below the lowest price to which international markets ever sink. The fund has become a regular part of government finances. It has been suggested that farmers at first responded positively to a guaranteed price, preferring as they did a steady, low income to wildly fluctuating earnings. But as time has worn on, production has been depressed by a system that pays farmers little more than their production costs and plows a vast amount of cash into general government expenditures.

The existence of a state marketing board still leaves plenty of scope for private-sector merchants between the point of production and the government's buyers. This intermediate gray zone is marked by a variety of practices, ranging from state-licensed Lebanese firms to an army of petty traders. It is also an area rife with complaints about abuses on the part of licensed agents, usually involving credit advances, withholding of payments, and the like. But any kind of market competition at the ground level is better than total administration of distribution by a government body manned by personnel selected for their political allegiance and usefulness to the party. Under those circumstances there are no checks whatsoever on abuse of the producers, and corruption is notorious at all levels in the hierarchy.[7]

Where there is a strongly entrenched mercantile network, it is not always easy for the state to acquire a monopsony. Examples of persistence in the face of state pressures would be the Lebanese merchants in much of the rice-growing belt on the western coast and the Hausa merchants who control northern Nigeria's groundnut crop. Moreover, the opportunity to smuggle crops abroad and get higher prices for them is a partial check on state aggrandisement at the expense of farmers. The relative prosperity of the Ivory Coast, Liberia, and the Gambia has been assisted by the smuggling of goods out of Ghana, Guinea, Sierra Leone, and Senegal, where state monopsony (and potential bankruptcy) is deeply entrenched.

Large-scale agricultural projects

Numerous excellent studies have pointed out the organizational and economic deficiencies of large schemes in Africa. De Wilde (1967), Chambers (1969), and Lele (1975) have all offered the same points of criticism, without apparently shifting development practice a great deal. Frankel (1938) made similar criticisms of colonial schemes shortly before World War II, and Dumont's advocacy of the peasant against capital-intensive, mechanized agriculture has been a persistent feature of the last two decades.[8] I agree with this overwhelming consensus that large projects do not work and do waste money. The tales of farmers obliged to pay too much for fertilizer they do not need and sinking into a morass of indebtedness are wholly credible; and they evoke a standard ethical response from all humanitarians. But I have already explained why in some sense all these criticisms miss the mark.

When an institution persists in the face of its own glaring inefficiency, we need to ask what interests it *is* serving. Clearly, if the aim were to increase output by the most efficient means available, or even if it were to bring advances in social welfare to rural peoples, this method of satisfying such aims would not be chosen over and over again. I stressed earlier that one dominant interest served by these large projects is the strengthening of state rule in the countryside, with the corollary that government revenues may accrue as a result. There is, of course, an external dimension too: Large projects generate a great deal of work for foreign businesses and professionals. In the case of the Office du Niger, it seems to have been part of a retirement plan for noncommissioned officers from the French army (Suret-Canale 1971; Magasa 1978). Today, international construction firms and development bureaucracies vie for shares of what usually turn out to be very lucrative projects for all concerned (including government officials) – lucrative, that is, for everyone save the farmers whose work on the land can never possibly generate a surplus large enough to pay for all these overheads.

The problem of graft or "skimming off," whereby those in power take a percentage of the funds disbursed in projects employing foreign contractors, is impossible to quantify. Occasionally a reformist junta will expose the corruption of its predecessors, only to be exposed itself after the next coup. These revelations, and the confessions of international corporations at congressional hearings, constitute our main sources on this important issue. Because such payments are illegal, they cannot be written in as overhead expenses and therefore must come out of monies earmarked for the essential workings of the projects involved. The economic viability of large-scale schemes is thus undermined doubly by this larcenous conspiracy, whose persistence makes a mockery of the pretense that their aim is the improvement of the livelihood of the masses. Small projects using local initiatives and perhaps a diesel pump for the irrigation ditches do not generate anything like the same payoffs to foreign capital, to development consultants, and to indigenous public officials. No doubt that, too, is one reason why unviable large-scale projects continue to be unveiled in West Africa.

There is another possible reason, more speculative and less culpable. Large-scale water projects are a powerful symbol both of mastery over nature and of social progress in the western United States. So too are they in West Africa. Dams such as the hydroelectric scheme at the Volta River in Ghana, creating the longest man-made lake in the world (over 300 miles) and generating enough electricity for the industrialization of three countries, are a majestic symbol of West Africans' determination to conquer an environment that has dominated them in all previous history. The sheer daring of shutting off a major river in order to irrigate millions of acres of dry land is breathtaking – and difficult to turn down in favor of some cheap, small-scale peasant scheme. The new states of West Africa need opportunities to prove to themselves, to their subjects, and to the world that they, too, can harness the forces of nature on a grand scale. And who is to say that the region's peoples will not benefit in the long run from their persistence in these efforts? Obviously, there are obstacles in the way of successful large-scale projects; perhaps, instead of pointing out over and over what they do wrong, we might find out what they do right and build on that. At the moment they stand as a shining beacon to the new states, offering a way to bring at least some parts of the economy up to the scale and level of operations at which the government itself (but little else in West African society) is constituted.

Cooperatives and public credit

Where farmers are working for themselves as small-scale producers, the best the state can hope for is to organize them into cooperatives. Such cooperatives may or may not be linked to marketing monopsonies, and they may also be attached to government land reclamation and irrigation schemes. More often they are based on existing "traditional" corporate organization, such as a village or a more extensive territorially defined group. These cooperatives give the government an opportunity to enter village economy in several capacities: as monopoly distributor of farm inputs, such as machinery for hire, fertilizer, seed, or tools; as principal source of local credit, that is, as a banker who also sells to and buys from the peasants; and, of course, as a political agent in village life, distributing patronage to followers and offering employment on the basis of party support. Usually cooperatives coexist with other arms of government, like the normal agricultural extension services, and this makes for some confusion at the local level. If some international agency gets involved, the high turnover of expatriates merely adds to the confusion.

This picture of West African cooperatives is perhaps unnecessarily one-sided. There have been occasions on which villagers made use of these institutions to their own benefit. In one case, for example, cooperatives were adapted to the marketing needs of members in ways that went beyond the role the government had designed for them (see, e.g., Guyer 1980). More typical of the literature, however, is this account of cooperative rice schemes and their failures:

They watch the tractors get stuck on the land because they were ordered too small for the size of trees and the strength of roots; the delay in planting until after the rains have started; the birds eating more than half of the crop; the rice becoming overripe and dropping out of the ears; and rodents and insects devouring much of what remains . . . As long as wage and salary earners continue to constitute the bulk of the membership, there is not the slightest chance for co-operative development. [Seibel and Massing 1974:135–6]

Most West Africans are by now quite jaded in their attitude toward cooperatives, and they invest as little of their energies in them as they can afford to without offending government officials. This pattern need not have become the prevailing one: Cooperation was once a vital part of customary work organization; and anyone who has worked in a team knows that it is more enjoyable than doing the work alone. Quite apart from that consideration, there are economies of scale in distribution that any farmer can see might be worthwhile if he benefited from them. But all too often the priorities of cooperative movements focus on anything but improving the payoff to producers – on elaborate buildings, uneconomical machinery, government profits, rhetoric without substance. Farmers often end up being expected to work harder for a smaller return, and when they withdraw their efforts, they are accused of being stubborn and reactionary (Clower et al. 1966:33).

I can illustrate the point with an example drawn from northern Ghana, the area in which I did fieldwork.[9] In the early 1960s, soon after independence, Ghana acquired a jute-bag-making factory, an important input to the cocoa industry that would reduce imports from East Pakistan. The country needed more raw hemp to be grown locally, and it was suggested that rural members of parliament might urge their constituents to do something about it. The local MP in this instance returned from Accra inspired with loyalty to his president, and explained to the local people that they would grow hemp for this great new national enterprise. A cooperative was formed to farm in the dry season, using wet bottomlands. Response from a number of villages was remarkably good: Some forty men presented themselves for work at the appointed time. They were told that profits from final sales would be shared equally among them and that they would receive some advance payment to tide them over the period until harvest. No money ever arrived, but most of the cooperative's workers stuck with the hemp crop until it was ready. Unfortunately, many other MPs had been just as inspired, and the bag factory was inundated with more raw material than it could use. Worse, northeast Ghana was as far away from the factory as it is possible to be, and supplies were bought from near at hand. So the hemp was left to rot and local wiseacres said, ''I told you so.'' Months later the cooperative's members received five shillings each (less than one dollar) for all their dry-season labor. Needless to say, the next time a cooperative scheme was put forward, even though it was a much better planned affair, it fell on deaf ears.

The point of this cautionary tale is to suggest that, although West Africans have no intrinsic objection to cooperatives, especially if they offer them tangible benefits, they are quick to withdraw active support from initiatives that let them down or simply exploit them. Often cooperatives are a means of incorporating independent economic activities into a framework of government control; and when they are routinized, they often become an instrument of almost absolute state power in the village. The state even manages to become a usurer under these circumstances, offering credit that draws ever more peasants into a nexus of indebtedness built on buying cheap and selling dear. In order to defend the rights of their members successfully, cooperatives need to be built on an existing base of some measure of collective autonomy such as is generally lacking in the West African countryside. There are, of course, no traditional antecedents for modern cooperatives.

Education, extension, animation rurale

The state is above all else an educator these days. What follows is a brief note on the massive topic of the educational, practical, and ideological impact of the state on the countryside.[10] Educational advancement is the principal means of entering the state apparatus itself; and opportunities for bureaucratic employment and for higher education do not lie in the countryside. State schools, focusing on literacy and numeracy, have thus been seen as a powerful stimulus to rural emigration. But to focus on rural education is to confuse cause with effect: The cause of the exodus from West Africa's villages is the concentration of economic benefits elsewhere, first in the export-crop areas and now increasingly in towns formed around the growth of the state. Nor is it the case that rural illiterates are less likely to migrate than their better-educated peers, for the towns offer them, too, the best chance of improving themselves (Hart 1974). The young must seek their fortunes abroad regardless of education, as long as farmers are overtaxed and city dwellers are subsidized. Moreover, suggestions that rural school curricula should be modified to help peasants' children learn what peasants ought to do is callous and elitist. Literacy is the best defense a peasant has against rapacious bureaucracy: To deny him the chance of being able to read is to condemn him to second-class citizenship. The argument most often heard against this rejection of dual schooling standards is that school replaces customary socialization and leaves children fit for nothing but hanging around employment exchanges. But this is to take a very short-term view. A literate rural labor force may not be essential to an agrarian revolution, but under modern conditions it probably is essential to the kind of social development that alone can provide a secure basis for one; and there should be no turning back now just because of a temporary disjunction between rates of education and the structure of employment opportunities.

The new states of West Africa have seen the necessity of leading the mass of their citizens to the threshold of modern rationality; their colonial predecessors never did, preferring rather to limit education to the perceived needs of likely employers. But the drive to literacy is a huge social movement that pushes the state forward rather than the other way round. Whatever else they may aspire to, the governments of West Africa are compelled to continue to provide formal schooling to as many people as possible.

Advice to farmers thus takes place largely outside the school curriculum. The history of extension services in West Africa is uneven. Some would say that the great export-crop innovations took root and flourished here without or even despite the advice of European agricultural experts (Green and Hymer 1966). Others stress the importance of research stations, zoological gardens, and similar institutions brought to the region by colonial regimes (Faulkner and Mackie 1933). The truth is probably somewhere in between. Certainly the evidence suggests that cocoa was developed through independent African experimentation and perhaps contrary to expert advice. In other instances, it can be shown repeatedly that peasant rationality is superior to the extension officers' knowledge, so that these officers spend their time finding out what the peasants know already. In the postcolonial period extension officers often have been poorly trained and have known or cared little for local circumstances. Often extension efforts have been organized around selling one way of doing things to the farmers, though it is obvious that a more rounded approach is usually needed. But such a description is a caricature. The colonial period saw the groundwork laid for the development of a scientific agriculture. Many sound innovations originated from the experimental stations, and extension work emanating from this source has often been excellent, if sometimes slow and unglamorous. The colonial heritage of universities and research institutions is a proud one, and it has been carried over into the present period. One of West Africa's great assets is its trained manpower: Given political and financial support, agricultural scientists and extension workers can continue to play a major part in the region's coming agrarian revolution. There are major questions to be resolved concerning tropical soils and the effects of plowing, for example. Research and extension are thus an essential branch of state involvement in agriculture, and they are not likely to be carried out except under public auspices.

The notion of *animation rurale* or rural revitalization has been very much a preoccupation of the French and their successors (see Goussault 1970). The basic idea is to select likely individuals for preferential treatment and instruction concerning a limited number of policy goals in agriculture; these persons are then let loose on the other members of their communities as agents of diffusion or, one might say, as inspirations to others. The danger is that more effort is put into whipping up enthusiasm than into efficient organization or solid economic benefits. There have been some positive results, however. The term *animation rurale* avoids the presumptive neutrality of ''agricultural extension,'' and indeed, technical advice offered under its rubric is normally inseparable from the blatantly ideological activity of political parties in the countryside. Quite often, the specific work of promoting a given rural program is undertaken by international firms (usually French) contracting with the government to supply both personnel and program design. It is unfortunate that expatriates have to be employed in such tasks at this time in West African history, but indigenous participation has often been disastrous too.

There is, of course, much more to public administration in rural areas than I have touched on here. The important point is to see the overall pattern as it affects agricultural development. On the one hand, there is a surface commitment of the new states to an active program of improvement in the countryside. Some of these initiatives are directly beneficial to the targets of government intervention (education and extension, for example). But most, on the other hand, are not; the underlying function that they serve seems to be only that of strengthening the state's presence in its rural territories (cooperatives, projects, marketing boards, land regulations, etc). The result is a growing discrepancy between self-aggrandizing public institutions and a depressed agriculture whose depression is exacerbated by the weight of state rule. The easy response is to cry "hands off!" and denigrate the state's present role. But much of what is going on is necessary to the evolution in the long run of a high-productivity economy. What would the economies of the West be without the period of absolutist monarchy (or Weber's patrimonial regimes)? More to the point, how could West Africa develop without an enhanced role for the state? The problem is obviously loaded with contradictions. I will merely conclude with the observation that foreigners whose priority is to free West African peasants from these new forms of bondage play into the hands of international forces that would benefit from keeping the region's political development at its present stage of fragmentation and backwardness.

The imbalance of state expenditures

Most of the emphasis so far has lain on the sources of revenue and organizational requirements of the new states. But the overall pattern of their expenditures also has a significant impact on agriculture that we must consider briefly.

Table 3 shows some recent figures on central government expenditure patterns for those West African countries whose fiscal accounts were available to the World Bank.[11] Drawing strong inferences from these results is a hazardous enterprise, but the evidence they present reveals both considerable homogeneity in some respects and marked diversity in others. All figures are percentages of total expenditure, unmodified by any consideration of the absolute amounts involved. Of course, anything the Nigerian government does is more significant for West Africa as a regional population than is the combined expenditure of all the rest put together. (To take an extreme case, the Gambia spent in 1977 one three-hundredth [0.3 percent] of Nigeria's outlays.)

The pattern is markedly different from the norm in the case of the Ivory Coast and Nigeria. The Ivory Coast is the highest spender by far on defense, health, and social services, which together account for over three-fifths of its budget. (Mali, the next highest on these items combined, spends only 30 percent; five countries spend less than 20 percent). Ivorian priorities seem to center on security, with the lowest degree of emphasis on education, agriculture, and economic services in general. Nigeria's spending on services to industry and transport/communications is astonishingly high by regional standards – almost two-fifths, when the majority spend less than a tenth. This is especially true of industry, which gets 15 percent in Nigeria, whereas all the rest devote 2 percent or less to this sector. (The Gambia and, to a lesser extent, Ghana, Liberia, and Niger devote significant sums to nonagricultural economic services as a whole.) Nigeria spends a good

Table 3. Government expenditure by function in eleven West African countries (in percentages)

The richer countries	Ivory Coast	Nigeria	Liberia	Senegal	Ghana	Togo
Defense	38.9[a]	17.9[a]	4.5	10.3	3.8	9.6
Education	8.3	9.6	14.8[a]	18.2[a]	19.5[a]	13.7[a]
Health	4.2	2.2	7.9[a]	5.7	7.4	5.8
Social security & welfare	17.8[a]	1.1	1.5	8.4[a]	7.9[a]	5.4
Housing & community affairs	0.9	3.2	2.0	1.7	—	0.1
Economic services	9.5	45.8	20.1	13.3	21.3	15.9
Agriculture	0.7	2.6	8.1[a]	5.0	9.0[a]	6.4
Industry	1.3	15.2[a]	0.7	—	2.4	2.0
Utilities	0.9	2.2	0.1	1.0	0.1	0.1
Transport & comm.	1.7	23.3[a]	9.3[a]	0.9	8.6[a]	6.9
Others	4.8	2.5	2.0	6.4	1.2	0.6
Other	24.9	20.2	49.1	44.2	40.0	33.0

The poorer countries	The Gambia	Sierra Leone	Niger	Upper Volta	Mali
Defense	—	3.9	6.1	11.0[a]	19.3[a]
Education	10.0	15.2[a]	23.3[a]	19.7[a]	25.0[a]
Health	9.1[a]	5.2	6.0	7.8[a]	6.9
Social security & welfare	3.0	1.7	2.9	6.2	4.1
Housing & community affairs	0.5	0.6	0.1	0.1	—
Economic services	39.6	23.7	19.6	14.8	13.3
Agriculture	15.6[a]	7.8[a]	6.6	7.0	8.4[a]
Industry	—	0.9	2.2	0.2	0.1
Utilities	2.6	1.5	1.7	0.1	0.3
Transport & comm.	19.6[a]	5.0	8.5[a]	4.4	4.0
Others	1.8	8.6	0.6	3.0	0.4
Other	37.8	30.1	46.1	40.5	32.9

[a] High priority.
Source: World Bank (1980).

deal on defense, but even at the height of the civil war, this outlay did not reach the proportion that is current in the Ivory Coast. Like the Ivory Coast, Nigeria spends little on agriculture and education, but it also spends the least on health and social services. The two richest economies, therefore, differ immensely from the rest in their pattern of public expenditures, particularly in their relative neglect of education and willingness to spend huge amounts on arms. Where one is embarked on a course of state-promoted industrial expansion and infrastructure development, the other shores up its social security system in several ways.

The state in agricultural development

The largest single category in eight of the eleven cases is education. It is notable that three poor Sahelian countries (Mali, Niger, and Upper Volta) head the list in this respect, with expenditures of 20–25 percent. Apart from the upper echelon in defense expenditures (Ivory Coast, Mali, Nigeria), three countries – Upper Volta, Ghana, and Togo – spend around 10 percent on arms and the rest much less. With the exception of the Ivory Coast at 23 percent, seven countries spend 11–17 percent on health and social services, and the three others less than 10 percent. The Gambia gives unusual support to agriculture (16 percent); the rest, apart from Nigeria and the Ivory Coast, spend 5–9 percent. The combined expenditure on services to industry, utilities, and transport/communications (in which Nigeria and the Gambia were abnormal, with totals of 41 percent and 22 percent, respectively) was on the average slightly higher than that for agriculture, with five countries falling in the range 7–12 percent and four below 5 percent. Nevertheless, government spending in the agricultural sector is far from insignificant.

These observations are marred by the size of the unidentified portions of government expenditures (the last two lines of Table 3), which vary from under 30 percent (Ivory Coast and Nigeria) to over 50 percent (Liberia and Senegal). A good deal of this expenditure will be transfers to other parts of the government and debt financing. Despite this handicap, however, the figures give a rough order of magnitude to our general discussion of state expenditures. After debt-servicing charges (now mercifully curtailed for some of the poorer countries), the main expenditures of West African states are on social services, especially education. Thus six countries currently spend about one-third of their budgets on this "social" sector (Ghana, Senegal, Mali, Upper Volta, Niger, and the Ivory Coast), four spend about a quarter (Liberia, Togo, the Gambia, and Sierra Leone), and Nigeria spends only a sixth. In some countries military expenditures are high, but rarely does the army use up as much as the systems of schools and hospitals.

I have already commented on the effects of this educational policy on agriculture; almost as significant is the cumulative impact of public health measures. Full utilization of productive lands in the region depends on sanitizing the infested river valleys and coastal swamps. Major international programs exist now to combat onchocerciasis and bilharzia, the main water-borne diseases. If they are successful and the states can stand the strain of all the additional infrastructure expenditures necessary to make these reclaimed lands inhabitable, the prospects for agriculture are good.

This task is one far beyond the present fiscal limits of West African states: It is a laborious process, full of frustration and setbacks. In other parts of the world, great civilizations of past millennia tamed the river valleys; West Africa has waited until the present century. It is a process that the colonial powers refused to tackle head on; the successor states cannot avoid it if they are responsive to the needs of the region's peoples in a world that sets ever-escalating standards for modern civilization. These processes of transformation through state-led initiatives are heroic when judged by West Africa's recent history. We should recognize this heroism before exposing the manifest flaws in the ways in which development programs are operationalized in the region.

In practice, urban areas, areas with concentrations of population, get a higher standard of services from the state than remote rural areas (Gugler and Flanagan 1978). It is not uncommon to see 40 percent of government expenditures being spent on that tenth or so of the population which lives in the biggest cities. Roads are more frequent there and better maintained; schools and hospitals are larger and more advanced; intricate water and sewage systems are heavily subsidized. Prices of urban consumer goods, including imported foodstuffs, are subsidized out of funds acquired from rural agricultural exports. The quality of the administration in the countryside is inferior, because there are fewer checks on bad bureaucrats. The result is that rural areas appear to be neglected in comparison to the main towns, and the flow of people out of agriculture remains unabated. It lies within the power of governments to change this pattern by emphasizing the quality of services and infrastructure in the countryside. Some of the schemes referred to in the last section of Chapter 3 go some way in this direction in the name of integrated rural development.

It is possible that more West African governments will see their future stability as lying increasingly in capital investment and current expenditure programs favoring rural areas. But a shift of this sort is almost unthinkable under existing political conditions. The short-term preoccupation of West Africa's rulers is with the immediate danger of an unsatisfied urban mob.[12] Long-term planning for the countryside is entirely incompatible with the siege mentality of politicians, soldiers, and bureaucrats who are literally counting the days before they lose their power (and lives) in the face of growing anger over hunger, inflation, ostentatious wealth, and civic indifference. This anger means most in the major cities; it commands constant attention and the award of temporary palliatives, one after the other, all adding up to the relative impoverishment of farmers. The necessity of reversing this emphasis is an urgent message of my book; but a political prescription for achieving a dedicated government capable of withstanding all the institutional pressures that militate against success in this aim must await historical circumstances that do not yet obtain in West Africa. We will take up this issue again in Chapter 7.

The problem of order

Every state must establish a boundary defining itself as a territorial entity and must maintain control within that boundary, so that, from its own point of view, there is a higher degree of order inside than outside. Boundaries are relatively new to West Africa, given the weak definition of territorial states before the modern period; indeed, movement of people and goods then knew no frontier from Angola to Cape Verde and Lake Chad. Imperialism in the nineteenth century did not alter this state of affairs. But colonization by four Western powers implied drawing up boundaries on a map, and that is indeed what was done in the decades preceding World War I. Colonial boundaries were not seriously intended to stop the continuous flow of people and goods across them. They defined rights of exploitation and control of a given territory, but in view of the often arbitrary nature of the lines drawn and the small numbers of armed forces available, the authorities could not expect to patrol the borders very effectively.

These new lines on the map did, however, have a decisive impact on settlement patterns, movements, and production. Pélissier (1966) suggests that Africans may have moved to settle near a convenient border. The advantages were great: Variations in the weight of taxation and forced labor between neighboring regimes could be dealt with by hopping across the border to the more lenient side; if prices were controlled, smuggling allowed people to take advantage of serious discrepancies; escape from conscription or punishment was easier near the border. All in all, boundaries of this new kind added to the repertoire of West African farmers – much to the annoyance of their colonial masters. The Gambia was – and is – a notorious example of this kind, stretching deep into Senegalese territory; others included the French territories surrounding the Gold Coast and the common borders of Sierra Leone, Liberia, and Guinea. The further balkan-ization of West Africa as the price of independence has only increased the problem of borders by multiplying them. Evasion of government-controlled prices by crossing the border is the farmers' main weapon in the struggle to keep the West African states honest, and it is likely to remain so. The costs, in terms of a distorted pattern of settlement and production, are considerable.

Nigeria, with its large and relatively prosperous national market, stands in stark contrast to the rest of the region. Here, and to a lesser extent in the Ivory Coast, too, people and goods are drawn by centripetal force from their weaker neighbors. Thus, when Nigeria recently reduced the tariffs on imported cattle, the government of Niger was precipitated into a crisis overnight, as it were, because it immediately lost a sizable proportion of its herds across the border. Modern governments must attempt to keep separate economies whose divergence is the result of an uneven pattern of historical development and whose populations find it easier to move between them. Under these circumstances the weaker countries will be forced eventually to harmonize their economic policies with those of the stronger.

The only means available to the new states for close control of imports and exports are the sea and air terminals. But the growing volume of overland smuggling has reduced even that bulwark of the old mercantile system. Through such smuggling West African middlemen and producers keep alive the reality of a regional free-trade area that governments would prefer to keep fragmented.

Control over borders, however, is not the only problem of organization facing the new states: They have a problem of internal order, too. Administration of a high quality is essential if goods are to flow along the economic circuits designed for them by governments (i.e., taxes, buying and selling, financial arrangements). Bureaucratic standards lie very lightly on West Africans, who, for a number of historical reasons, normally choose to behave in a manner that, from the standpoint of law and civil service ethics, would be considered corrupt. Not to mince words, public administration at all levels in West Africa is riddled with corruption. This has a profound effect on commercial agriculture: It means that the principal determinant of profit and loss is often successful negotiation of illicit administrative channels. Distribution becomes more problematic than production, and entrepreneurial ingenuity is directed into black-market activity at the expense of increased technical efficiency. At least one breakthrough into mechanized rice agriculture collapsed into a mess of smuggling, payoffs, and barter (known as "the *Kalabule* economy") that left the market mechanism in ruins and respect for the law perhaps irretrievably damaged (Goody 1980). The colonial administrations in varying degrees established the institutions of lawful government within which commercial agriculture could flourish. Some of the postcolonial regimes carry on that principle – Senegal, for example – but most do not. The job of government is to defend a nation from its enemies, to provide a lawful framework for the activities of its residents, and to perform those tasks of economy and administration that are best carried out by public agencies. Many West African governments represent in themselves the single greatest threat to their citizens, treat the rule of law with contempt, and multiply hasty public schemes designed principally for their own private and collective enrichment. It is difficult to know how the situation can be reversed, but responsible politicians must deal with the matter urgently. Without extensive reform of the government apparatus itself, talk of commercial development in agriculture is unrealistic.

In contrast to the virtual anarchy of much that passes for government in West Africa stands the rhetoric of state policy, which mirrors the ideological trends of the modern world more closely than local realities. Most West African states call themselves socialist. Partly this is because Third World countries that were exploited under colonialism and now find themselves excluded from the wealth being piled up in the West turn easily to a political stance of opposition to "capitalism." But more important is their commitment to a greater degree of state control over economic life than is normal in the traditional market democracies. For a time, around the period of decolonization, they were able to mobilize a good deal of popular support for what later evolved into fairly monolithic regimes, run by single parties, apparently immobile presidents, or, after the mid-1960s, military juntas. The pretensions of these regimes are colossal relative to their capabilities. The reality consists of a decentralized economy, chaotic administration, weak control, and an increasingly disenchanted populace. In stark contrast, the government maintains a steady flow of expansive speeches, state documents, plans, high-level negotiations with visiting foreign bureaucrats, new political initiatives, and international conferences. The United Nations is fed a continuous supply of plausible statistics; planners conduct highly technical discussions with officials from the World Bank, AID, the French foreign ministry, and so on; budgets are drawn up and appraised. After this public display the money ends up in the usual pockets.

It is hardly surprising, in light of this pattern, that rural West Africans experience "development" as a world of words and numbers detached from material and social realities. The "book" is today as powerful a symbol of domination by a remote civilization as it was when Islamic marabouts inspired fear in West Africans and respect for written learning, or when colonial rulers taught them that getting their names written in a book meant taxes or labor conscription or probably both. Literacy in this context is not just an instrumental means of getting on in the world; it is the dividing line between those who exercise power and those who do not.[13] Almost everything that the new states do in the name of development means the intention at least of forcing the diversity of remote rural lives into an iron grid of title documents, accounts, censuses, and tax lists – words and numbers. The fact that they are not very good at it should not blind us to the enormous social force of this confrontation: It is the essence of the process that draws West African farmers into the modern world.

The international donor agencies

What part do the sources of foreign aid play in the development process? Although all donor agencies share certain common orientations to West African development, they do often adopt different postures reflecting variations in their concerns.

The main supranational agency working in the region is the World Bank, once the International Bank for Reconstruction and Development, (henceforth "the Bank"). It takes a global view of development, and particular countries have often found themselves pointed toward projects replicated in other nations at the same time. If promotion of oil palm or beef is in vogue at the Bank, such is the range of its influence that many countries find themselves making a contribution to what all parties hope will not be a glut in the world market. It should be remembered that the World Bank is a bank, not just the charitable arm of Western capitalism. Projects are evaluated according to their internal rates of return; and these have often been remarkably high.[14] It should be noted that lending, even when aimed at producers on the ground, is always channeled through the nation-states themselves. Indeed, all donor agencies deal directly with the state when it comes to transferring funds, personnel, or technology. In recent years, however, awareness of the failings of indigenous governments has led the Bank into a role akin to that of a floating international welfare state. MacNamara's 1973 call for a greater concern with equity in development has seen the Bank supporting programs aimed at improving general welfare levels in the countryside. This shift has sometimes caused Bank personnel to take a more direct supervisory role in the administration of integrated rural development programs linking agriculture, health, roads, artisan production, and so on. Analysis of the evolution of the Bank's political role in the West African region is beyond the scope of this book. Suffice it to say that its influence in the sphere of agricultural development is large and apparently growing.

AID, unlike the Bank, is strictly in the handout business. Although its activities are subordinate to U.S. foreign policy, the recent mandate from Congress to use its funds to help the poorest of the poor means that AID is likely to be found operating in countries that are of less than average strategic significance. West Africa is full of such countries, and AID has become a prominent presence in the region, especially since the early 1970s and especially in the Sahelian states. At the same time, the technical experts and agricultural economists usually involved in aid programs have been supplemented of late by a number of anthropologists. This addition may reflect a trend away from deployment of abstract specialized expertise learned mainly outside Africa toward use of persons with highly localized general knowledge, including an ability to communicate with Africans in the vernacular. Certainly it reflects an increase in the critical tone adopted in some AID reports toward the institutions of government with whom aid personnel must work. Committed to enhancing the lives of the poorest and reinforced in that commitment by an informed empathy with local people, some AID personnel might, not surprisingly, see the successor states and/or the impersonal forces of international capitalism as the main villains of the piece. It would be compatible with such a view to advocate reinforcement of peasant agriculture and the inefficiency of large projects. It should be pointed out, however, that what is lost in this particularist version of humanitarianism is a coherent view of how West Africans are to be helped to emancipate themselves from the trap of low productivity and low income.

The other main donor agencies in the region are linked to the ex-colonial powers and are embedded in a much more complex set of institutional relationships between the West African states and the countries that gave them their present shape, public language, and much else. Here the dominant emphasis is on maintaining the political ties and economic circuits between metropole and former colony. From the point of view of the French (especially because they have always placed considerable emphasis on the idea of Greater France) and the British, the rising influence of AID and of the U.S.-dominated World Bank represents a threat to their former duopoly, a threat backed up, moreover, with a great deal of money, which they cannot match. This sets the scene for both cooperation and rivalry in rural development, as agencies and state administrators vie for control of a process in which they are all supposed to be disinterested collaborators, concerned only for the welfare of the people.

Much more could be said about international aid in the postcolonial world. Some observations are commonplace: that much of the money goes, for example, not to the poor countries, but to firms operating out of the donor countries themselves. Gaud's 1968 study claimed that 93 percent of AID funds were spent directly in the United States (p. 605, quoted in Mende 1972:93). The transfer of "free" goods and services to Third World countries is often more of a handicap to their development than a benefit. Real aid would open the West's markets to the emergent manufacturing industries of Asia, Latin America, and Africa. This is perhaps the strongest argument for devoting aid to the maintenance of a peasant economy in Africa: If capitalist development were genuinely to occur there, it would accelerate demands for access to those markets. In reality, costs of production and transportation would probably be too high at first for there to be a real threat, but the potential challenge to jobs at home (especially at a time of world recession) would be a powerful incentive for the industrialized countries to keep productivity levels low elsewhere and to restrict the sales opportunities of any nascent industries that do not become competitive. The international donor agencies thus have a rather complicated role to play in the future of West African agriculture: Whatever development strategies they endorse will have important consequences for the region's chances.

Historical variations and regional prospects

The foregoing generalizations do not capture the variety of political configurations in West Africa. Moreover, the particularity of each state is probably the single most important variable influencing the development of commercial agriculture in the country. This whole discussion has been an attempt to show how much the material and social conditions of state formation shape the forces at work in rural economies. We should remember that this is a region that includes as near neighbors the two tiny states of Guinea Bissau and Liberia. In the course of a guerrilla war against the Portuguese, the nationalist leader Amilcar Cabral (a hero of global Marxism and an agronomist by profession) directed a switch in rural production away from groundnut exports to rice for home consumption.[15] This was so successful that for a time rice was exported to neighboring Guinea. But when Portuguese resistance collapsed, the absorption of the coastal towns into the nationalist-controlled economy soon eliminated any commercial rice surplus. Nevertheless, Guinea Bissau has continued to aspire to a more self-sufficient national economy, rejecting export-led growth as a solution to its dilemmas. The contrast with Liberia could hardly be greater. The Americo-Liberian ruling elite has built its autocratic system of government on an economic basis of unfettered export production by Firestone Rubber and more recently some iron-mining companies. So externally oriented was the agricultural economy that a major academic study termed the impact of this formula "growth without development" (Clower et al. 1966). Others see Liberia (along with the Ivory Coast) as an oasis of sane capitalist development in a sea of socialist protectionism. Differences between Guinea and the Ivory Coast were at the center of the AOF's failure to survive decolonization as a political entity. The story could go on, but there is no room here for discussion of all the states.

The political economy of West African agriculture

Moving down from the regional level to specific comparative investigations of public policy toward agriculture is the obvious next step, if any focus on the evolving political framework of economic development is to be made more concrete. Research along these lines should be given a high priority, and it may be an appropriate conclusion to this chapter to indicate how a multilevel approach to questions of state and economy might be posed in the West African context. The key question facing West African states is how to choose between self-sufficiency and integration at the various levels relevant to economic decision making. At one extreme is the world market, a sphere in which many Third World states feel exposed, dependent, and exploited; at the other is the subsistence household of peasantizing mythology, a closed circuit of self-reliance. Between these poles lie the following levels, presented as a hierarchy of levels of inclusiveness: (1) international trading groups outside Africa, such as the European Economic Community; (2) international commodity-producing cartels; (3) neo-imperialist dependence on the USSR, United States, France, and so on; (4) the Organization of African Unity (OAU); (5) the Economic Community of West African States (ECOWAS); (6) clusters of West African states, such as the "entente" states;[16] (7) the nation-states formed by decolonization twenty years ago; (8) regions within a state, including the Nigerian states; (9) rural areas with a dominant ethnic identity; (10) districts (rural and urban); and (11) villages. Most economic decisions permit a shift either to a more inclusive level or to one lower down the hierarchy.

The modern theory, backed up by the major powers and all organizations like the United Nations and the OAU, is that (7), the nation-state, should be the dominant economic unit. We have seen that, whereas this is in practice the case in West Africa, the claims of other levels are strong, and national economies are weakly developed. In the new states of West Africa the name of the nation is often not something that the mass of country dwellers have yet internalized as referring to themselves. It is rather an imposition, an additional layer come to exploit them. To the people I studied, "Ghana" was a concept similar to the "European Common Market" as it appears to many Englishmen – a remote and punitive bureaucracy. In the case of Germany and Italy, whose history in the nineteenth century was the crucible of modern nation-state theory, consolidation of a national market preceded national unification, only to be given a further boost by the formation of a single state. Western European political integration since World War II likewise lags behind the processes of economic integration. In West Africa national boundaries on the map are a poor indicator of levels and directions of economic integration, and the new states proclaim a national unity for which little groundwork has been laid.

Faced with their history of producing for the world market under colonial and neo-colonial conditions, some ruling elites have espoused policies of greater national self-sufficiency. This does not mean a retreat into peasant subsistence; quite the contrary, for in order to compensate for lost revenue on overseas trade, there has to be a corresponding growth in the home market. Nor should rejection of traditional metropolitan markets imply withdrawal from other forms of international collaboration like ECOWAS. Again, withdrawal of a small country from generalized involvement in the world market often means that a neo-imperialist replacement steps in to pay the bill. Abstract talk of reversing patterns of dependence through greater self-sufficiency is meaningless without specification of the entities involved and of their interrelationships. In other words, the appropriate political units for economic development in West Africa are still a moot point. It is unlikely that the fifteen non-Nigerian states will retain their present shape for long; and it is not revolutionary to suppose that political developments will be the most significant determinant of agricultural prospects in the various parts of the region. Nevertheless, the class interest of existing rulers (politicians, bureaucrats, soldiers) and the support of international agencies have so far conspired to remove the question of further state formation in West Africa from the agenda of development policy.

5

The market and capital in agricultural development

The problem of the future will be to deal with the native capitalists when they arise, as they will desire to oust the State from control of industry. This is the crux of the matter and it awaits determination.

Allan McPhee, The Economic Revolution in British West Africa (1971:280)

If the problem of the state can be treated as a separate topic for analysis, it is rather more difficult to isolate the role of the market and capitalism in West Africa's agricultural development, because these issues pervade this whole book. So the present chapter is short and even less descriptive than most of the others. It addresses four issues: the central mechanism that has led to the explosion of commercial agriculture in the modern period; the organization of marketing and transport, which together have produced a commercial revolution in modern times; money, that is, the forms of wealth and capital accumulation; and the question whether proletarianization of rural labor has laid the grounds for an agrarian revolution along classical capitalist lines.

Why did West Africans produce for the world market?

I have already indicated that the market was a significant feature of West African economies before the modern period. It was restricted in its development, however, by the low density of population, high transport costs, the self-sufficiency of local agriculture, the high import content of effective demand, and the low degree of specialization in the division of labor.[1] I suggested that social barriers were erected by those who benefited most from trade, so that the mass of Africans were not able to participate fully in the market. In the case of the Atlantic slave trade, it was the slave-raiding aristocracies whose political monopoly, luxurious consumption of imports, and war-making proclivities put a brake on generalized commodity production. In the countryside as a whole, village elders managed the circuit of trade goods in such a way as to maintain their control over women and young men, by linking trade to the marriage system of bridewealth payments. The merchant class was often ethnically separated from the local population, a factor that inhibited the investment of merchant capital in produc-

110

tion. Only in the Sudanic heartlands of the Hausa, Dioula, or Mande diaspora was the market economy integrated into an advanced division of labor involving the clear-cut separation of town and countryside. A partial exception was to be found on the coast, where indigenous merchants (including forerunners of the "market mammy") and a specialized division of labor had grown up around the European forts.

Very little of this commerce involved agriculture: Slaves and livestock were favored because they could walk themselves; and metals, ivory, and gums had a high unit price. Only market gardening on the coast and near the savannah towns permitted a degree of agricultural commodity production; elsewhere local markets existed for the circulation of products in minute quantities. The interesting question is how the market has penetrated into the bulk of West African production during the modern period.

How and why were West Africans first drawn into commercial agriculture on a scale that has since given their economies a definite external orientation that did not exist before? There are two possibilities: Either groups who were committed to the existing trade (mostly in slaves) switched to agricultural products, or groups who were previously excluded from trade entered as agricultural producers of commodities. The first explanation is extremely plausible. West Africans offered slaves to the world market because they had nothing else of value to sell in bulk (if we overlook ivory, gold, pepper, etc.). The world market took a sharp turn from slaves to industrial raw materials in the nineteenth century, and it was discovered that West Africa could supply vegetable oils more cheaply than could any other region. At the same time the political autonomy of the slave-raiding classes was actively undermined by the beginnings of a colonization movement. What could be more natural than a switch to oil palm or groundnut production? This is certainly what happened in Dahomey and Senegal (Coquery-Vidrovitch 1971*a*; Klein 1977). In some cases the slaves were set free as tied tenants; in others they were employed directly by their masters. The rubber and cocoa booms at the end of the century were a continuation of this process of dismantling the slave economy and deploying accumulated wealth in agricultural production. Other agents in the slave trade, such as coastal merchants, also played a part in the first great speculative upsurge of export crops.

What of the masses, the excluded peasantry? My guess is that their participation in commercial agriculture was at first secondary, delayed, and in a different capacity. The really major producers in the new export trade were men with access both to capital and labor. Their prior commitment to the export-oriented sector gave them a head start on other producers, who might find it hard to break in, especially because West African middlemen would often be in control of the trade. Peasants would therefore be restricted to cultivating small amounts near their homes for sale to merchants, or – and this was especially true for the interior population – they could offer their labor for hire, often in areas a long way distant from their homes. Clearly the mobilization of the coastal hinterlands would occur only after an initial period of exploitation by agents situated near the seaports. None of this is definite, however. For example, the destiny of freed slaves outside Senegal and Dahomey is still a moot point (see Coquery-Vidrovitch 1971*a*; Klein 1977; Suret-Canale 1971). The point of significance is that, when we discuss the transition to an export-cash-crop economy, we should recognize that the differentiation of the West African people prior to the modern period must be incorporated into any account of their supposed motivations.[2]

We explain the beginnings of this massive social movement into export agriculture first by the collapse of the market for slaves and the concomitant rise of demand for vegetable oils. But after that, what was in it for the West Africans themselves? The coastal and near-coastal elites badly needed to restore their income, maintain their prestige, and find a new place of power in the emergent European-dominated system. Their slaves probably had little choice but to take whatever role their masters allocated to them, unless they could make their way to a major town under European protection. The merchants obviously entered these new trades as a profitable way of turning over their money and possibly also of acquiring property for their descent groups. What about the peasants? They had shown no unwillingness to migrate or sell commodities before: There already was a domestic exchange of forest products (kola, oil palm) for savannah animals that involved large numbers of ordinary people at some stage in the process. The standard liberal argument, that people sold their goods and labor in the hope of raising their living standards, acquiring a wider range of consumer goods, and perhaps investing in property, is more plausible for West Africa than for almost any underdeveloped region. I believe that such an account would be true for most of the population who entered commercial agriculture in one capacity or another during its initial period.

It has been suggested often enough that force was the midwife of West African commodity production (Suret-Canale 1971; Amin 1973; Rey 1969; R. Thomas 1973). This case rests on the measures taken by early colonial authorities (especially French) to find labor for public works, mines, and sometimes commercial agriculture. Money taxes were introduced in order to compel subsistence producers to sell their labor or goods. Here the needs of commodity economy are conflated with those of administration, and it is difficult to determine which interest serves which. In general, though it is always possible to coerce labor from a population, force has the opposite effect from that intended when it is applied to the unsupervised production of commodities. So whatever may have been the excesses of early colonial rule, reliance on free production of indigenous cash crops sooner or later[3] ousted forced labor as the principal mechanism in colonial political economy. This export-crop economy was fueled in the beginning by West Africans' enthusiasm for new opportunities. The penetration of the market into agriculture did not rest on force.

We have only to compare the brutality that accompanied the establishment of plantation colonies in Kenya and Rhodesia, for example,[4] with West Africans'

112

experience of the trading houses and their associated administrations, to realize that any reduction of these major variations in the impact of colonialism would be seriously misleading. The Ivory Coast had a fairly oppressive colonial history, linked to a late-starting plantation economy, and it has become the capitalist showpiece of the postcolonial era. In this respect, and for reasons that go beyond the requirements of this argument, it resembles Kenya more than it resembles, say, Ghana, where capitalist production never took root in the countryside and the postcolonial political economy has been, to say the least, fragile. As Luxemburg (1951) pointed out, the invasion of commodity economy into backward areas may be peaceful (by trade) or violent (by armed subjugation, compulsion of labor, etc.) Capitalism is not intrinsically wedded to either method, except that it is always cheaper to have people hand over their goods and labor freely than to pay thugs to beat them into unwilling submission. The style of intervention depends on the form of capital (mercantile or industrial/agricultural); the urgency, power, and national culture of the capitalists; and the relative strength of the social forces they have to overcome.

In West Africa the idea of a forced transition to capitalism, which has even been elevated to the level of theory by Rey (1973), is mostly a mirage in that, no matter what violence may have been inflicted on the indigenous population, the forms of commodity production are still overwhelmingly precapitalist. Moreover, the British colonial authorities, at least, throughout their short period of rule, were ideologically convinced that the use of a repressive military apparatus to maintain exploitative systems of labor relations and land tenure was both out of the question and unnecessary, in view of the natives' evident willingness to increase their involvement in the commercial economy at a rate far in excess of the capacities of the expatriate capitalist class. The very success of this strategy, from both points of view, is the reason why most West African states find themselves today a long way from the agrarian revolution that they undoubtedly need.

The organization of marketing and transport

If there has been a revolution during the last fifty years, it has been in transport. When 80 or 90 percent of the consumer price is taken up with costs of distribution – as it often was in nineteenth-century West Africa – there is not much point in striving to reduce the costs of production. What the regional economy needed first was more efficient transport and larger, integrated markets; then competition would whittle down traders' margins and the stage would be set for capital to enter production with a view to improving the efficiency of labor. The plan has not worked out quite that way, but not for lack of initiative in the marketing and transport sectors.

The main entrepreneur in the construction of transport infrastructure was the government – colonial and, to a lesser extent, postcolonial. Railways, docks, bridges, and roads all dramatically reduced the cost of shipping bulky materials like agricultural products. The development of the steamship from the 1850s had an enormous effect on the structure and volume of coastal trade (A. G. Hopkins 1973). There is still much to be done; the inland waterways, for example, could be made more suitable for bulk transport. The means of transport, on the other hand, have been supplied by thousands of small firms, most of them African. Cars and trucks are, of course, imported; but indigenous enterprise keeps them running in West Africa. One group that played a crucial role in the early days of motor transport was the small cadre of Levantine businessmen who linked up the coastal European enclaves with the interior network manned by Muslim merchants of the savannah. As a result of their common religion and Arabic language, these "Syrians" were able to establish a region-wide system of truck parks that serves today as the basis for overland trade and internal communications (Hart 1970).

The markets served by these cheap transport networks have seen a great variety of trading firms. First there were the huge merchant houses of Liverpool and Bordeaux, themselves merging into what amounted almost to colonial monopolies – United Africa Company, Société Commercial de L'Ouest Africain, Compagnie Française de L'Afrique Occidentale, and so on (Coquery-Vidrovitch 1975). Out of the groundwork prepared by these distribution giants came the postwar marketing boards, later to be the basis of nationalized merchant groups. We saw in the last chapter how much these monopsonies have squeezed the life out of commercial agriculture. Some of the Levantine trading firms grew quite large and were able to survive French and British attempts to drive them out of business. Hancock (1941) believed that they were more efficient than the colonial merchant houses, and he was probably right. Today the Lebanese have a reputation with Africans for being unscrupulous and antinationalistic; at least, that is the image that nationalist antimarket politicians promote. Then there are the Muslim merchants from the north. They have been fairly conservative, retaining control of internal markets in livestock, kola, and other traditional items. They also have competed successfully in some sectors of the export market, such as cotton and groundnuts in northern Nigeria. These constitute the upper echelons of the trading hierarchy: government, European firms, Levantines, and Muslim merchants. The relationship among these groups oscillates between uneasy symbiosis and explicit confrontation. Many postcolonial governments, in particular, have sought to dominate (*maitriser*) the market of colonial trading houses and foreign merchants in the name of rescuing oppressed peasants from the agents of commerce (B. Lewis 1980). Liberation through government monopoly is, as we have seen, often worse than the illness it was designed to cure.

Most imported consumer goods and a high proportion of domestically produced commodities are marketed by a horde of indigenous traders (Bohannan and Dalton 1962). Some are specialized both as to commodity and as to function (wholesale/retail, rural/urban). Most are flexibly located over a range of market-ing capacities, which they switch and combine readily. Many are women, for reasons outlined in the next chapter; and specialization by ethnic group is common. The dynamism of West African markets is largely a function of the willingness of millions of people to fill out and expand commerce in those zones left untouched by the larger operators. As a result, market economy has pene-trated to the heart of every village; and after 150 years of expansion on the back of the export economy, West Africa's home market has now reached a level of integration that makes internally oriented commodity production a genuine foun-dation for economic development.[5]

Money and wealth

What part has money played in this commercial revolution? Before colonization, West African trade proceeded via the medium of special-purpose currencies: Metal bars, cowrie shells, pieces of cloth, cattle, slaves, and tokens from merchant houses were all employed as measures of exchange value in restricted commercial contexts (A. G. Hopkins 1973; Bohannan and Dalton 1962). Barter of a fairly direct kind (e.g., groundnuts for cloth, via the trader's accounts if the two items were not present at the same time) also persisted well into the colonial period (Suret-Canale 1971). The amount of general-purpose money in circulation remained quite small until after World War II, when more liberal monetary policies were adopted by the colonial powers and by their successors. Ghana is the first West African country to have reached Latin American rates of inflation, and the economy is fast receding into a nexus of barter and special-purpose currencies (such as cans of gasoline). But in countries with more restrained governments, there has never been a time when money was more available and pervasive in economic life than now. This means that money capital, liquidity in general, and credit are at levels never before achieved in the West African economies. Commercial agriculture is thus less constrained by capital shortage than it was during the colonial period.

There are two financial circuits in West African countries. One consists of the government, international firms, a few large corporate enterprises with local roots, and the banks (either government owned or foreign owned). To these we should add the international donor agencies and foreign governments, whenever they spend money inside West Africa itself. This "formal" circuit is highly corporate and bureaucratic and is backed up by state law enforcement. Its loans may be very large and its interest rates are low (reflecting international standards); loan collateral must be property with a realizable cash sale value. Needless to say, very few Africans qualify for the credit offered in this circuit, although they are encouraged to deposit their cash savings, and some government institutions make small loans for specific purposes (e.g., the purchase of fertilizer and machinery).

The political economy of West African agriculture

The other financial circuit is the flow of money between West Africans outside the corporate banking sector. It is highly personal and barely documented, and it is practically beyond the law. Loans are usually small and interest rates are astronomical; loan collateral may take the form of pawned consumer durables. Interest rates of 25–50 percent a *month* are normal in this circuit. Obviously, loans undertaken at this rate are more often for consumption than for investment purposes. Credit from traders normally carries the same rate of interest. What this reflects is the shortage of liquidity in the lower echelons of the West African economies; predictably, it also reflects an extremely high default rate (up to four out of five loans in some cases; see Hart 1970, 1973).

Interest rates are high in West Africa, not because the people cannot figure out an economic rate, but rather because they can. The institutions of an advanced market for money either are absent altogether or do not impinge directly on the transactions involved. Production conditions vary widely, and markets are erratic. Enforcement of loan payments is always a problem. So when governments make agricultural credit available at the low interest rates normal in international financial circles, they are bound to take a loss, especially when the loans are tied to specific investments the failure of which (the usual result) will encourage farmers to put the blame on the government, and therefore not to accept responsibility for repayment. There is perhaps an inverse relationship between the social standing of the moneylender and the probability of repayment: Indebtedness is a measure and sanction of public support and deference. Why would politicians want villagers to pay off their debts?

The interest-rate revolution, whereby the improved efficiency of money markets drives the price of capital down to a level set by the rate of profit in industry, has not occurred in West Africa – for the good reason that money markets are not efficient and capitalist industry has not yet emerged. But because the official money market is responsible to international expectations, an enormous dualism has been created. This discrepancy must lead to a steady leakage of funds from the upper circuit to the lower by means of channels that we would probably label "corruption." This leakage could be – and often is – an avenue whereby public funds enter commercial agriculture as capital. For the mass of ordinary West Africans, the liquidity shortage is a perennial feature of their lives that leads many of them into indebtedness and penury. The main source of their salvation is that they cannot sell their land to pay their debts.

What processes of accumulation have accompanied the expansion of the market economy? What are the main forms of property in which money capital has been invested? First, a fair amount left West Africa in the pockets of European firms. Second, the successor states have grabbed the lion's share of the proceeds from export agriculture and much else. Indigenous accumulation has therefore been based on the leavings, and if more of the money that West African producers generated had come back into their hands, I would be telling a very different story today. But the leavings were still substantial, and the home market

116

is a sector from which neither foreign capital nor the state has yet learned how to skim off the profits.

The early export-crop producers invested wealth earned from the slave trade and similar activities. Commercial farming has remained a principal investment medium ever since. Although land cannot be bought, money can be spent hiring labor to establish a farm from which rental income will in future be derived (e.g., on a sharecropping basis). It is possible to specialize in farming and accumulate substantial enterprises, but most people who enter farming as investors choose to diversify their profits into other channels. Many build houses in towns, again as a source of rental income, and also as a source of family prestige and security. Many purchase motor vehicles both for their own use and as commercial enterprises. Trade, from which many family fortunes originated, is still considered a lucrative investment medium; and for all its risks, so is usury. Most manufacturing enterprises require specialized commitment, and very few West Africans have accumulated wealth as industrialists (see, e.g., Kilby 1969). So the hallmark of concentrated wealth is rentier investment in a diversified portfolio linking agriculture, housing, transport, trade, and services (Hart 1970). There has been no transfer of occupied land into the hands of a few concentrated property owners. Nor has there has been a significant entry of indigenous money into capitalist production units. The partial exception is agriculture, where the option to take a direct (rather than rentier) interest in managing a farm worked by paid laborers has long existed. For the time being, however, commercial agriculture has not been a vehicle for cumulative capitalist investment, nor has the logic of such accumulation governed agriculture's dominant pattern of organization.

Forms of labor: an agrarian revolution?

Because it is known that many West Africans sell their labor for wages in the rural economy, the question naturally occurs whether new classes have been formed by the process. The key term is "proletarianization" (Sandbrook and Cohen 1975). By the term "proletariat," Marx meant a class that has no property save its own labor power, which it must sell for wages in order to find the means of subsistence.[6] The conversion of production to a system of wage labor is momentous in three ways: First, production of commodities by means of commodities vastly expands the scope of the market – people consume more commodities, because they must sell their labor; second, the scope for improving the output of human labor in productive enterprises immeasurably increases the rate of capital accumulation over that possible in nonproductive forms of investment; and finally, capitalists and workers are driven by an inexorable logic to a polarized class struggle.

In the case of West African commercial agriculture, the dominant form of labor is not that done for wages, but that done by a family worker farming on his own account. This worker is not free from complex social ties: He may be

117

embedded in associations derived from membership in a descent group, and he is almost certainly working alongside his wife and children in a setting that is domestic. He may be a sharecropper, splitting his product with a landlord who does not "own" the land and who may be a senior kinsman. He may be working on a settlement regulated by the government or by a religious order. All of these are variations of peasant farming and they still predominate.

There is also a class of rural labor that consists of work done for wages. This category divides into two basic kinds: migrants who enter a wage contract for a fixed length of time, usually a season or even a full year; and people working as daily wage labor in communities where they have homes. The first type is classically found in the migrations of savannah youth to the forest export-crop zones (Le Bris, Rey, and Samuel 1976; Hart 1974; Amin 1974*a*); the second type is found there, too, but more characteristically in areas of intensive cultivation such as Hausaland (Hill 1972; Raynaut 1976). In addition, there are large-scale public- and private-sector farms that hire migrant and local labor much as they would if production were industrial rather than agricultural. In most cases the forms of payment are mixed, and the workers can be found at different times in most of the available roles. Thus Hill reports for the Hausa village of Batagarawa that farm laborers are paid partly in cash and partly in porridge and are sometimes offered grain instead of cash. Domestic servants, "most of whom have sought refuge from their poverty by a partial withdrawal from the economy, are mainly renumerated with food" (Hill 1972:30). The communal labor system (*gayya*) has largely given way to farm laboring for some kind of wages (*kwadago*). Elsewhere, it has been pointed out for the Nupe of northern Nigeria that communal forms of labor sometimes persist despite the invasion of wage labor into village farming (Nadel 1942). Examples could be multiplied; the more important question is whether they add up to an emergent rural proletariat in West Africa.

The answer to this question has several aspects. First, only a few of these wage laborers will spend the majority of their working lives as wage laborers. Second, they are not yet torn from the ancient nexus of property and social relations that provides them with long-term security (this holds for migrants as much as those living at home). Third, they are rarely landless, and they can usually aspire to possess land, even while they work as wage laborers. Fourth, they normally produce their own food and thus remain in part subsistence farmers. Fifth, they are rarely subjected to the work discipline expected in industrial capitalist firms, even, or perhaps especially, when the employer is a mechanized government operation. Finally, they are rarely unionized and are incapable of conceiving of themselves as being in conflict with a class of capitalist owners, because such a class is nonexistent. In sum, neither the economic nor the political dimensions of proletarianization are visible in the West African countryside. This small mercy is the region's compensation for failure to generate a capitalist agriculture out of its export-commodity boom.

The main force driving West African commercial agriculture thus seems to be the rationality of peasant farmers allied with the judicious investment of rentier capital by various kinds of absentee farmers. This force at times has been supported by the state and more recently has been almost throttled by it. This may be an appropriate place to offer a comment on peasant rationality. Indigenous producers always know what they are doing, and they usually know how to get what they want better than outsiders, however expert the latter may be. Two quotations from the literature make the point well. The first was written almost half a century ago: "True he (the native farmer) often prefers a method that is slow rather than one that is quicker but involves harder work for a shorter time. This is due to the fact that he does the labour himself and therefore regards it from a different viewpoint from one who pays for it by the day or hour" (Faulkner and Mackie 1933:6). The other comes from a trenchant indictment of Liberia written in the 1960s: "Even the most eloquent advocate of economic progress cannot demonstrate the advantage of growing two grains of rice where only one flourished before if the prospective grower knows that both grains will go to someone else" (Clower et al. 1966:33). These remarks point out the absurdity of a bowdlerized economics whose "rationality" forgets the centrality of distribution in classical political economy, in this instance the contrast between wage and peasant labor and the effects of exactions by the state. Peasants do not lack intelligence: They understand these matters better than most development economists. What they lack is political power and material resources. They are acutely aware of their local environment and of nuances in the organization of production. They are less knowledgeable about processes whose focus lies elsewhere, like the market and the state. But any decent anthropologist will be able to discover that a given peasant population is finely tuned to the needs of the local economy and, on its own terms, more rational than a foolish bureaucrat with a development plan to sell. Some anthropologists delight in doing just that. Nonetheless, when nations set their sights on development, what is rational to a peasant may be sabotage to a plan. And in West Africa's case, 150 years of peasant rationality have left the region in a backward economic condition and with a precarious political future. It is no use claiming that colonialism produced this mess. Even if it did, the successor states are now nominally sovereign, and it is their responsibility to devise an escape route.

After a transport revolution and a commercial revolution, the next item on the agenda is an agrarian revolution. There is no point in having an industrial revolution with an inefficient agriculture and overpopulated countryside; no industrial revolution ever took place before rural productivity had been substantially improved (W. A. Lewis 1978*a*). So the question is whether and how a transformation of agriculture can take place soon in West Africa. Because this is the main topic of Chapter 7 I will make only a brief comment here.

It is clear that the principal source of capital in any agrarian revolution will be the state, either directly as a public body or indirectly through the wealth of its main beneficiaries. This is just as well, for without the reliable support of a functioning state apparatus, capitalist agriculture cannot survive. There is enough capital and expertise in West Africa now for the entrepreneurs to be indigenous, although foreign corporations may play a part in establishing large-scale enterprises. What of the other factors of production – land, labor, and technology? Land scarcity is now real enough in some places to encourage intensive exploitation by high-productivity labor. Labor is obviously available in large quantities; semiskilled and skilled labor can easily be attracted from the unproductive public sector. Technology has to be imported, as does the energy used by the machines: This need will lead to many experiments to find the most appropriate mix of local and imported supplies, but it should not inhibit the drive toward higher levels of efficiency. Finally, demand already exists, in the shape of a huge food-importation bill, the needs of home industry, and the world market for foodstuffs and agricultural raw materials. There are thus, in principle, no technical obstacles to the entry of capital into agricultural production with a view to revolutionizing the productivity of farm labor. Equally, there is no historical necessity for the occurrence of such a development in West Africa during the 1980s.

6

The social impact of commercial agriculture

Our facts do more than illumine our morality and point out our ideal; for they help us to analyze economic facts of a more general nature, and our analysis might suggest the way to better administrative procedures for our societies.

Marcel Mauss, *The Gift* (1967:69)

Labor mobility and the rural exodus

The impact of modern developments on West Africa's rural societies is manifested in a number of ways, none of them easy to measure. Those who consider the commercialization of agriculture to be an enormous source of various pathologies would emphasize the impoverishment, class contradictions, and social disorganization that they imagine to be characteristic of rural life today. These judgments imply a comparison with earlier times that is even harder to make concretely. Not everyone would express his or her opinion as decisively as Polly Hill (1977:172): "This miserably inefficient, competitive, ill-equipped rural economy, where most men work far less hard than they would wish, shuffles along much as it did forty years ago – only relieved by the migration of some married men and their dependents." But in this chapter I will pursue such themes with some degree of analytical interpretation and rather less documentation. Probably no topic captures the vicissitudes of recent changes in the countryside more completely than the massive shifts in population that have accompanied urbanization since World War II. This section describes the migration phenomenon and then deals first with the causes of rural emigration, next with the part played in it by commercial agriculture, and finally with the consequences for the general welfare of the people of a shift toward urban areas.

The aggregate statistics of regional migration patterns are somewhat elusive. West Africa's population has increased four or five times since the late nineteenth century, and urban centers now contain a fifth of this much-expanded total. This means that rural populations are now at least three times what they were. Some villages may have stayed roughly the same in numbers, with people trickling out gradually as a kind of homeostatic regulator; even so the majority of villagers have had to go and live elsewhere, mostly still in the countryside. Moreover, a skew in the age and sex distribution of those who move (among whom younger men predominate) can leave the local division of labor badly disorganized despite stability or even growth in the size of a given rural population. Suffice it to say that all this mobility in a period of extraordinary growth is both a significant economic resource (freeing labor as a commodity in large quantities) and a cause for some political disquiet.

There have been two great movements of population in West Africa (Amin 1974a:introduction). The earlier, which is over a hundred years old, is from the savannah interior to export-cropping zones nearer the coast, notably the forest belt. This rural–rural migration pattern is still important, but extremely difficult to quantify, because rates of natural population increase also vary widely within the region. The second movement, which is substantially a feature of post–World War II history, is the rapid growth of West African cities, especially capital cities (Gugler and Flanagan 1978). Annual growth rates for the region's urban centers have been consistently higher than overall growth rates of 3 percent, being 4–10 percent in various countries and 5–6 percent on the average for West Africa as a whole during the period since 1950. The number of West Africans now living in urban areas (30 million) is about six times what it was three decades ago, and the urban share of the population has more than tripled to its present level of 20 percent (see Table 1, in Chapter 2).

The concentration of this growth in a few centers of government is revealed by an index of primate urbanization based on the ratio of the first- and second-largest cities in each country (Gugler and Flanagan 1978:41). Thus in six countries (Senegal, Guinea, Guinea Bissau, Liberia, Mali, and Togo), the capital city was six to nine times bigger than the next-largest city at the beginning of the 1970s. In another four (the Gambia, Sierra Leone, the Ivory Coast, and Niger), it was four to five times bigger. And in five countries (Nigeria, Benin, Ghana, Upper Volta, and Mauritania), it was less than double the size of the second city. Of this last group, Mauritania has an urban population that has been growing at the rate of 15 percent a year for over a decade; the capital city of Benin is not the largest city; Ghana is the most urbanized nation in West Africa; and Nigeria's several regions are all densely populated, with over half of West Africa's major cities distributed among them. In general, the tendency since decolonization has been for more migrants than ever before to make their destination a handful of national capitals. Thus Dakar, which before the war had a population of 54,000, reached 800,000 by 1976; Lagos grew from 126,000 to 2.5 million in the same period; and Abidjan increased from 10,000 in 1931 to 555,000 in 1970. Less spectacularly, Monrovia went from 10,000 to 164,000 in forty years, and Accra's population increased a mere tenfold to 636,000 in 1970. Some of the smaller capital cities had the most dramatic increases: Niamey from 2,000 in 1931 to 108,000 in 1972 and Lomé from 7,000 to 193,000 in the same period. Guinea's capital, Conakry, managed to grow to almost sixty times its original size between 1934 and 1972, from 9,000 to 526,000 (nine times the size of the next-largest city). These figures show that, in the post-World War II period, West Africa has acquired for the first time a genuine urban basis for its regional economy, one that has been fueled by massive growth in the total population and, in equal measure, by the migration of country dwellers from their villages to the new urban agglomerations that mark the rise of the postcolonial state.

The mobility of West Africa's population has thus been a highly visible feature of the region's modern history. Some would find in it a measure of instability and dislocation, mass exodus from the countryside being seen as an index of rural malaise. But this mobility is neither novel nor dysfunctional, for migration and movement were intrinsic to the indigenous population's way of life even before the concentration of economic opportunities on the coast set up today's asymmetrical drift from savannah villages to forest plantations and city slums. Warfare and slave raiding produced continuous population movements on a large and a small scale. Shifting agriculture allowed for micro-variations in settlement that over time could amount to substantial demographic change. Migration for political, religious, and trading purposes was common well before the *pax colonica*. Rules of exogamy created well-dispersed affinal networks through which people could travel long distances. The development cycle of domestic groups routinely produced forces for residential fission that might occasion relocation either nearby or farther away. Migration was *not* encouraged among slaves and married women, who made their residential moves prior to assuming those statuses. For others, though it was sometimes fraught with danger, migration was normal, expected. I mention this as an antidote to any lingering belief that colonialism jerked a static indigenous population into a nomadic existence to which it was wholly unaccustomed.

There are two main types of long-distance migration. In one the migrant is a settler; this type is more likely if his destination is a rural setting, for he can readily establish there the conditions of reproducing himself and his family for the duration of his own lifetime and beyond. The other type is circulatory migration, in which the migrant expects to return to his home village sooner or later; this type may involve long or short stays in town or countryside (Hart 1974). Labor circulation, a prominent feature of West African rural settings on a seasonal, annual, or longer-term basis, is the dominant mode of migration to the cities. The reason is simple: None but a few securely employed and affluent city dwellers can expect to find in urban areas the long-term life-support system they need. Residential flexibility and a way of life linking the migrant strongly to his home area are thus normal in West Africa. This means that the rural exodus, which has gathered momentum since 1960, should not necessarily be understood as the countryside's permanent loss of population. A shift in the balance of population in favor of the cities would occur if the rate of rural–urban circulation increased in the population as a whole and if the average length of absence from the village increased. It would not need to mean that the volume of new urban *settlers* had significantly increased, although it is undoubtedly true that the number of city dwellers without effective links to the countryside is growing all the time.

The mechanisms of mass migration both now and in the colonial period are a subject of considerable debate. Some writers (notably Amin 1974*a*), reacting against liberal models of rational decision making in a free labor market, have emphasized the elements of compulsion in modern West African migration – the use of force by colonial armies and recruiters, the imposition of money taxes, and pressure from village chiefs (today, famine, loss of land, and rural impoverishment might be enlisted under a similar rubric). Though there is a valid case to be made against neglect of these considerations, it is my opinion that the bulk of migration can be understood as having taken place within the framework of a "free" labor market (in the legal rather than existential sense). Obviously the case of the Ivory Coast before World War I differs somewhat from that of southwestern Nigeria today in that regard; but if a general characterization has to be made, modern West African migratory movements have been largely voluntary. This conclusion may affect our evaluation of the rural exodus. It leads me to describe the large picture as that of West Africans voting with their feet, if somewhat tentatively, for city over village life; others might understand the process as the ejection of an unwilling population from a rural setting that they would otherwise prefer.

One partial antidote to these polarized discussions about the causes of population movement is to stress the significance of studying rural social structures themselves to see how they differentially affect the release of labor (Le Bris, Rey, and Samuel 1976). We have seen that traditional social life is not without its contradictions. Further studies may throw light on the reasons why some peoples lose most of their young adults while others retain them. Both the "liberal" and the "compulsion" theories of migration tend to treat rural West Africans as a passive, homogeneous mass, whereas rural society has its dynamics and variations that need to be taken fully into account.

It is also important to keep a historical time scale in mind when thinking about labor-migration trends. If the depression of 1930–45 is anything to go by, a prolonged slump in the world economy today will reverse the shift of people out of the countryside that occurred in the 1960s and early 1970s. Certainly, as jobs become harder to get, the possibility of migrating on a seasonal basis is much reduced, and this change may compel migrants to choose between staying longer abroad and never leaving the village at all. These long swings in the labor market affect the balance of power between laborers and employers. Thus, when a boom takes off, demand for labor exceeds supply, wage levels rise, work conditions are determined by what keeps the workers happy, and turnover and mobility are high. When there is a recession, labor supply exceeds demand, real wage levels fall, workers take any conditions they can get, and turnover and mobility are much reduced. We have a tendency sometimes to think of migration as a linear growth curve; the evidence of the last century in West Africa is that a long-term upward trend is masked by significant fluctuations in the medium term. The chances are that the early 1980s will constitute a downward fluctuation.

To what extent is commercial agriculture responsible for the rural exodus? Obviously, commercial agriculture, as in the classic examples of cocoa and groundnut farming, has played a significant part in drawing population away from the savannah hinterland to areas most suitable for export production. But this shift constitutes a redistribution of rural population, not a loss to the countryside as a whole. There are two main ways in which it could be said that commercial agriculture has contributed to rural emigration. The first would be instances where concentration of capital, land, and technology has displaced rural workers and forced them to seek their livelihood elsewhere, let us say in the cities. As we saw in the previous chapter, there is scant evidence that any such development has yet taken place on a significant scale in West Africa. It is in another way that the commercial evolution of the countryside has encouraged emigration, and then only indirectly: Export-crop agriculture has been the economic basis for state aggrandizement in the region. The wholesale transfer of agricultural surpluses from rural areas to states whose expenditures are biased overwhelmingly in favor of urban areas is the main reason why more and more people make unfavorable economic comparisons between their own villages and the nation's principal cities. If income generated from agriculture stayed in the countryside there would be a much-reduced rural exodus. Country statistics show variation within West Africa from urban populations of less than 10 percent to several of more than 30 percent. Figures as large as the latter imply a massive alteration of national economic structure. Importation of cheap food from abroad has delayed the commercialization of food production for the home market that ought to accompany such a demographic shift. I shall argue later that urbanization on this scale presents enormous opportunities for the West African economies. But the prevailing opinion is that cities are dangerous and unhealthy places that represent both a drain on the public purse and a threat to the political status quo, to the extent that the swollen urban masses cannot find adequate work.[1]

The fact is that the quality and quantity of material amenities are much higher in the cities than in most villages. Moreover, when people are concentrated in central places, markets are bigger and services can be delivered more cheaply on a per capita basis. Village life has its solid virtues, but economic horizons are necessarily limited there, and that limitation matters to a large number of people, especially young adults. The rulers of states, whose own economic behavior draws villagers in thousands to their capital cities, may sometimes regret their presence so close to the corridors of power, where they do more damage if they become upset. But they can hardly claim that these people would be better off to stay in the countryside, unless they match the claim wih a massive redirection of state expenditures. Judgment on this issue is as much a matter of philosophy and politics as it is of the economic and demographic record.

The standard of living, social security, and reproduction

The question is whether, as a result of commercial developments in agriculture, West Africans are now materially better or worse off. Leaving aside for now the issue of unequal distribution of social costs and benefits, the question still poses formidable difficulties. If we examine the life-style of a community before and after it makes the shift to a significant level of production for sale, the organization of time changes. Activities that were relatively undifferentiated become identified as separate forms of labor, each with a market price. Thus child care and socialization may have been casually intermeshed with the ordinary web of daily life, but the introduction of schooling makes them educational services that have to be paid for. Agriculture in the traditional economy was guided by the rhythms of family and community life: We have seen that West Africans spent a relatively small number of man-hours per year on acquiring their food, whereas by European standards they may have spent an extraordinary amount of time on funerals. Who is to say that the maintenance of relations between the living and the dead is less important than growing plants? But when agriculture is commercialized, the evaluation of time spent on it is necessarily transformed; for it becomes specialized labor with a value that can be realized as purchasing power. Then attending funerals can be portrayed as wasteful, both of time and of money. The point is that one way of life cannot be evaluated by the standards of another. At least one cannot compare, as by a single measure, the value of two distinct patterns of *consumption*. It seems that a shift to commodity economy means that West Africans "work" harder and have access to a wider range of goods and services, but it is impossible to say whether their time would have been better spent in the old way. Perhaps the two patterns of production may be judged according to their effectiveness in dealing with the hazards of the material environment and the needs of physical survival.

Nutritional level is a poor measure of changes in a whole way of life, but it is vitally important when people are living at the edge of starvation. I shall not present detailed statistical information on nutrition here, both because of the difficulties of evaluating it and because time-series data of any historical time depth are hard to come by. So we will rely on impressions and logic.

The last decade has been notable for the publicity given to ecological deterioration and famine in West Africa (Copans 1975a; Dalby and Church 1973; Dalby, Church, and Bezzaz 1977). It seems that aridity has increased of late, with the result that the Sahara has effectively moved South. This has happened before, and there is no certainty that it is irreversible; but it has never happened before under modern conditions of world markets and nation-states. Famines are more visible today than even at the time of the last major disaster in 1913–14. Suret-Canale (1971:130–1) quotes a 1938 article by Henri Labouret ("Famines et disettes aux colonies"), who reported that the famine of 1914 was preceded in 1912–13 by a drought, which was followed by a bad harvest in the whole Sahel region from

126

Senegal to Chad. The Tuareg "invaded" south in search of food. Parents pawned their children for a handful of millet. Granary reserves were eliminated. Colonial taxation made things worse for everyone. Slaves were abandoned by masters who could not feed them. Grain prices went through the roof. The relatively new European regimes sat back and watched the people die. We should not therefore leap to the conclusion that recent events are a greater or lesser human disaster than previous episodes in West African history. We know only that the social precipitants and consequences are likely to have been different, because the political economy is different. The Sahelian relief efforts are too familiar to require elaboration. More generally, as concern with food supply in the Third World has grown, people have noticed that it is not uncommon for West Africans to go hungry. For example, savannah dwellers routinely experience "the hungry gap" between the last of one year's food supplies and the next year's harvest. Sometimes this can provoke a general crisis in whole village communities; more often it is responsible for a few deaths in certain families.

But has the commercialization of agriculture contributed to modern ecological and nutritional disasters? Some would say it definitely has. It can be argued that the shift in emphasis from food to export crops has made subsistence shortfalls and the rundown of food reserves inevitable. By becoming more individuated and less conservative, people have let old social mechanisms of distribution and collective survival under crisis conditions weaken to the point of ineffectiveness. Moreover, commercialization has in some cases led to wanton land-use practices that accelerate long-term damage to the terrain for the sake of immediate profits.[2] Nor are the new states and international agencies exempt from criticism: It is they who have led rural peoples into these dangerous ways because of an insatiable need for increased commodity flows.

This argument would be more convincing if it could explain the crass neglect of their own interests exhibited by the peasants themselves in this instance. Why do they use their groundnut sales to buy trinkets, when more food would save them from starvation? It is not as if food deficits were a novel feature of their lives, reintroduced suddenly after decades of uninterrupted prosperity. One possible explanation is that the market offers a more reliable safeguard against famine than any social mechanism that West Africans were able to devise before modern times. Improvement in transport facilities and the flexibility of commodity economy mean that pockets of people suffering from serious food shortage, who would previously have been isolated and left to starve, can now usually find some measure of relief. The dangers of the market mechanism will be considered later on in this section.

The link between hunger and death is as often as not disease: West Africa is one of the most unhealthy regions in the world. Concerning the relationship between commercial agriculture and epidemiology, the briefest of sketches, again, will have to suffice. Responsibility for improvements in mortality rates may be laid at the door of modern medicine; but general nutrition and improved social organization (e.g., the peaceful administration of modern states) are more profound causes of what has been a substantial reduction in West Africans' exposure to the threat of premature death. (Life expectancy of around forty-eight years is twenty-five years less than the rate for advanced countries, but still a major improvement on nineteenth-century rates in West Africa.) Even so, disease is still rampant in the region, and some have suggested that alterations to watercourses in the name of irrigation or power supplies may expose the rural population to higher levels of malaria, schistosomiasis, and onchocerciasis (e.g., Suret-Canale 1971:279). Usually, agricultural intensification – which involves bush clearing and higher population densities – would reduce exposure to the tsetse fly and hence trypanosomiasis. Some of the old agricultural techniques in the forest, it must be remembered, were very dangerous (e.g., climbing to the top of palm trees), and modern commercial methods of cultivation may reduce these risks somewhat. To the extent that trade and transport are linked, commercialization has brought a new category of death (by road accident) to the countryside. All of these associations are not sufficiently clear to permit a satisfactory grasp of the relationship in question.

In general, any attempt to draw up a balance sheet on the link between agricultural commercialization and the most severe manifestations of West Africans' vulnerability to their material environment would seem at this stage to be a recipe for premature expression of prejudice. My belief is that, on balance, any advance in the social organization of production and distribution toward higher levels of regional, national, and international integration reduces the material vulnerability of rural peoples. I can find evidence to support that view in West African history; but then the imperfections of commercial mechanisms are such that others can argue with some apparent justification that these peoples would be better off relying on more localized and customary subsistence strategies.

Once we move away from dire extremities, we face the problem of measuring quantitative changes in material well-being, usually conceived of as *income levels*. Here I must take time out to explain something that is very poorly understood. In any economy people do some things for themselves and buy other goods and services on the market. (They also pay taxes for public provision of some services, but I will leave that matter for now.) Economists, if they bother to measure them at all, would normally value subsistence activities at market prices – assuming that the equivalent can be bought as a commodity. This is the normal practice in West Africa, too, and it is inherently plausible, because most household heads frequently face the option of withholding subsistence crops from the market or selling them at the going price. What such an approach neglects is the dynamic effect of levels of commercialization on the market price in the first place.

To take an example from western economies, what is the value of a housewife's labor? It is possible to break down the many components of her daily routine into services that are also provided as commodities by specialists – chauffeur, cook, educator, and so on – and to cost them at market prices. The result is predictable: The market value of what she does is astronomically high. This is so because very few people can afford such specialist services; when they do purchase them, they do so because the specialist's price is lower! Indeed, now that fast food is really cheap, fewer housewives spend every day in the kitchen. Moreover, as long as her labor is functionally undifferentiated, the housewife does not really have the option of selling her services in the market, because that would involve specialization to the detriment of her performance of the subsistence role *in toto*. Hence, when women do go to work (and it is invariably at wages much lower than the notional "price" of housework), they find that they must still do most domestic duties themselves, and in much less time than before.

The lesson from this analogy is that pricing subsistence activities by their current market equivalences *inflates the money value of nonmarketed goods and services*. Thus, if an individual farmer releases part of what is predominantly a subsistence crop onto the market, and if the price he gets is used to value what is not sold, the overall value of his "income" will be much higher than if all farmers sold all their crops at the same time. Witholding goods from the market acts to keep their price up. This practice, known under other circumstances as hoarding, is not foreign to economists; yet they persist in pricing subsistence goods as if the market were indifferent to the fact that these goods are in fact being withheld.

The case of crops that have both commercial and subsistence value is more clear-cut than that of those West African subsistence practices which are more directly analogous to a housewife's labor. How can a price be given to tasks like carrying water? It is embedded in the daily routines of village women; no one can make a living being paid to do it for them. In cities without household water supplies, workers pay carriers to bring water for their baths, cooking, and drinking, and commercial water carrying can then be costed on a man-hour basis; but what relevance does that have to estimating village living standards? Would the women be any better off if the market price for water carrying went up in the cities? When people do most of what they need for themselves, what matters is reduction in the labor time necessary for performing their various tasks. A year-round government standpipe in each village would free rural women from a time-consuming walk to a faraway pool or stream in the dry season. That would be a real improvement in their living standards, and it would reflect a *reduction* in the social cost of providing water. But calculations of the money value of subsistence activities in terms of market prices measure mainly the level of labor specialization and market demand, not relative living standards. Nor is there much point in measuring the value of food stocks, which do sometimes appear on the market, while omitting the value of housing, which in rural West Africa almost never comes on the market. Under these circumstances, talk by economists about growth or decline in rural real incomes is just that – talk.

But we must persist in our search for reliable indicators of rural poverty trends. If the consumer utilities of subsistence and commercial goods are incommensurable and price comparisons are fraught with difficulty, are there alternative yardsticks? Degree of control over one's material circumstances might be one: This would stress the powerlessness of the poor. Another might emphasize the range of options open to an individual, counting the opportunity to travel in a car rather than walk a measure of prosperity. Freedom from drudgery or the amount of hard labor endured in an average day might be yet another index. These are selective and qualitative standards of evaluation, but it is well to be explicit about them because they often enter covertly into our judgments. My inclination would be to use a measure of labor efficiency or productivity (i.e., output for a given amount of labor input) as an indicator of standard of living – to ask, that is, how much labor it takes to produce food, clothing, heating, light, housing, child care, medicine, and so on. But then labels of this sort mean such different things in various cultures that an index along these lines would be bound to be arbitrary.

In the light of this discussion, can we say that commercial agriculture has benefited or impoverished West Africa's mostly rural population? What of all those who have ended up in city slums? Many of them know destitution, but they know periods of relative prosperity, too. They do not starve. To the extent that they work in large impersonal organizations, they exercise less control over their own labor than they did in the countryside. If they work in the "informal sector" of urban employment (Hart 1973), they increase their control over work conditions, but have less predictable earnings. Certainly the range of opportunities open to city dwellers is very wide, even if few succeed in bettering themselves substantially. They probably do less physical labor than at home and have access to more labor-saving devices (such as electric light). They have more money to spend, but almost all their material needs can only be satisfied by cash and they rarely have enough.

In the rural areas, those who retain a subsistence base have a measure of security in their guarantee of access to the land; but they are more vulnerable to the vagaries of nature than are city dwellers. They often subsidize the food needs of relatives in the city, hoping to receive commodities in return. Commercial agriculture normally involves harder work than traditional agriculture, with the consequence of increasing access to marketed goods and services. Landless laborers are bound to be worse off than they used to be in the savannah, probably less so in the forest. Indeed, to the extent that savannah dwellers have moved to the coastal/forest zone as a result of commercial agriculture, they are probably better off than before, at least in the sense of having reliable access to food at a lower labor cost. Unfortunately, this discussion of rural poverty in West Africa is fatuous, not so much for any lack of knowledge as because the criteria of evaluation are so imprecise. Econometric studies of the problem that purport to supply quantitative evidence must be spurious until we have made more progress in specifying what we are talking about and how it should be measured.

For most West Africans, the issue that shapes long-term strategies is the framework within which they expect to carry on both their own lives and those of their descendants. Insurance and security are no less a concern for them than they are for Americans. In fact, West Africans have more reason to feel insecure, because the state and corporate businesses have not yet developed well-organized social security schemes that will apply to most people. One recent study of Mali shows how emphasis on the continuity of village institutions, inspired in part by security considerations, can lead to a restriction of market participation (J. V. D. Lewis 1979a). This pattern of subsistence solidarity is reinforced by the evidence from surrounding villages that are more individuated and commercialized: Farm failure is more devastating in these communities, because people have no wider associations to fall back on when they are in need. There can be little doubt that collective adhesions of a traditional sort, founded on a common relationship to the land and to production, represent the best available mechanisms of social insurance at this time, and most West Africans are well aware of the fact.

Commercial farming is not, however, in itself a necessary dissolvent of close ties based on kinship. Indeed, it may even be the opposite, providing the glue that holds people together, as several studies of West Africa testify (see, e.g., Nadel 1942). It is true that a shift to commodities and money seems to increase the potential for family discord and domestic fission; but as we saw in Chapter 1, there was no guarantee of solidarity in traditional kinship organization, where conflict and dispersal have always been normal.

In both traditional and modern settings, men have always turned toward political patronage as a source of security for themselves and their families: The principle of redistribution, whereby the poor receive material benefits from the rich in return for their loyalty as followers, is as alive today as ever. The vast scope for circulating surpluses is such that income differentials are often substantially reduced by a tendency for economic goods and political support to flow in opposite directions. So far, more advanced attempts at state pooling mechanisms – pensions, social security schemes, unemployment benefits, and the like – have had little effect.[3] Moreover, there is no capital market in which people can invest their savings. As a consequence, increased opportunities to make investments in small commercial enterprises managed by themselves – in farming, housing, transport, and so on – reduce the dependence of some affluent West Africans on social relations that trade freedom of maneuver for long-run security (Hart 1975).

Finally, it bears repeating that extension of the market *reduces* the insecurity of farmers by making the supply of foodstuffs less hazardous than when it depended on extremely localized climatic conditions. So here, too, there appears to be no clear-cut conclusion that can be drawn about increased or reduced material security owing to the commercialization of agriculture.

Let us consider now the demographic evidence. The one indisputable fact bearing on the material welfare of West Africans is the quintupling of their population in less than a hundred years. From a figure of around 30 million in the nineteenth century (and only 36 million in 1910), the region's population has reached approximately 150 million in 1980, over half being concentrated in

Table 4. West African demography

Country	Crude birth rate per thousand		Crude death rate per thousand		Life expectancy (years)	
	1960	MRE[a]	1960	MRE[a]	1960	MRE[a]
Nigeria	52	50	25	18	39	48
Benin	52	49	27	19	37	46
Togo	51	50	27	19	37	46
Ghana	49	48	24	17	40	48
Ivory Coast	50	50	27	19	37	46
Liberia	51	51	25	18	37	48
Sierra Leone	47	46	27	19	37	46
Guinea	49	48	28	21	35	44
Guinea Bissau	48	46	33	23	31	41
Senegal	48	48	27	22	37	42
Mauritania	51	50	27	22	37	42
Mali	50	49	30	22	37	42
Upper Volta	49	48	27	22	37	42
Niger	52	52	27	22	37	42
Sub-Saharan Africa	47	46	24	17	40	47
Developing countries	42	37	17	12	47	54
Industrial countries	18	14	10	10	69	73

[a]Most recent estimate, normally 1977.
Source: World Bank (1980); these data exclude the Gambia and Cape Verde.

Nigeria's territory (see Table 1, in Chapter 2). The most rapid expansion has taken place since World War II. The technical explanation for this explosion is the juxtaposition of high fertility and low mortality rates. The demographic transition that has accompanied industrialization in the more-advanced sectors of the world's economy consists of a shift from a pattern of high birth rates and high, but erratic, death rates to one in which both rates are low and stable (McKeown 1976). Historically, death rates have fallen faster than birth rates; the result is a transitional period of abnormally high growth in the total population before fertility adjusts to prevailing expectations of mortality (Cipolla 1978). One consequence of this shift is a rapidly aging population, revealed as higher life-expectancy tables. West Africa, as Table 4 shows, is far from matching the demographic performance of industrialized countries, but the evidence suggests that the region is at that early phase when death rates have begun to fall drastically and fertility has not yet been adjusted downward.

It can be seen that, since 1960, birth rates have remained stable around 50 per thousand, with a slight trend toward reduction by 1 or 2 points. Death rates, on the other hand, have fallen sharply in less than two decades from just under 30 per thousand to around 20 per thousand. This represents an increase in the crude annual growth rate from 2 to 3 percent, almost all explicable by changes in mortality. At the same time, between 5 and 9 years have been added to the average life expectancy of West Africans. In displaying this pattern, the region is similar to sub-Saharan Africa as a whole, although birth and death rates are both slightly lower for the continental population. This difference is even more accentuated when West Africa is compared with all developing countries, the difference in birth rates being most marked. But the industrialized countries offer a stark contrast: Fertility is here on the average a quarter of West African rates, mortality a half, and life expectancy half as much again. This difference between rich and poor countries is matched in some degree by variations within West Africa. Compare the figures for the top seven countries in Table 4 (the richer, forest-belt countries) with those for the bottom half (the Sahelian or dry savannah countries). Average death rates are 3 points higher in the latter group, and life expectancy is 4 or 5 years lower. Improvements in life expectancy since 1960 have averaged 9 years in the southern coastal countries, only 5 years in the Sahel (against 7 years for all sub-Saharan Africa). Demography is a rough index of improvements in general economic welfare, but it is a powerful one.

The pressure toward high birth rates already existed in traditional attitudes to parenthood: The lineage is a fertility machine whose fuel has clearly not yet run out. Why are death rates now lower? Obviously, pressures that had operated for millennia in West Africa have been suddenly removed. These must include vulnerability to disease, and modern medicine no doubt has had a significant effect. But West Africans would also seem to have been better fed; and that means – recent well-publicized famines notwithstanding – that nutritional deficiencies now make less of a contribution to mortality rates than before. Another factor would be reduced risk of death by violence, now that warfare and slave raiding have been eliminated. The sheer stress to human life caused by living an arduous countryman's existence has been alleviated for many, either completely or in part, by new employment opportunities and the spread of public amenities.

Many may ask whether the population explosion is not indeed a "time bomb," causing unmitigated hardship for the teeming millions who inhabit the Third World. In West Africa's case nothing could be further from the truth. It is one of the most sparsely populated regions in the world: Historians of all persuasions are united in attributing its economic underdevelopment in part to a low density of population, which has inhibited growth of the market economy, state formation, intensification of agriculture, and so on (A. G. Hopkins 1973; Goody 1971). Now that the demographic conditions for the establishment of a progressive political economy are beginning to emerge, it is perverse to suggest that population growth is deleterious to the region's well-being! The most prosperous parts of West Africa are the most populous – Nigeria is the most obvious example – and they are certainly nowhere near bursting point. When England's population increased by 50 percent in the nineteenth century, it was taken as a measure of material improvement; in France, promotion of the birth rate has never gone out of fashion. It is surely advantageous to West Africa today that its land area is at last beginning to be filled up; the epidemiological benefits alone will be epoch-making. There may be a few pockets of land, particularly in densely settled former refugee zones of the savannah, where population growth appears to have exacerbated already depressed local farming conditions.[4] But it should be said, first, that these are atypical of West African settlement patterns and, second, that they will eventually be relieved either by voluntary emigration or by circulatory migration.

We will return to these matters in Chapter 7. Here it will suffice to point out that West Africa's demography offers irrefutable evidence that its people have broken through Malthusian checks on their growth in the middle decades of this century, having been able in millennia of previous occupation to reach a population of only 30 million. To the extent that this growth coincides with agricultural commercialization and absorption into the world political economy, we must conclude that the principal effect of such a change has been one of overall material improvement.[5] This general position is valid even though we may recognize some negative consequences of the shift to commercial agriculture.

How harmful have been the vagaries of commodity markets? West Africans have had plenty of experience of the boom–bust cycle of world trade. They underwent decades of depressed prices in the late nineteenth century and, after the early colonial boom, the shock of world depression in the 1930s and 1940s. More recently they have suffered from the twin attack of global inflation and giddy swings in commodity prices.[6] So even though some people may have been caught once by becoming overly reliant on the market for one export crop, most West Africans are now aware that they should keep their options as open as possible.[7] This is doubly important because, when there is a global shortage of grain or oil, the price goes up and those least able to pay often have to do without. When the commodity is food and there are no local substitutes available, West Africans are among those most likely to starve – although the region is not a Bangladesh or even an Ethiopia. It is one of the most striking features of West African agriculture that commercial farming has usually been combined with a variety of subsistence production patterns. It is true that grain has to be imported from abroad, but then the population has been growing much faster than food production. There can be little doubt that commitment to commercial production is risky under current world market conditions, but West African farmers have in large degree offset the potentially damaging consequences of such a commitment by pursuing strategies to secure food supplies for themselves by other means. This partial retreat into subsistence, however, only exacerbates the nonagricultural population's reliance on overseas food supplies. A lasting solution to the problem will come only when a specialized segment of West African agriculture produces food for the home market.

This discussion's necessary inconclusiveness is accounted for by the lack of unequivocal standards for measuring material progress. By international standards, West Africans undoubtedly consume more commodities than they used to. They are probably better fed, clothed, and sheltered than their ancestors. They listen to radios and go to school, where before they sat at their grandfathers' knees. Their horizons are wider; they are more fully part of the human community. In my judgment they are better off, but the means of resolving an argument with anyone who disagrees lie beyond the scope of this book.

Growing inequality?

It is now widely recognized that programs of agricultural commercialization, such as those promoted under the rubric "Green Revolution" in the 1960s, made some people richer than others (see, e.g., Mellor 1966, 1976). In 1973, Robert MacNamara made a famous speech at Nairobi enjoining World Bank staff (and indeed all of us) to pay greater attention in future to considerations of "equity" in dealings with Third World nations. Distributional goals have become so prominent at AID, following a mandate from Congress to seek out "the poorest of the poor," that leveling out differences of wealth could now be said to rival development itself as the agency's principal concern. Domestic jibes about the taxes of U.S. workers finding their way via overseas aid into the pockets of corrupt Third World elites must only reinforce what in any case may be a philosophical preference of many of those who now enter employment in the international donor agencies.

A proper concern with social justice (equity) is a necessary corrective to the old "development or bust" mentality; but overzealous egalitarianism may be both damaging to West Africa's prospects for economic growth and misleading in the sense that the perceptions of well-intentioned people are unnecessarily distorted. Equality and equity are not the same thing; nor is the political goal of equality of opportunity to be confused with economic equality in fact. As de Tocqueville pointed out long ago (1863), the United States is the last place on earth where one would expect to hear the argument that reductions in wealth differences are essential to the well-being of the citizen body. Yet it is not uncommon to read in development-agency literature pejorative references to the fact that some farmers have become enriched as a result of aid programs.

Of course one's political and moral sensibilities are outraged by systematic neglect of the disenfranchised poor, by oppression and landlessness in villages ruled by a new landlord class, by unconscionable looting of the public purse on a grand scale. These are matters that should be opposed wherever they occur, and prophylactic measures should be built into the administration of programs supported by international agencies. But awareness of these possibilities should not lead us into judging every minor variation in income levels to be a social injustice. The fact is that the only way to keep income levels as equal as they are now in West Africa is to keep the people as near as possible to a subsistence level of self-sufficient economic organization. Any shift toward higher productivity or income growth in the population as a whole must increase the range of wealth differences. Moreover, the population will become more differentiated as production becomes more specialized and as social organization becomes more complex. There will be losers in this process; there always are, and there have been for millennia of West Africa's history. In the end, economic development offers more hope for a just social order than does stagnation.

The question is, How much social inequality can be tolerated, that is, considered reasonably equitable? This broad question cannot be answered here; but it may be more appropriate to ask whether inequality has increased in the countryside. Chapter 2 has already shown how basically unequal were the traditional societies of West Africa. The societies of the Sahel and Sudan, in particular, were as rigidly stratified as many in India, which is widely (if perhaps unfairly) recognized as the world leader in social inequality. Even the so-called stateless societies were rendered homogeneous by their relations with the surrounding states, who victimized them as a reservoir of potential slaves. Moreover, as has been pointed out before, when social organization and economic production rest heavily on kinship, the development cycle of family growth and decline in itself generates considerable material inequalities through time. In many rural communities the rich are older men with large mature families; the poor are struggling young families, often with some chronic defect like an ailing or missing spouse. This is the case in most parts of the world, but it is especially significant when production depends heavily on the recruitment of family labor. Much modern inequality in the countryside is thus the same as the old inequality, except that some contemporary trends may have acted to reduce the power of monopoly exercised by elders over their juniors.

If economic differentiation is inevitable, it is certainly recognized as such in most West African cultures (Lloyd 1974). As long as wealth may be attributed to personal good fortune (the Hausa term is *arziki*),[8] or to the hard work, skill, and so on of affluent individuals, no one considers it to be an affront to a sense of social justice. West Africans value positively the pursuit of personal enrichment and often deny that good fortune can be inherited from a rich father. What they are less keen on, and this is revealed in the traditional customs of many indigenous peoples (as well as in the force of present-day public opinion), is the transmission of enduring privilege between the generations.[9] In this they share the sensibilities of most Americans: There is general agreement that all citizens should have the same property rights and broadly the same access to a means of livelihood; if some individuals prosper, they may seek to pass on some advantage to their children, but the institutions of society do not guarantee that those children will end up enjoying a life-style and set of opportunities starkly superior to those which are the lot of other children in the society. The savannah civilizations often departed from this norm; and everywhere strangers, slaves, and their descendants held inferior rights, usually political and ritual rights (especially rights to office), rather than economic. But as long as the matrix of social life was the land, and access to the land was freely available to all group members, property in the means of production could not be – and was not – a basis for social stratification.[10]

The social impact of commercial agriculture

Having said all that, I will turn to a brief discussion of the ways in which social inequality has come to manifest itself in West Africa. Differentiation within the countryside itself cannot be considered in isolation from the larger polarizing tendencies in the world today, of which the most significant is the growing gap between rich and poor nations. Nor should inequality at the village level be treated separately from the major forces for stratification within the region and its component states. We will consider these aspects of the problem before turning to the question whether rural class formation is a significant issue for West Africa.

The main class opposition in the world today is that between rich and poor nations. Global industrialization has generated both a widening productivity gap between north and south and a net transfer of resources in the former's favor. The result is that differences between these groups of nations are overwhelmingly more significant than inequalities within any one state. The poorest U.S. citizen would stand out as a man of wealth in Mali. U.S. involvement in the Sahel, as a result of famine relief programs initiated by Congress, uses up a minute part of the country's budget – literally just petty cash; but those few million dollars have turned the political economy of a country like Upper Volta upside down.

West Africa's total GNP of near $60 billion in 1977 (including figures for Nigeria, which accounted for over two-thirds of the sum) was shared out among a population that is about two-thirds of the United States' and that occupies about two-thirds of the United States' land area. But the GNP of the United States in 1977 ($1,900 billion) was some thirty-two times that of West Africa. In fact, what Americans spent on imported oil in 1977 ($55 billion) was close to the value of all the sectors of West Africa's sixteen national economies. Or, to take an even more bizarre example, West Africa's GNP is little more than twice the estimated street value of illegally imported soft drugs (cocaine and marijuana) in the United States. When U.S. (or British or Swedish) aid officials express concern about growing inequality in rural areas where the *annual* per capita income is about half what development consultants are paid *per day*, the situation is more than ironic – it is obscene.

If equity is part of our moral legacy as human beings, then the gap to be reduced urgently is that between rich and poor nations, not that within the poor nations themselves. Fundamental change in this global class structure can take place only through a combination of rapid increases in Third World *productivity* and massive transfers from the rich countries. Talk of equity in the absence of any such commitment is self-deception or worse. Let no one be in any doubt that the most tangible manifestation of social inequality in West Africa's countryside is any white face, even if it is attached temporarily to a hair shirt and baggy shorts. The history of the last hundred years and current global realities ensure that most West Africans would make such an identification of the basic cleavage in the distribution of privilege.

Turning to the question of inequalities within the region as a whole, these are mainly of three kinds. Today the biggest gap in West Africa – and it is growing –

is between Nigeria and the rest. This is partly, of course, because of oil, but not mainly so. The country's size and the long-standing market integration of its diverse population have contributed more durably to its economic prospects. It seems inevitable that people will gravitate further toward West Africa's only state with a recognizable future. Some states would like to see Nigeria take up a more actively redistributive posture toward its neighbors, but there has been little evidence of this happening so far, and there is unlikely to be more in times to come. The future pattern of Nigeria's hegemony in the region is uncertain, but it is likely that Nigerian citizens will enjoy marked privileges in relation to other West Africans.

The second principal inequality in West Africa has been that between Francophone and Anglophone states. The British colonies were more prosperous, especially the Gold Coast and southern Nigeria, partly because of their precolonial endowments and partly because of a more felicitous agricultural policy than was followed in French territories. The result was a substantial flow of population from French to British territories, with the immigrants enjoying rather low status in their host societies. Postcolonial developments have tended to alter this pattern somewhat, with the rise of the Ivory Coast, the strengthening of franc zone currencies, and the decline of Ghana. The recent concentration of American aid effort in Francophone areas is a further push in this direction. But it has to be said that the five Anglophone states (Nigeria, Ghana, Sierra Leone, the Gambia, Liberia) still account for three-quarters of the region's GNP and 70 percent of its population, though they cover less than a quarter of the region's land area.

Perhaps the most perdurable inequality within the region as a whole is that between coast/forest and interior/savannah populations. The interior savannah peoples have a proud and ancient civilization, strongly Islamic and highly stratified. Their links with the Mediterranean Arab world ensured their maintenance of a cosmopolitan outlook rarely found elsewhere in sub-Saharan Africa. The forest-dwelling peoples were culturally backward and pagan; they never founded a mercantile tradition comparable to the region-wide networks of Hausa and Dioula traders. But as we have seen, European imperialism induced a strong shift in West Africa's economy toward the coast and forest agriculture. Today the forest peoples, swollen now by many immigrants from the savannah, are still more prosperous and more westernized. The savannah areas are universally poor, with the exception of parts of Senegal and Hausaland. Differences of climate and environment, of economy and culture, will ensure that this historic cleavage remains a persistent element of class conflict in West African distributional politics at both local and more inclusive levels.

There is no room here to discuss all the minor regional and ethnic divisions that exist in West Africa. But it should be said that these, taken together with the three large categories of inequality just listed, often have provided the framework for the expression of social conflict arising out of perceived exploitation and inequality in West Africa. This does not mean that they are not class conflicts;

rather, it indicates that they gain added impetus from the congruence of economic and other primordial alignments. It is an explosive ingredient in labor relations if the boss and his workers speak a different language, profess antagonistic religions, and cannot stand the weather in each other's home area.[11] That is why so many struggles take on the structure of an ethnic division between people of local descent and strangers. Within the West African nations, the principal class cleavage is between those with privileged access to state power and those without. Closely associated with this division are the oppositions between literate and nonliterate and between town and countryside. None of these oppositions was foreign to West Africa before colonization, but colonial rule and more especially the two decades of postcolonial government have generated a growing gap between an urbanized, highly educated elite, drawing its power and its principal employment from the state, and the rest, a relatively undifferentiated class of poor workers and their families straddling the gap between town and countryside. The main means of upward mobility in West Africa is still education. Hitherto, recruitment to bureaucratized office via higher education has been relatively open, and therefore it is not judged by the excluded masses to be particularly invidious. But there is evidence that, with the end to postcolonial Africanization near at hand and stagnation in government budgets an inevitability, some rigidification of class position is under way.[12] Obviously, today's members of the state elite are in a better position to secure educational advantage for their own children than are the parents of children living in a remote savannah village.

Moreover, the state elite was for some time content to live indirectly off the countryside's agricultural surplus (see Chapter 4), but recently civil servants, soldiers, and other public employees have taken a more direct interest in controlling agricultural production, acting both as government officials (of marketing boards, cooperatives, irrigation schemes, etc.) and as private individuals interested in securing their future or even in amassing fortunes through farming (Adegboye and Abidogun 1973). Given the fusion of economic and legal practice, these people are in the best position to secure a pathway through government bureaucracy and win the support of local political leaders for their enterprises. The class basis of rural inequality is thus clearest when members of the state elite become landowners and absentee agrarian capitalists. If recruitment to that elite were more closed and its members more detached from a wide circle of lower-class kinsmen, we would have a fully fledged stratification system in the countryside. As yet, any such tendencies are only incipient in West Africa.

One country in West Africa has already reached the stage of possessing a wealthy landowning elite, and that is Liberia, where private land acquisition has long been proceeding on a scale rarely seen outside southern Africa (Liebenow 1969; Clower et al. 1966). In 1964 President William Tubman, who was no mean landowner in his own right, made a speech claiming that several members of the Americo-Liberian ruling class, as well as some chiefs whose services had been indispensable to the government, had acquired estates of up to twenty thousand acres for as little as fifty cents an acre. The stark polarization of castes in Liberia was a major aspect of the recent coup in which many leaders of the ruling elite were killed by soldiers recruited largely from the indigenous masses. Perhaps the remainder of West Africa's ruling classes will stop short of such obvious self-aggrandizement: A Swiss bank account may lead to exile, but a large estate is more likely to lead to the firing squad.

The gap between city and village is great enough, but the circulation of personnel between the two acts to reduce any perception of rural and urban populations as being fundamentally different. (According to one student of the urbanized northern Nigerian emirates [Nadel 1942], the cultural polarization of peasants and townsmen was probably greater before this century than is the case today, with higher rates of mobility.) There are certainly disproportionate amounts spent on urban infrastructure and subsidies to urban consumption. Moreover, in each country, opportunities in the capital city far exceed possibilities elsewhere. But for the mass of people, living standards are not greatly different between town and country; the main difference lies in the chance to break out of poverty in the city, a chance realized by only a few, but enough to keep the others hopeful. Village life is a dead end, and that is the main source of rural–urban inequality: It reflects above all the centralizing hierarchy of the postcolonial state.

And so at last we turn to the countryside itself, with the question whether agricultural commercialization has led to growing inequalities at the village level – perhaps even to class formation and class conflict. Some of the ground has already been covered in Chapter 5. Wealth differences have probably increased over the last century or so; but just as the main source of privilege was once political power and membership in a slave-raiding aristocracy, so too is modern privilege endowed by the state. Agricultural commodity production as such has not so far produced a significant rural gentry of capitalist farmers; farming is not yet the main avenue to personal wealth, being outstripped by bureaucratic employment, the army, trade, and the professions.

One case where capitalism and the state power came together in a potentially explosive combination was the development of large-scale private rice farming in northern Ghana in the 1970s (Shepherd 1978). It is of some interest that social protest against these new farmers (civil servants, soldiers, chiefs, merchants) was widespread, taking the form not only of litigation over land rights, but also of crop burning (Goody 1980). These acts were matched by burning of government-owned sugar plantations in southern Ghana at much the same time, and comparisons with agrarian protest in Britain at the time of the Industrial Revolution seem apposite. The temptation is to build on these incidents a theory of proto-class consciousness, but it is too early to tell whether such developments are systematic or isolated.

More common is the finding that rural West Africans are slow to perceive class inequality in their social relations. The French and English literature on Hausaland is unanimous in stressing the inevitabilty of inequality and an ideology attributing material good fortune to personal qualities.[13] Thus, despite the fact that Hausa society is distinguished by a rigid political hierarchy that has persisted through all the upheavals of the last 150 years; despite the advanced division of labor, the social separation of town and countryside, and widespread landlessness; despite the gulf that exists between ethnic groups in Hausaland – despite all this, this literature speaks of a pervasive individualism and asserts that life chances are not stratified by birth. Hill's case is a persuasive one, although M. G. Smith's earlier (1955) ethnography paints a less egalitarian picture of the Hausa countryside. It is probable that increased levels of commodity production and geographical mobility have acted to reduce social stratification in Hausaland, whereas the opposite trend may be true of areas that entered the modern period with more homogeneous social structures.

The important questions are whether landed property has grown in significance and – the corollary – whether ruinous indebtedness and landless penury are now more common in West Africa's villages than before. We may well be at a turning point where land is concerned, in that state guarantees of private property in land already exist in some countries and may be near at hand in others. But because rights in land are meaningless without access to the labor to work it, the more important question is how that labor would be organized – whether as sharecropping tenants or as supervised wage workers. Again, the evidence is not clear-cut. Nor is it clear whether landlessness is growing as a result of accumulation by others or merely as a spin-off from labor circulation.

Up to the present time, cash-crop expansion has been into areas with plenty of land to spare; there has been no expropriation. But it may be that this period is drawing to a close, so that further expansion can take place only at the expense of sitting farmers. This is already the case with many irrigation schemes: Flooding has been used to get more people off the land than have eventually been enabled to farm the irrigated areas. Abuse and neglect of the interests of settled populations in such cases has been standard. Usury and financial indebtedness is a serious problem; but because individuals do not have title to their lands and property, it is impossible for them to mortgage their means of livelihood and eventually lose them. The growth of commodity economy in general ensures that some will benefit disproportionately and others lose out. West African rural society is no exception, but there are many areas of Asia and Latin America where the plight of villagers is much worse (see, e.g., Taussig 1980). The main difference is that the social institutions surrounding lineages and their membership have not been destroyed in West Africa, and this structure has provided a bulwark against commercialization.

When West African villages are placed next to the centers of national and international power, their internal differences pale into insignificance. The overwhelming gap between the two produces a homogenizing effect, so that rural peoples really do seem to have become a mass peasantry. Until this century, West Africans lived in local groups with few significant external relations (and these generally intermittent). They relied on segmentary organization, which yielded vertical associations – such as named descent groups – as the basis for particular identities through which they differentiated themselves from others. Nor was the sale of produce by free farmers enough by itself to peasantize them. It is the modern state and the new weight of institutions bearing down on village life and deriving a living from it that have generated a true peasantry throughout the region, squeezing out all but those willing to endure a life of underprivileged drudgery. Chances for enrichment and personal advancement are increasingly monopolized by agencies external to the village itself. Hence what is remarkable in West Africa is the growing sameness of villagers, not their internal differentiation.

Men and women

All significant changes in the social life of a people involve alterations in the most fundamental of human arrangements – domestic organization, the productive and reproductive cooperation of men and women. In traditional West African societies, the sexual division of labor was pervasive; as we saw in Chapter 3, it covered more than cooking and farming. Moreover, it varied considerably within the region. Subsequent developments always seem to have been strongly influenced by these variable traditional sex divisions; so it would be unwise to make generalizations about West Africa as a whole.

One common pattern was described for the Nupe of northern Nigeria by Nadel.[14] Here the men traditionally farmed and controlled distribution of the grain that they grew, whereas women concentrated on preparing food, kept kitchen gardens, and were involved in local marketing on a small scale. Colonialism opened up new opportunities for commercial agriculture and wage labor, both of which were monopolized by men. But the growth of urban centers, with their predominantly male populations, generated a demand for goods and services that women were able to supply on a commercial basis, notably, prepared food and sex (Little 1973). Moreover, women began to fill the distribution gaps in trade beyond the local level, in an extension of traditional roles that greatly increased their independence. The upshot was that the men's productive activities did not yield much in the way of savings; wage laborers spent most of their earnings just living in the towns, and commercial agriculture afforded small profit to rural production units whose surpluses were quickly absorbed by taxes and bridewealth. Women's trade, on the other hand, became very profitable, and before long they controlled much of the liquidity in Nupe economy, lending money to their husbands, brothers, and sons when the latter could not pay their dues. The men apparently were not greatly pleased with these developments.

The general pattern has been replicated wherever male specialization in colonial wage labor was grafted onto an economy in which women were able to expand their traditional marketing role and move into the gap created by urban markets where no capitalist firms provided for the needs of the African population. Of course, sex imbalances in urban demography have now been much reduced, but the dominance of women in petty trade remains a prominent feature of coastal/forest West Africa. Some casual observers of the West African "mammy" believe that she constitutes evidence that women were not always dominated by men in traditional society; but as this account indicates, twentieth-century economic life is far from traditional.

According to a well-known hypothesis of Boserup (1970), West African women played a prominent part in the agricultural economy as hoe farmers, and they have been squeezed out of modern commercial agriculture by a male monopoly of new cash-crop opportunities, especially when agriculture is mechanized (a rather rare event). Thus commercialization of agriculture has reduced women's economic power and social status. Boserup has in mind the forest zone, where, before colonialism, women farmed while men fought and captured slaves; afterward, women continued to farm and some men turned to commercial exploitation of rubber, cocoa, and oil palm. I do not know whether this constitutes a loss to women or not, except that they might see more of their husbands under the new regime. Boserup's hypothesis is a reasonable description of the facts in some places and not in others. Yoruba women in southwestern Nigeria fit the general scheme, but the strength of their manufacturing and trading activities easily compensates for their low rate of participation in cocoa farming. It is always necessary to investigate what has happened to the division of labor as a whole, not just to commercial and subsistence agriculture.[15] For even when men do monopolize export-crop industries, women usually have considerable opportunities in the secondary and tertiary sectors of home markets opened up by the advance of commodity production, not just as retailers of imported textiles and similar manufactures, but as wholesale foodstuffs distributors, beer brewers, soap makers, and so on. This pattern is especially prevalent in the south, where men were often more interested in politics than farming and left much of long-distance trade to Muslim merchants from the north.

In the Islamized savannah interior, women of course often operate from behind seclusion. Here too, however, they control a great deal of the cash flowing through the economy, operating a "hidden trade" from indoors, largely through their children (Hill 1969). So highly commercialized is the division of labor here that women are said sometimes to sell food to their own husbands. It cannot be said that women enjoy an equal position in society with men, but trends in agriculture do not appear to have played a significant role in bringing about this inequality. By contrast, McCormack's work on Sherbro in Sierra Leone shows that women of the coastal rice-growing belt have achieved considerable independence in places.[16] They are frequently heads of cognatic descent groups, and they sometimes fill such local offices as chief. Again, the sexual division of labor varies greatly over short distances and is very sensitive to shifts in the balance of commercial opportunity; so that women may be found to outnumber men where the local economy favors their specialty and vice versa where male economic roles are more lucrative. Elsewhere in the rice-growing belt, rising commercial demand for what is often a women's crop is posing a strong challenge to the traditional ethos of sex divisions. These cases hammer home the point that trends in the fortunes of men and women vary a great deal in rural West Africa and can never be taken for granted.

The main cause of any deterioration in the position of women in West Africa is not cash cropping as such, but rather the overwhelming share of opportunities in modern – especially higher – education that have gone to men. Female primary education rates are substantially lower than those for male children and about half the average secondary education rates for boys, and in higher education women are outnumbered by men on the average six to one (World Bank 1980). In both the colonial and the postcolonial periods, government has been virtually monopolized by men, as indeed were precolonial polities (queen mothers notwithstanding). The post–World War II boom in lucrative bureaucratic employment is a men's affair; skilled jobs in the public and private sectors are filled by men; most trading firms requiring import/export licenses are run by men. We have a situation, then, in which the upper and middle classes are male; although the mass of the people are divided by sex in such a way as sometimes to give women the appearance of economic superiority at the local and domestic levels. It is ironic that the image of the female market trader is so often invoked by male representatives of government to explain inflation, food shortages, and general economic mismanagement.[17]

It does seem that the future of commercial agriculture in West Africa will be dominated by men, especially if mechanization proceeds much further. Women appear most frequently in this setting as cheap unskilled labor or as undifferentiated members of peasant households. Their best chance lies in encouragement of diversification in the local or national economy, because they have many marketable goods and services within their traditional repertoires. It is also imperative to check out sex divisions before acting on the basis of conventional assumptions about West Africa. The results of such an investigation will often be surprising.

I cannot leave this topic without entering a note on marriage. Throughout West Africa the most significant links between corporate descent groups were traditionally those forged by marriage (Meillassoux 1975a). Often these marriages were accompanied by bridewealth transactions involving cattle, cloth, and other valued goods. Control was exercised by village elders over these transactions and hence over an important part of the lives of women and younger men. Modern economic developments, including agricultural commercialization, have had a profound effect on this system. Once again, local patterns are highly variable. In some areas old men have retained control over the bridewealth system and have accumulated many wives themselves, thereby drastically raising the average age at marriage for younger men.[18] Moreover, the women and their children now have an increased value as agricultural laborers able to produce surpluses for the market. In other areas, elders complain that increased opportunities for the women and young men to earn money on their own account have eroded the elders' control over marriage. In still other places, young men complain that parents hold their daughters to ransom, inflating the bride-price and extorting side payments in cash. Everywhere, rates of marital breakdown appear to have increased, and women seem to be less willing to be used as pawns in political games played by older men. On balance, it could be said that the commercialization of agriculture has had a liberating effect for many women, in that they no longer need be as passive in the marriage system as they undoubtedly were until quite recently. But once again I must caution against failure to take account of local variations through time.

Changes in rural social organization

In traditional village life, particularly among the patrilineal peoples of the savannah, production depended on the periodic cooperation of men drawn from more than one domestic group. Thus cooperation was normally achieved either through the authority structures of lower-order lineages (which linked elders with their junior agnates) or through age grades (which established village-wide work groups of young men). Where neither of these options was available, more ad hoc reciprocal exchanges of labor took place.[19] And, of course, in many areas slaves supplemented or even replaced family labor. These forms of cooperation were especially crucial at labor bottlenecks in the agricultural cycle, and they were relatively efficient for heavy tasks like land clearing. Cooperation in production was also reflected in the distribution mechanisms and property forms linking households: Group labor often meant that the product was pooled centrally for allocation by someone with authority in the descent group; private production was limited to the hours after cooperative work on common fields had been completed.

It is frequently observed these days that commercialization and the growing volume of cash sales have undermined the traditional work groups, leading to individuation of production and the growing importance of private property. The authority of elders has been weakened because they are no longer pivotal in the division of labor, and social solidarity is much reduced. As a result, collective mechanisms of insurance against hardship have been eliminated, and families are left exposed to the cold winds of a market that they barely understand. Rural emigration, especially by young men, results from and in turn reinforces this process of social disintegration, leaving the countryside to be occupied by old men, women, and children. Needless to say, people who paint this scenario think it is on the whole a bad thing.

The picture is far too idealized to be true for all of rural West Africa. First, commercial agriculture has sometimes had the effect of increasing the size of cooperative farming groups, owing to the benefits of cooperation and division of labor in some sectors of an expanded market (Nadel 1942). Second, some villages have been able to retain the allegiance of their young men and the vitality of traditional work groups, taking advantage of the seasonal complementarity between savannah and commercial agriculture. Third, emigration normally is in fact labor circulation; and whereas village elders in the 1920s may have been justifiably frightened that they would lose migrants forever, urban conditions and the low prospects for marriage away from home have meant that by the 1970s most elders knew that their sons must come back (Hart 1978). Fourth, although it may be true that production is more individuated today, agnatic solidarities still often provide the basis for sharing of family responsibilities and exchange of goods and services between kinsmen living at home and abroad (Hart 1971, 1978). Fifth, there are many forms of cooperation alive in West African villages today that may not be traditional, but that have been generated spontaneously by rural people in response to present-day conditions (Seibel and Massing 1974). In summary, village institutions have proven to be far more resilient than is often assumed. Nor should we imagine that social solidarity was any greater in the nineteenth century than it is today, or that "individuation" is a negative process, especially when it means that more women and younger men are able to emancipate themselves wholly or in part from a kinship order that they find oppressive.

The most interesting feature of changing patterns of cooperation in village life is the introduction of *cooperatives*. Senegal placed much emphasis on development through cooperatives that were supposed to reflect traditional communal institutions. As in other countries, painful experiences revealed how great was the gap between modern political ideas and the realities of "collective" life at the village level. The Senegalese government has been particularly brutal in insisting on the purchase of expensive fertilizers and machinery at prices that have meant financial ruin for the farmers. More recently, the approach has shifted to a cooperative model that treats members as individuals, on the lines of schemes devised for peasants in postreform nineteenth-century Russia. Perhaps this will be more appropriate to the peasantized condition of Senegalese villagers. In general, it has proven difficult to deal with West African farmers as individual household heads, precisely because, although they do not belong to collectivist organizations, they are enmeshed in a series of supra-domestic ties and institutions that render their isolation as households sociologically problematic. In the long run, these ties will undoubtedly be weakened, and they are being transformed all the time; but the breakdown of village society into a collection of commercialized monads is still a long way off in West Africa.

What have been the effects on village social life of an increased commitment to commercial farming? It depends very much on the village: Not only is rural West Africa divided into hundreds of cultural/linguistic groups and dozens of ecological/climatic zones, but within any one "ethnic group" even neighboring villages whose social structure is entirely different can be found. Anthropologists who delight in discovering the endless diversity of human arrangements will no doubt be cheered by this state of affairs. It is, however, possible to select some general features for discussion.

Most of rural West Africa is still organized on the principle of descent-group membership. The origins of a settlement's inhabitants are always remembered; ascription by birth is therefore a durable principle of status allocation in village society. The main export-crop-producing zones, such as the groundnut belt of the Senegambia and the cocoa belt of the eastern forest, have had to assimilate very large immigrant populations into areas that were fairly sparsely settled to begin with (Haswell 1953, 1963; Pélissier 1966; Kobben 1956; Dupire 1960; Dunn and Robertson 1973). At first the indigenous peoples were happy to absorb the immigrants: They intermarried with them and took gifts, rents, and other revenues from them. The immigrants brought money and prosperity. But since World War II, things have changed. The indigens often feel threatened by the numerical superiority of the newcomers, and the latter have in turn begun to demand more solid political and property rights. The citizen–stranger problem is a pervasive one. If a clear-cut economic division is overlaid on this dualism, explosive conditions for rural class conflict arise. Confrontations between peoples organized collectively according to principles of common descent are likely to be a prominent feature of the commercial farming areas for some time to come.

The political organization of rural West Africa has penetrated deeply into its social structure. Usually, but not always, these political developments have been closely associated with commercial agriculture. I have touched on chiefship in Chapter 4. Undoubtedly the position of the chief in local social hierarchies has been strengthened by the need of outside agents to avail themselves of the land and labor to which he controls access. Local chiefs have also frequently taken the lead in promoting large-scale farming within their communities. In a case such as that of the Mourides of Senegal, a politico-religious hierarchy has become entrenched almost as a state within the state, through its capacity to organize followers as territorial segments of groundnut growers (Cruise O'Brien 1971, 1975; Behrman 1967). Elsewhere, the dominance of a single-party regime has meant that every village has its notables, tied into the central government often as agents in cooperatives and similar institutions associated with local agricultural improvements. And throughout the region, the rural areas are linked to the towns by absentee landowners, rentiers, and capitalist farmers who are themselves often employed by the government in some capacity. All these factors taken together point once more to the fact that social stratification in the countryside is the product of a conjuncture between state influences and agricultural commercialization.

It would therefore be wrongheaded to think of village social life as largely homogeneous and self-sufficient. The myth of village unity has wrecked more than one cooperative scheme. For it is not just the elements of political leadership and economic privilege already mentioned that undermine any conception of the village as a single collectivity, but much more the persistence of principles of segmentary organization in rural society. Factionalism is rife in West African villages, even within lineages and families. This is why some groups have developed village-wide secret societies and others clientship – in order to limit the divisiveness of kinship (Horton 1976). Most West African peoples were never beaten into submission to authority, and unruly administration is thus inevitable. Commercial agriculture has sown the seeds of an economic dependence on outsiders that may counter this anarchy in the long run; but there is still a great deal of autonomy built into all levels of West African rural social structure. The partial exception is the social organization of large-scale irrigation and land-colonization schemes. Here the authorities really hold the whip hand, and discipline is, at least in theory, quite reliably instituted in the political and economic fabric. No wonder West African states persevere with these projects and villagers do their best to stay away from them.

Some observers seem to think that the underpinnings of the traditional society and culture have been taken away by modern political and economic developments.[20] It is a difficult issue to settle, because sociocultural forms are continually being created, transformed, and abandoned. Indeed, the claim that any institution or behavioral norm is "customary" should always be looked at askance. Today's innovation is very soon tomorrow's custom, to be ceaselessly invoked by the innovator's successors as an immemorial tradition. We have seen that the events of the last 150 years – let us say the last six generations of West Africans – have witnessed considerable upheaval in the region. Many of the traditional authorities in the area are nineteenth-century upstarts, and most chiefs came into their own as a result of their elevation by the colonial powers. Rights to land are equally debatable, given the restless mobility of whole populations up to the modern period. Practices that are today sometimes described as unthinkable under traditional law turn out to have been merely suspended during this century (an example would be land sales in certain densely settled parts of the region). Traditional custom is thus a chimera, a manipulable sanction through which present-day interests justify their actions. In the sense that it is routinely invoked in conflicts over land, political office, and similar matters, traditional culture has never been more alive.

The liveliness of traditional culture is attested to also by the frequent references (especially in the French literature) to the significance of customary expenditures in modern rural settings (Nicolas 1967; Raynaut 1972). Nicolas, Raynaut, and others writing of Niger (Maradi) emphasize the sheer volume of "ceremonial" spending, which ensures that a large part of villagers' earnings from cash crops is spent on wasteful celebrations ("potlatches") rather than on investments in improved production. Although their judgment is curious, these authors do bring attention to the importance of redistributive networks and of rituals such as funerals in which West Africans maintain their social relations. The way they occupy themselves in the dry season, the way they choose to invest their lives with meaning – in all this villagers demonstrate that they are still very much

148

captive to ancient folkways and beliefs.[21] And why not? They still have to break the soil with a hoe; they still have to account for the death of a child; they still have to prove that their descent group should have won the chiefship. Selling groundnuts does not end all this; not even famine ends it. In this case, too, we see that customary life flourishes under partially commercialized conditions; the fundamental character of rural society has not been undermined. Nicolas's studies (especially 1965*b*) incidentally show how ceremonial circuits both provide insurance for the poor and validate the status of the rich. It is precisely because they have not lost their function as the principal social security mechanism for rural and urban dwellers that West Africa's villages remain a vital repository of social and cultural life.

Finally, despite the penetration of Islam and Christianity into the region, many West Africans remain attached to an animist religion linking relations between living family members to the ancestral dead (Goody 1962). They also often adhere to cults of the earth and local shrines that celebrate their attachment to particular descent groups and territories.[22] These considerations are still extremely important in shaping the attitude of West Africans to the land and to their kinsmen. When they perceive their links to either to be threatened with rupture, they are likely to respond aggressively, even violently. Any planner who expects to flood land or remove a people without the most deeply felt resistance will be surprised. Crop burning is just one manifestation of what happens when traditional sentiments are aroused. So it can be said that traditional culture is alive in this sense, too.

Commercial agriculture may intensify collective attachments even as it assiduously erodes them. To the extent that village life is not now self-sustaining (if it ever was), commercialization has undermined the framework of rural social life. The division of labor and the centers of relevant social power are instituted far beyond village boundaries. But in the continuing evolution of West African society, traditional culture is still very much a dynamic force to be reckoned with. The abstract categories of sociology and economics will not capture West African realities; true comprehension of rural development problems requires an intensive knowledge of local cultures as well as analysis of cost–benefit ratios and administrative hierarchies.

Nor is it clear that the ethical issues raised in this chapter are capable of normative resolution. The problem was highlighted by Oscar Lewis' (1951) reinterpretation of a Mexican village studied by Robert Redfield (1930): Where one found harmony, the other found only discord; one's integration was the other's pathology. In the present instance, it seems to me that the main predisposing variable is what one thinks of capitalism in the context of West African development. I have been unable to wrap my observations in fabricated moral or political certainty; the account that I have given will have to stand as its own assessment.

Even if we can identify phenomena that all agree are to be deplored – such as the famine of the early 1970s – the remedies against such ills are not as obvious as some writers appear to think (see, e.g., Comité d'Information Sahel 1975). Thus the famine has been attributed to the Sahel's involvement with world capitalism: International corporations grow fat while West African pastoralists die, and so on. The inference to be made is that withdrawal from the system of commerce linking the region to world markets will reduce the risk of famine. I have already indicated that the risks of being involved in the market are probably less than those of being left to the mercy of the elements and of whatever protection subsistence organizations may afford. But if we are genuinely open-minded, it would surely be worthwhile to explore the historical evidence and all the practical possibilities that exist for combining security and growth. The point is that productivity and the division of labor must advance further in West Africa; yet many sensitive observers are already worried about the costs inflicted on human lives by developments so far. How can agriculture contribute to social progress in the region, and what mechanisms, if any, exist to alleviate the social pain of mass dislocation? These questions will be considered briefly in the final chapter.

7

What is to be done?

The most important item on the agenda of development is to transform the food sector, create agricultural surpluses to feed the urban population and thereby create the domestic basis for industry and modern services. If we can make this domestic change, we shall automatically have a new international economic order.

Sir W. Arthur Lewis, *The Evolution of the International Economic Order*
(1978a:75)

West Africa's international significance

There are three criteria by which the big powers evaluate their interest in Third World regions such as West Africa: in descending order of significance, (1) global strategy, (2) economic resources, and (3) humanitarian concern.

West Africa is clearly a region of low strategic significance. It is far removed from the Middle East and southern Africa, the nearest centers of global conflict. But the sixteen West African nations play a part in both through their membership in the Organization of African Unity and other international organizations. And Nigeria is a state with the potential to play a dominant role in the affairs of the continent as a whole. Nigeria is one of the few OPEC countries with a large population; it is a major oil supplier of the United States and an important market for both the United States and Britain. France has an obvious interest in maintaining close ties with her ex-colonies in West Africa, as part of a long-term plan of informal expansion in Africa. The USSR has diminished ties with socialist countries such as Guinea and Mali, and appears to have lost interest in the region, with the exception, of course, of Nigeria. The time when West Africa's prominence in the decolonization movement brought on itself all the focus of the Cold War has long gone. The region has sunk back to what it always was in world history, a backwater. This means that, when aid tied to foreign policy objectives is being handed out, West Africa will get little of it. The United States and France seem to have the strongest interest in the region.

With the notable exception of Nigeria's oil and Niger's uranium, West Africa is not a producer of any strategic raw material. It has a dominant share of the world

151

market in only one item, and that a luxury food – cocoa. The colonial trading economy locked West Africa into an exchange of raw materials used in industrial manufactures and processing (groundnuts, oil palm, cocoa, rubber, cotton, and some minerals) for imported European manufactures (mostly consumer goods) and Asian rice. There are many substitutes for the region's vegetable oils, both natural and synthetic, produced in all kinds of climates around the world. West Africa has only three competitors as a tropical forest zone: East/Central Africa, Amazonia, and Southeast Asia (including Papua New Guinea). It could be that the flora typical of this kind of ecology – tropical hardwoods, plants for medicine, and the like – will become an increasingly scarce global resource. Moreover, even in the case of the present staple export crops, West Africa has an advantage of being close to North Atlantic markets. When it comes to mineral resources, there are some deposits of tin, gold, diamonds, bauxite, phosphates, and manganese; but these are not large, and they are, in several cases, due to be exhausted shortly. Liberia and Mauritania have substantial deposits of iron ore, the world's most common metal. These raw material exports mean more to West Africa than they do to the industrialized countries; the region's collective withdrawal from the world market poses a serious threat to no one. West Africa has not yet begun to manufacture anything that would have a substantial market overseas; so here, too, the region poses no threat in the immediate future to the industries of the West. Finally, West Africa does have the capacity to be a major food exporter, with rice and beef the probable staples.

A development strategy of strengthening production for the home market in foodstuffs, raw materials, and labor-intensive manufactures would not deprive the powerful countries of existing markets (much of what West Africa imports is produced in other Third World regions, such as Southeast Asia); and it might serve as a launching pad for new, less precarious staple exports to the world market. In general, however, the use of West Africa's material resources is an issue of greater concern to West Africans than it is to anyone else. This is both a handicap and an opportunity for the sixteen states concerned.

Last, there is the matter of humanitarian concern for West Africa as a reservoir of some of the world's poorest people. Because so many of the world's poor are out of reach of Western charity (mostly in Asia), West Africa's 150 million are a suitable target for aid. There are special reasons why the United States should feel charitable toward West Africa, because the ancestors of so many of its less-privileged citizens came from there in the era of the Atlantic slave trade. Indeed, the congressional black caucus played a significant role in Sahelian famine relief during 1973–4 when U.S. aid commitments to the region began to be raised substantially above previous levels. Moreover, in West Africa a small amount of aid (by U.S. standards) goes a long way: Any serious commitment by the American people to this region could have a massive effect on the development prospects of sixteen countries. It should be remembered, however, that aid as transfers sometimes stifles development by interfering with internal market mechanisms and depressing prices. The other industrialized countries are unlikely to spare the resources to make much of an impact on West Africa through development aid. So West Africa's main claim to significance in U.S. foreign policy is that, apart from containing the United States' second-largest supplier of oil, it is the spiritual homeland of American blacks. This combination of strategic irrelevance and sentimental attachment may serve the region well. At least no foreign power is likely to fight a war there, and a limited amount of aid *in extremis* seems to be assured. The job, then, is to develop the region for the sake of its own people; and in this, too, West Africa's position out of the mainstream of global resource flows and conflicts may be an advantage.

The priorities for development policy

This book has been an attempt to depict the present as a moment in the long-drawn-out process of West Africa's history. The last 150 years have seen a massive commitment of African labor to export agriculture, alongside a revolution in transport and commerce. I have suggested that, although some wealth has inevitably been generated by this process, the productivity of labor has not been much improved. This is principally for two reasons: It has been profitable for West Africans to harvest the fertility of an abundant virgin land area; and the state has appropriated most of the surplus for its own unproductive expenditures. The result of this latter process has been a growing imbalance between town and countryside, fueling a rural exodus that has increased its pace since decolonization twenty years ago. The low productivity of the rural economy is manifested in the cumulative discrepancy between West African production and the rates achieved in industrialized and industrializing countries: This is the basis of the region's underdevelopment. And it is manifested in the failure of commercial agriculture to supply the growing home demand for foodstuffs and other raw materials.

Some see the burgeoning cities as a threat to peace and economic stability. But their emergence constitutes a glorious opportunity for dynamic exchange between town and countryside. At the moment a low-productivity countryside and an almost wholly parasitic urban sector are locked together in a mutually damaging reinforcement of each other's stagnation by the dominant economic force in West Africa – the successor states. The ruling classes are generally inimical to private initiatives aimed at raising productivity in either the rural or the urban areas. Their own proclivities ensure that money is drained off from the sector that could use it most profitably (agriculture) and spent in ways that merely encourage wastefulness. Something will have to be done, but by whom and with what interest in mind? Let us suppose that enlightened opinion may play a part. My proposals are addressed, somewhat half-heartedly, to such a possibility.

153

Above all else, development policy must be geared toward raising agricultural productivity. It is wholly inappropriate to emphasize measures that will stabilize the population at existing income levels, when they fall so far behind the standards of the civilized world. Aid to the poorest would be most effective if it were aimed at improving productivity levels in the economy as a whole, but especially in agriculture. I believe that a continuing flow of people to the cities is a good thing, but only if it is sustained by rising productivity in the countryside. When an agrarian revolution has set resources free for industrial development, it will then be appropriate to talk about an industrial revolution. I am convinced that the stages of economic development through which all industrialized countries so far have passed must be recapitulated (with appropriate modifications, of course) in West Africa, if the region is to break the nexus of its collective poverty.[1]

Agriculture linked to simple technology manufactures for the home market is the appropriate emphasis at this point in West Africa's history. But for this strategy to be realized as an effective force for development, existing political structures will have to be drastically changed: The boundaries on the map will have to be redrawn to permit more inclusive political and economic units to emerge; and the composition and priorities of the entrenched ruling classes will have to be altered. My prediction is that many West African states will subside into a form of preindustrial stagnation presided over by increasingly repressive regimes. But I do believe that such a pattern can be broken in the 1980s, through a convergence of social forces that would include Nigerian leadership, the support of international agencies, and the rising dissatisfaction of West Africans themselves with a system that benefits so few, so extravagantly, at the cost of the economic emancipation of the many.

Alternative approaches to agriculture

It may be appropriate to tackle the policy alternatives in West African agriculture through a review of five broad approaches to the problem of rural development:

1. Attempts to provide basic needs through maintenance of the subsistence system
2. Promotion of smallholder cash cropping within the existing framework of land tenure or on schemes organized by the government
3. Establishment of large capital-intensive estates (publicly or privately owned)
4. Emphasis on linkages among agricultural improvement and crafts, infrastructure, health, and so on, in integrated rural development programs
5. Encouragement of rural emigration

Though combinations of these strategies are both possible and desirable, they may be seen as antagonistic alternatives. Thus (3) and (5) stand at an ideological pole opposed to (1), and (2) and (4) may be combined with either extreme. I will consider the implications of each strategy in order.

What is to be done?

Basic needs

No one could fault the humanity or the necessity of directing efforts toward meeting the immediate food needs of populations subject to famine and other crises. Improvement of subsistence grains will continue to be valuable for a long time in West Africa. But it should be recognized that any emphasis on subsistence food production (supplemented perhaps by minimal social services – the so-called basic human needs approach [Mellor 1978]) can serve only as a stopgap. It is an attempt to freeze local populations at a standard of living that has become unacceptable in most parts of the world, and as such it is a step backward. Associated with this strategy is an emphasis on population restriction, in order to reduce the demand for income transfers to the poor. The essence of this "development" policy is to keep as many people as possible in the countryside, even if this means maintaining them at a subsistence level with scant hope for participating in the commercial economy.

The immediate context for a renewed emphasis on this strategy is world economic recession. Thus, in the 1930s, mindful of earlier disasters in the West Indies and Ceylon when a proletarianized peasantry came to haunt its political masters in the cities during a slump, colonial regimes suddenly discovered the virtues of traditional rural life. Having promoted an export-crop boom after World War I, they now celebrated the subsistence flexibility of immemorial peasant traditions in village agriculture. It is the same today, when rural West Africans are hit the hardest by high energy prices and deteriorating market conditions.[2] Now the international agencies, who spent the 1960s encouraging wholesale commitment of land and labor to commercial production, profess themselves to be concerned with "equity" and the preservation of rural communities (see, e.g., MacNamara 1973). In this way development policy swings through its great cycle – liberal in times of boom, conservative when the bust comes. We can be sure that scant attention will be paid to the needs of smallholders when the next upswing arrives.

In the meantime, while the world market is in surplus, West Africans are encouraged to forget the rhetoric of modernization they were fed twenty years ago and content themselves with living the lives of their grandfathers. Such a strategy is sustained by fear of the consequences of social disintegration in the face of continued commercialization of agriculture, leading to an accumulation of concentrated, poverty-stricken masses at the urban centers of government. We will consider this point more fully in the discussion of rural emigration. There are a number of pragmatic reasons for wanting to keep the poor in subsistence agriculture and out of the cities: It costs less to maintain them there, for they can grow food and the land offers a degree of social security; they pose less of a political threat when dispersed away from the metropolis; inequalities and class conflicts are reduced if they all remain poor; and retardation of commercial developments (and population growth?) in the Third World buys the industrialized countries some breathing space, now that a downswing of the trade cycle makes breakneck export growth no longer so convenient.

Those who advocate a subsistence strategy, however, generally hold to one or more of the following ideological positions. First is a humanitarian concern for the food needs and basic physiological deficiencies of people whom they see as victims. From this point of view, long-run development strategies take second place to a temporary holding operation, and nuances, such as recognition that charitable handouts or surplus American grain might have negative economic effects on the growth of local markets, are ignored. Second is a romantic attachment to the virtues of "traditional" social organization, usually accompanied by an aversion to the idea of commerce. Leaving aside for now the realities of village life in West Africa, or indeed anywhere, it should be said that such opinions are likely to be held by disenchanted expatriate members of the professional middle classes, whose alienation from their own society leads them to fill the ranks of overseas aid organizations. Anthropologists may be expected to sustain enthusiasm for the authenticity of "their" people's way of life. Few Africans, outside the overseas-educated elite, will be found to share these views. The third position holds that West Africa will not follow Europe's development path; that it is ethnocentric to suppose that agricultural modernization and industrial development offer the only means whereby societies can emancipate themselves from gross vulnerability both to the forces of nature and to the predations of other men – famine, high mortality, dependence on climate, disease, warfare, and conquest. The idea of self-sufficiency is epitomized by subsistence agriculture; but it implies a continuing poverty and backwardness that runs counter to the human aspirations of the region's people.

If Third World governments choose not to modernize agriculture *or* industry, there really is not much left. Hospitals and schools are expensive in real resources that someone has to produce; and a large services economy can only be sustained by a productive agriculture or industry. There is only one way of escaping from the nexus of social fragmentation and material vulnerability, and that is by turning to commodity production (the market). The question is how far the commercialization of agriculture should involve large-scale or small-scale methods of production; and, as a corollary, how much effort should be devoted to preserving the continuity of rural social organization.

Smallholder cash cropping

Smallholder cash cropping is the route that West Africa has already taken over the last 150 years; and it has served the region well in laying down the political and economic basis for the next stage of commercial development, which in my view should be more capital-intensive. The stage of petty commodity production in export agriculture has been fairly painless. Although it has been argued for some time that participation in the "money economy" is disruptive of existing social arrangements, the evidence is that petty commodity production is compatible with a very wide range of social structures. Certainly social continuity is a well-attested feature of rural areas that have committed themselves heavily to commerce in one way or another.[3]

The problem with smallholder cash cropping is that labor productivity remains roughly the same as in traditional food agriculture. This allows resources to be switched flexibly from one sector to the other; it gives peasants the opportunity to purchase commodities not available to them in the local economy; it generates accumulation and enterprise on a small scale. But it does not establish a long-run dynamic of economic development through labor specialization, capital investment, and productive innovation in the sphere of technology and organization. Labor is merely shifted from subsistence to commodity production, and this invariably causes a demand for food imports, because productivity in the food sector is not high enough to fill the gap left by the new commitment to nonfood agriculture. (The forest areas are better placed than the savannah in this respect, because the labor requirements of food production there are relatively low.) Obviously, any negative effects of this process are exacerbated by migration to the towns, which is due as much to the growth of the state as to the growth of the commercial economy.

Smallholder cash cropping may take one of two forms: with or without direct government control over the basic conditions of production. The latter type has accounted for the vast bulk of developments so far, although independent farmers have increasingly come under government control, first at the level of marketing and then in the supply of production inputs (fertilizer, seeds, tools, credit, etc.). Government projects involving land colonization, immigration, and resettlement have been sporadic and generally ineffective; but the prospects for smallholder rice production on large government irrigation schemes should be taken seriously. After all, the government is the only institution with access to capital on that scale. The advantages of such schemes are twofold: Annual productivity per man can be raised significantly on these projects, thanks to the use of water in the long dry season; and the state strengthens its economic control over the countryside, a matter of some importance in view of the administrative anarchy that is normal at the present stage of West African development. But there are drawbacks. Organizational difficulties have meant up to now that the agricultural potential of these schemes has not been realized. And as long as peasant families control immediate production and subordinate it to the diffuse labor pattern of their annual reproduction cycle, intense concentration on rice would probably constitute an unacceptable degree of specialization. In any case, it is doubtful whether the discipline required for high-yield irrigation can be achieved in West Africa on the basis of smallholder participation.[4] We should not, therefore, look to such projects for the main solution to the region's commercial food problem.

As for the rest, there is no need for West Africans to desist from producing

157

export crops by existing or improved methods. They seem to enjoy a world monopoly in cocoa, the demand for which should outstrip supply in the long run. Groundnuts and cotton – the export staples of the savannah – have a future, the one as part of a peasant intercropping system, the other as an irrigated crop farmed under smallholder or estate conditions. Some (but not all) of the tree crops would benefit from plantation methods of production, especially because indigenous small-scale methods seem to be inadequate to cope with growing problems of farm deterioration, maintenance, and replanting. So far we have witnessed a harvest of the virgin forest's natural fertility, without systematic planning for the renewal of that fertility; the next stage of exploitation will require less haphazard methods. This message has been repeated continuously since the colonial era, especially in relation to rehabilitation of the forest's oldest industry, the oil palm. Yet West Africans have maintained a reasonable share of the world market against plantation competition elsewhere. The question is whether more of the same will be enough in the 1980s.

Smallholder production is bound to be at the center of West African agriculture for many decades. Many branches are more adapted to small-scale methods under local conditions than to mechanization on a large scale. Farmers can improve productivity in significant ways without resorting to high technology, and these small advances, multiplied by millions, are essential to any vision of a more prosperous future for the region. In order to be competitive in world markets, West Africa will have to continue to rely on smallholder production; for capital-intensive farming would probably require the protection of production for home markets – as large, it is to be hoped, as the West African region itself – in foodstuffs and industrial raw materials. In the long term, tariff protection could be reduced when this large-scale agriculture was more robust, and West Africa would then be able to export food to the world market on the Southeast Asian pattern. Meanwhile, however, thoughts of such possible developments should not distract planners from encouraging the present peasant staples – cocoa, groundnuts, and the like.

Capitalist farming

The case for large-scale capitalist estates (let us assume for now that they are privately owned) rests basically on a classical argument shared in various forms by Steuart (1767), A. Smith (1776), Mill (1909), Marx (1959), Lenin (1974), and W. A. Lewis (1978*a*). It goes roughly as follows: As long as the bulk of the population produces what it needs for itself, the scope for development of new branches of production is very restricted. A process of specialization must occur in which people forgo production of part of their needs in order to produce a narrower range of goods to sell as commodities, the market value of which may be used to satisfy those other needs. This stage of petty commodity production was reached in West Africa long ago. In its fullest form, specialization has each man selling his labor to one specific productive enterprise, using his wages to buy commodities produced by others like himself. The combination of capital and machines made possible by this expanded circuit of commodities vastly enhances both labor productivity and the range of consumer wants satisfied. The big question is where to start in this process.

The key is agriculture, which contains the bulk of the population in a matrix of natural forces and local social organization. Somehow a good deal of that labor has to leave food production and start producing something else needed by the remaining food producers (or by some other non-food-producing population). Even if those who leave agriculture appear at first to produce nothing, but merely exist as parasites in the towns, they thereby provide a market for agricultural producers, who must then spend their earnings on commodities, produced, it is hoped, in the towns to which the rural emigrants have come; in this way nonagricultural production is stimulated, and more farmers are encouraged to leave the countryside. As the proportion of urban dwellers grows beyond the level of up to 10 percent that preindustrial economies are able to support, food producers *must* raise their productivity significantly. And now we get to the controversial bit: How can the proportion of farm workers be reduced and their productivity increased?

In the first industrial revolution it was done in part through enclosures, which allowed large-scale agrarian capitalists to organize highly productive farms that displaced many rural folk from occupancy of the land, thereby swelling the ranks both of vagrants in the countryside and of seekers after urban wage employment. It should be remembered that the burgeoning urban industrial sector could not absorb this rural exodus at first: The rate at which the countryside has yielded up its peasants has usually been in advance of urban labor demand. There can be no doubt that the process of industrialization both caused a great deal of hardship at the time and laid the foundation for the wealth that we now enjoy.

What are the prospects for capitalist production aimed at the home market in West Africa? The region's national economies are both small and open, a condition that increases the scope for intersectoral disequilibria in the development process. Thus farmers import fertilizers and machinery, and all groups purchase imported consumer goods, including large amounts of food. Yet the urban population is between a tenth and a third of the whole and growing. There already exists, then, a substantial home demand for agricultural products that is not being met, and this stands as an indictment of smallholder food farming or of the public policies that have dampened its growth. Perhaps it is not economical to produce this commodity on the existing scale of food-producing operations and at present price levels; perhaps food production is not geared to the market on any significant scale. In any case, it seems necessary for national governments to create the conditions under which a high-productivity commercial agriculture could emerge.

The most difficult problem is to engineer a price rise in foodstuffs. The

159

mercantilist Sir James Steuart (1767) was well aware of this priority when he observed that economies of the sort he was familiar with prospered under a regime of high agricultural prices. High prices stimulate the bulk of producers (i.e., farmers) to realize a portion of their output as commodities; they need a market, essentially of local consumers, protected from cheap imports; and the money they earn will be spent on the products of local industries, provided that they, too, can earn some respite from foreign competition in order to defray the relatively high costs imposed by local food prices and by their neophyte standing. Steuart made it clear that this protected exchange of agricultural and industrial products was necessary in order to generate a dynamic commercial division of labor in a country whose economy was initially backward and stagnant. When the infant commodity-producing sectors grew stronger, they could be exposed to the downward spiral of prices and costs of which Steuart's successor, Adam Smith (1776), made so much, a spiral that is widely assumed to accompany laissez-faire conditions of international competition. Then the cry would legitimately be for low food prices, which would reduce the local cost of wage labor and enhance the competitiveness of local firms in world markets. This transition is very hard to achieve, especially when most economists are either free-market liberals under all circumstances or devoted to protection as a universal panacea. We would do well, however, to remember that the transition begins, according to eighteenth-century theory and experience, with high agricultural prices.

The situation is not very different for West African countries today. The mechanisms are clear enough – tariffs, import quotas, removal of price controls, rejection of free food aid, and even a total ban on food imports (as in Ghana in 1973). The benefits, too, are obvious: High food prices would carry the infant farming industry through its initial phase of mechanization, and wages would be good enough to attract labor in the absence of dire compulsion. The problem is that West African governments have historically pursued a cheap food policy for an urban population that represents the most politically powerful constituency within the state (B. Lewis 1980). The prospect of food riots is in itself sufficient to discourage most governments from favoring commercial food agriculture, unless they stumble into the policy by accident, owing to lack of foreign exchange or some similar economic catastrophe.

Assuming that this hurdle could be overcome by some combination of political forces, production would focus on rice in the coastal swamps and the savannah and on maize and cassava in the forest. The first commercial boom, in export crops, took place in a land-abundant environment, and it is still possible that relatively underused land could be taken up for cereal cultivation. It would be better if alienation of existing farming land were kept to a minimum, if for no other reason than that the labor supply would be more reliably fed if it came from surrounding villages that still retained some economic viability. Agricultural wage labor in West Africa will have to farm a good part of its own food for some time yet. It is interesting to speculate about the difference it would make if these rice estates were controlled by governments rather than international corporations or local individuals; but we cannot go into the matter here.

Obviously, if commercial food farming were to stand any chance of success, its encouragement would have to be linked to selective protection of other home industries, such as agricultural production of raw materials for processing and manufacturing industries, as well as basic consumer industries like fishing, production of textiles and drinks, and soap manufacturing. The main priority for imports would have to be transport (vehicles and petroleum), machines, and farm inputs such as chemical fertilizer. Foreign exchange for these imports would be generated by extractive industries (timber, oil, and minerals) and continued sales of export crops; reduced food imports would release some foreign exchange. The first stage, then, is one of a higher-productivity agriculture geared toward the home market and linked dynamically to industrial manufactures of low-technology mass-consumption goods. The challenge of building high-technology manufacturing plants for agricultural and industrial capital goods would follow later. The main priority is to bring down the price of food once agriculture has become more efficient and to take advantage of a low-cost urban labor force to establish home mass-consumption industries. Moreover, it is clear that the concept of the home market should be widened as fast as possible to embrace local associations of nation-states and ultimately the region as a whole (ECOWAS). This process could start with progressive removal of tariffs on movements of agricultural products within the region.

The snags in all this are patent; but without some such strategy for agriculture, the economies of the West African nation-states will continue to stagnate.

Integrated rural development

One strategy for rural development, currently favored by such bodies as the World Bank and the Regional Fund of the European Economic Community, emphasizes the need for linkages between agriculture and the other sectors of a local economy (World Bank 1973). It is based on the recognition that a single-minded concentration on one export crop misses most of the significant interconnections that will probably determine the success or failure of the project. This is a welcome change, drawing attention as it does to vital linkages (examples would be the service to plow agriculture provided by blacksmiths, the feeder roads needed for cash-crop agriculture, or the health facilities required by an irrigation labor force). In one sense it leads international agencies to take on the functions of regional government that have been neglected or abandoned by the state claiming nominal responsibility for the welfare of rural areas. By recognizing that the development needs of a locality are multiple and interrelated, this strategy points up the lack of coordination normally found among existing agencies, both national and international.

Integrated development packages, embracing agriculture, crafts, local urban service centers, health facilities, water supplies, roads, and so on, are indeed attractive in that they treat people from a holistic point of view and aim at some kind of economic development for the rural areas. As such the strategy is an improvement over the basic-needs approach, which offers no hope for development at all. Yet its emphasis on restriction of the concept of self-sufficiency to a local level of economic integration, which must be supplemented by dynamic intersectoral linkages, may be unnecessarily limiting. There is much to be said for decentralization and for the spread effects of many rural towns, especially if a major concern is with maintenance of the fabric of rural societies. But the main argument against integrated rural development is that the market is too restricted. How important are cleavages brought about by specialization in the regional division of labor? Is it necessary to separate agriculture and industry physically into countryside and town for rapid economic development to occur, or can much the same effects be achieved through local integration of these two main branches? The answer I favor is large-scale specialization, both urban and rural, aimed at the largest market available, home and abroad; but pragmatic resort to decentralized integrated development schemes in the rural areas has an obvious complementary role to play within such an overarching strategy.

Rural emigration

The weight of my policy conclusions favors an exodus from the countryside. In 1800, the world's urban population was under 3 percent; it is now over 40 percent and growing at a log-linear rate. There is no point in supposing that West Africa will buck this trend and a great deal of point in making a virtue of it. A rural exodus is necessary for the development of a capital-intensive food agriculture geared at first toward the regional home market and eventually to a world market, one that will sustain high levels of demand into the foreseeable future. There will be an inevitable surplus of workers over the labor requirements of the organized urban economy, but the excess population will be supported by the trickle-down effect of government expenditures and by the inherent economic dynamism of concentrated urban markets, which generate an almost infinite range of activities based on commodity exchange (Hart 1973). Eventually this work force will be absorbed into enterprises requiring cheap labor in considerable amounts. Then these, too, will give way to more capital-intensive enterprises. There are several ways in which this transition could be managed. France and Japan, for political and military reasons, as well as perhaps through social foresight, maintained large peasantries until the 1950s. Japan's agricultural population did not decrease in absolute terms through the early phase of its most rapid industrialization (Mellor 1976:25). Yet since World War II the rural population has declined from 60 percent to 15 percent of the total. In Britain, the United States, and Germany, the rural–urban shift took place at different rates and phases of the industrialization process. So West Africa does have options that, however long term they may be in their effects, should inform policy now.

Maintenance of rural societies cannot be justified as a policy goal. The existing pattern of settlement and land use is not dictated by criteria of agricultural efficiency, being rather the product of a series of ad hoc, often recent, pressures, usually political in nature. Nor do the customary social ties linking most West Africans to the land originate much beyond the last hundred years. For example, so-called stateless people were concentrated at high densities in remote areas as refugees from political and military forces; similarly, slaves were herded into savannah areas where they could be put to effective work on the land. The warfare and population mobility that characterized the nineteenth century produced a pattern that was artificially frozen by colonial rule. Since then, redistribution of population into the coastal forest and towns has continued. Conditions are deteriorating in the Sahel, and not just because of commercial exploitation and greed. The situation everywhere is fluid and nowhere optimal. Though some people reasonably cling to what they know as their only security, government should be rewarding those who leave home, not those who stay there. What are the arguments, beyond local chauvinism, for artificially maintaining people in an unsuitable area? It is better for population to be concentrated in places where it can participate effectively in economic development, even if that means rural disintegration in the less-favored areas. The richest countries in West Africa today are those with the largest, most densely settled populations. The association is not coincidental: West Africa's economic backwardness as a region is largely attributable to the fact that its population is small and dispersed; the growth, redistribution, and concentration of that population in areas favorable to economic development is essential, if it is to break out of a nexus of continued underdevelopment.

Mobility does not necessarily mean permanent emigration. The normal pattern of labor circulation between town and country in West Africa permits immigrants to retain a stake back home while they are away. Membership of home corporations based on kinship ("lineages") provides absentees with a rural safety valve and long-run security. Where such institutions exist, policy may be served by encouraging their continuity. But in many areas emigrants cannot maintain rights in home land, and elsewhere the land available is simply not big enough to reabsorb absentees if they were all to return. So the best safety valve would be a voluminous source of cheap food for urban areas and abundant government revenues for supplying the rest of the people's needs in extremity; neither of these goals will be served by shoring up decrepit village social structures at the expense of developing a high-productivity agriculture.

Probably the most contentious issue concerns property rights, especially in land. Because large amounts of land are still held collectively by kin-based corporations, it may be worthwhile to register these corporations as legally entitled landholding units to which recruitment is by birth. These units could then lease the land to capitalist farmers, farm it cooperatively themselves, or make other choices. Absentee members would retain their rights and a share of property income, if any. This seems to have been the Japanese solution to agricultural modernization since World War II: A multitude of peasant proprietors were encouraged to form cooperatives; before long capitalist farmers using advanced equipment came to occupy most of the land through leasing arrangements; and the peasants now live in high-rise apartment buildings in Osaka with a steady income from land rent.[5] It would be nice if West Africans could retain a stake in the land while they were being displaced by farmers better equipped to cultivate it efficiently.

Finally, does this whole argument fall on the incapacity of West Africa's cities to absorb the rural exodus? I think not. The evidence is that urban economies in the area are very vital and capable of evolutionary growth. They are not yet entirely dominated by formal business and government concerns; their commerce is dynamic and, to an increasing degree, integrally linked to the surrounding countryside. The dualism of the colonial enclave economy is slowly, sometimes rapidly, giving way to the formation of national home markets. Yet these same cities are often represented as stagnant pools of underemployed and unemployed refugees from a crisis-stricken countryside. Some historical perspective may throw light on the matter.

A century ago, writers such as J. S. Mill compared London with ancient Rome's consumer proletariat – a drain on the public purse, a cancer at the heart of the state. Yet as Alfred Marshall predicted, the unwashed masses of London's East End had been fully absorbed into the wage economy within a few decades.[6] In the 1960s the cities of Southeast Asia were a prime example of what was then called "overurbanization": They were flooded by rural migrants who seemed to find very little that was productive to do there (Reissman 1964; McGee 1971). Some of those same cities now spearhead the region's emergence as a major center of industrial capitalist development, only a decade later. This is a process entirely consistent with the classical theory of development on which this book, perhaps idiosyncratically, is based.

Conclusions

As I understand it, the general development policy of the international donor agencies at this time is to favor peasant agriculture as both a subsistence and a commercial activity. An explicit corollary of this is the attempt to reduce flows of population to cities, which are thought of as centers of social pathology, material deprivation, and political danger. But can the threat of an economic evolution such as that which I have advocated here be so great as to justify systematic attempts to maintain rural economies at or near their current pathetically miserable level of efficiency and real income? One may be excused for supposing that aid distributed under these auspices is cosmetic rather than constructive.

I have emphasized the striking need for rapid improvements in labor productivity during the 1980s and in doing so I have concentrated on the possibilities for capitalist agriculture, progressively substituting machines for human labor. Agricultural modernization is not as far away in West Africa as some might suppose – not as far, for example, as the New England smallholders of the last century from the midwestern farmers of a few decades later. But this extreme view should be modified to take account of the many intermediate ways in which West African agriculture could be put on a path of steadily rising productivity. Export agriculture may benefit from rehabilitation and improvement of cocoa and other crops that are not best suited to combine harvester or plantation methods. Peri-urban livestock, poultry, and egg production is well suited to small-scale methods, as are most forms of market gardening. Integrated rural development programs offer hope for improvement across a broad front. I do not oppose, but rather welcome, all of these possibilities. Small-scale commodity production was a prominent feature of the industrialized countries until only recently, and it will be intrinsic to West Africa's development for some time to come. But I have sought to counter the view that the region's economic development can be satisfactorily promulgated by exclusive reliance on small agriculture. A dynamic, capital-intensive sector aimed at home consumption needs would become the engine driving the small-scale rural and urban sectors. Without it, we are left with large-scale government and services financed by an agriculture whose individual members can barely break even. It is not merely that income levels will be unsatisfactory; without a productivity breakthrough in agriculture soon, the political economy of West African nations will collapse in the 1980s. Faced with the prospect of a dozen Haitis[7] (there are one or two in the region already), who among us can afford to remain indifferent to West Africa's plight?

This book has conveyed a general picture of West African commercial agriculture. It is obvious how I think the material welfare of West Africans would be best advanced in the long run. I have chosen to demonstrate how rural economy is part of an integrated historical process linking it to the state, to urbanization, to international capitalism, and to much else. Any substantial attack on the region's development problems would have to begin with reversing priorities in rural and urban expenditure, a process that involves central government policy. Yet most of the development advice given by economists starts by assuming the political status quo as given. This pusillanimous deference to governments whose behavior often barely warrants the title ensures that the problems underlying West Africa's economic backwardness will never be touched on. Development is a contradictory process, and it should be recognized as such. Thus states whose need for revenues from agriculture makes them act so as to destroy rural societies are threatened by the urban discontents that their own policies of proletarianization produce. Capitalism impoverishes and enriches as it liberates the forces of human production. The anodyne formulas of an economics wholly innocent of contradiction serve only to perpetuate a make-believe world of conferences and press releases. Indeed, to the extent that economics is a source of legitimacy for government actions, the modern discipline constitutes in itself a major obstacle to development in backward regions.

I have argued that political forms are the principal determinants of agricultural development and stagnation. Equally, every political form requires minimal material conditions in order to flourish or persist. It does not matter which side is emphasized as prior – West Africa is evolving modern state forms that both accord with agrarian backwardness and reinforce that condition. A functionalist theory would note the positive feedback loop in the system and conclude that there is no escape from this vicious circle of poverty. But the system generates and absorbs power; and power is predicated on its absence, the lack of power, which in turn can become its negation, resistance. Only a dialectical theory of historical struggle can restore to West Africans the freedom to conceptualize and fight for their own political emancipation from the dead hand of preindustrial despotism. The issue is compounded by what amounts to a worldwide conspiracy to sanctify the political boundaries of the post-1945 international order, holding every petty nation-state inviolable. Economic development requires political evolution of a kind that it is almost sacrilege to contemplate these days. How long can West Africa continue in the form of one big fish, two or three minnows, and a dozen tadpoles? Political fragmentation, therefore, as Kwame Nkrumah used to preach in the heyday of decolonization (e.g., Nkrumah 1963), will be the enemy of Africans' search for social progress. The forces that may be capable of defeating such an enemy seem farther away now than they did then.

Notes

1. Introduction

1 Karl Kautsky's *Die Agrarfrage* (1902) is the most theoretically comprehensive work on this issue. Unfortunately, it is available in most European languages, but not in English.

2 An up-to-date compilation for all countries is World Bank (1980); see also *United Nations Statistical Yearbook, United Nations Demographic Yearbook,* and the annual reports of such publications as *Africa Economic Digest* and *Economist Intelligence Unit Reviews.*

3 See Evans-Pritchard (1940), Leach (1961), Fortes (1970). I am grateful to Skip Rappaport for the chance to see his unpublished manuscript on the subject.

4 Goody (1958), Fortes (1970), Robertson (1979). There are analogues in the previous work of the economist Chayanov (1966) and the biologist Thompson (1917).

5 Some Marxist anthropologists have debated whether this fact makes kinship roles the basis of class opposition in West African rural societies: Meillassoux (1975*b*), Terray (1972), Dupré and Rey (1978). Fortes (1949) provided the clearest ethnographic account of this form of conflict.

6 I have written several unpublished papers on "commoditization," including one for Esther Goody's forthcoming collection in the Cambridge Papers in Social Anthropology series. My main inspiration has been the work of Marx (1959, 1973) and Mauss (1967).

7 Myint (1971) revived the term "vent for surplus" from Mill's (1909) critique of Adam Smith (1776). Whereas the latter saw export demand as an opportunity for mobilizing unused factors of production, Mill deemed it a vulgar theory, a relic of mercantilism. In this book, "mercantilism" is not the dirty word it was for classical economists. See Keynes (1936).

8 For the history of the "marginalist" revolution, see, e.g., Schumpeter (1954).

9 Polanyi (1944) devotes some time to exposing the big lie that the liberal state was not an active political agent in economic affairs.

10 Schumpeter's (1954) treatment of the preclassical period of economic thought is indispensable.

11 See many of the articles in Gutkind and Wallerstein (1976) and Hecht's (1978) review of this and several other recent contributions to the radical African literature, by no means all of them to be subsumed under the heading "dependency theory."

12 Proposals range from cutting ties with the West to the formation of more autonomous regional economic units. Probably no one has in mind another Cambodian experiment in self-sufficiency, but the rhetoric sometimes sounds as if that were the intention.

2. Economic backwardness in anthropological perspective

1 For a selection of the best attempts to overcome mere speculation, see Ajayi and Crowder (1976).

2 Spearman's rho was calculated for a comparison of West African states ranked according to degree of urbanization (percentage of the population that is urbanized), income level (annual per capita income in dollars), and population density (persons per square kilometer of national territory). Rho for urbanization and income level gave a correlation of 0.64 (significant at the 1 percent level); population density and income level yielded a rho of 0.38 (not significant); and urbanization and population density yielded a rho of 0.14 (not significant).

3 Modernization theory, which was hegemonic in the Anglophone world during the 1960s (see, e.g., Apter 1963), was driven underground by the fierce attacks launched against it toward the end of that decade by, among others, Frank (1969). Since then, radical critics of the underdevelopment process have held the stage (see Gutkind and Wallerstein 1976) and, freed from a serious external dialectic, have multiplied their various positions to the point where it is no longer feasible, if it ever was, to characterize them with a single label.

4 I have found White and Gleave (1971) the most useful textbook on West African geography.

5 By the time Miner (1953) studied Timbuctoo, there was not much to look at; but the city already supported an intellectual life equal to northwestern Europe's in the fourteenth century.

6 Several good collections on slavery were produced in the last few years: e.g., Meillassoux (1975a), Miers and Kopytoff (1977).

7 Fortes (1945, 1949), Bohannan and Bohannan (1968), Paulme (1940). Meillassoux's famous study of the Gouro (1974a) spans the division between forest and savannah (see also Terray 1972).

8 The most impressive forest state was probably Ashanti (Wilks 1975); see also Terray's work on the Abron kingdom of Gyaman (e.g., 1974, 1976).

9 Meillassoux (1971a) stresses their positive and negative role in his introduction.

10 Our witnesses were the early travelers, such as the nineteenth-century German explorer Barth (1857).

11 A good general discussion of this is Hicks (1969).

12 See n. 7 to this chapter and n. 5 to Chapter 3. Horton (1976) makes a sophisticated effort to build a model for West Africa's stateless societies.

13 Reciprocity and redistribution are terms popularized by Polanyi (1944); see Bohannan and Dalton (1962).

14 Bohannan and Dalton's 1962 study contains several descriptive case studies.

15 Hill (1972:40) points out that the *gandu* relationship of trust between Hausa fathers and sons was also extended to slaves: "A well-trusted slave, known as *sarkin gandu*, was often in charge of the farmwork, having authority over sons and slaves alike and maybe himself avoiding heavy work." (Cf. M. F. Smith 1964.) Klein (1977:355) also speaks of the continuity between the *jaam* (slave), *navetane* (migrant worker), and junior male kinsman among the Wolof: "In the most widely noted form of tenure the *navetane* simply assumed the obligations of a *jaam* or an unmarried son. The owner gave him a field, a hut and food. The *navetane* owed in exchange five days of labor from sunrise to about 2.00 p.m. He worked for himself evenings and on the other two days." The forms of domination or *Herrschaft* (Weber 1978) were similar in that all three groups were unequally linked to the master of the house.

16 See n. 15 to this chapter and also Rey (1971).

17 The basic theory for the declining labor value of underdeveloped countries' exports is outlined in Emmanuel (1972).

18 Meillassoux (1971a: 10–12) summarizes a complex literature.

19 And to color French writings about colonialism: See, e.g., Suret-Canale (1971), Rey (1971).

20 "Official interest in the development of African agriculture was motivated less by dreams of empire than by the mundane necessities, first, of creating a taxable income within the territory; second, of creating demand for expensive transport systems, the prime object of which was to serve administration; and third, of producing agricultural goods and particularly, of course, cotton for the industries of the metropolis" (Elliot 1969:123–4).

21 Hancock (1941) satirized this tendency of colonial trading capital.

22 Kaye's (1972) assemblage of documents and tables for the Gold Coast graphically illustrates this point.

23 Leys (1976) summarizes and extends the Marxist debate on the postcolonial state.

24 Amin's 1971 study used the term "neocolonialism" when it was published in English in 1973.

25 Gugler and Flanagan (1978). I have addressed the topic in several of my published and unpublished papers.

26 B. Lewis (1980) provides an extremely competent review of the food problem and its West African literature, including the Stanford University rice project's findings.

27 The phrase is, of course, Wittfogel's (1957).

28 Cleave (1974:34). "The African often provides himself with food on his savannah clearings with less expenditure of calories than the Asian on his irrigated ricefields" (Dumont 1972:124).

3. The organization of agricultural production

1 The Hausa are perhaps the best-documented West African people for our purposes. See M. G. Smith (1955, 1978), Hill (1972, 1977), Hogendorn (1978), Raynaut (1969, 1972), Nicolas (1971), Nicolas, Doumesche, and Mouche (1968), Norman (1967).

2 Also Fulbe (the language is called Fulfulde) and, in Francophone areas, often Peul.

3 See Nadel (1942) for an account of traditional urban guild craftsmen.

4 "No really satisfactory and definite substitute has yet been developed for bush fallow" (De Wilde et al. 1967: I, 36–7). De Wilde believes that, in consequence, conservation of soil fertility is Africa's number one problem, especially when rotation ceases for technological, demographic, or economic reasons.

5 This account is based heavily on my own fieldwork among the Tallensi of northern Ghana. I have tried to incorporate elements from Nadel (1942), Bohannan and Bohannan (1968), Meillassoux (1974a), and several other monographs.

6 I have generally eschewed listing figures on current export volumes and values, because they are meaningless unless compiled in the form of comparative time-series data, and this task seemed too onerous for its exegetical worth.

7 Two case studies on eastern Nigerian farming communities are Fogg (1965) and Olowusani, Derna, et al. (1966).

8 Berry (1975:29) reports that rubber exports from Lagos were 56 pounds in 1893, 5,867 pounds in 1894, and 5,069,557 pounds (value £269,863) in 1895. After five years the trade collapsed "apparently because wild supplies near the coast were exhausted by destructive tapping measures."

9 The English brokerage firm Gill and Duffus is the leading astrologer in the magical

world of cocoa futures. The magazine *West Africa* and the quarterly reviews of the Economist Intelligence Unit (one series of which I composed for three years) faithfully report the latest signs.

10 Hill (1963*a*), Dupire (1960), Berry (1975). Stavenhagen (1975) is one well-known derivative account.

11 I am indebted for much in these paragraphs to my conversations and correspondence with Polly Hill and Sandy Robertson. I offer thanks to both.

12 It is a major point of Hill (1963*a*) that these companies were normally based on partrilineal kin ties, whereas family-based farms were often matrilineal. This may reflect the different origins of Krobo and Akan settlers, the former being both partilineal in kinship organization and long involved in business enterprise.

13 Hill (1963*a*, 1970) has always preferred to call cocoa farmers "capitalists." My use of the term is based on Marx's much more restrictive definition, summarized in the noted sentence.

14 Dunn and Robertson (1973) describe the timber-producing area of Ghana known as Brong-Ahafo.

15 See Comité d'Information Sahel (1975), Copans (1975*a*), Dalby and Church (1973), Dalby, Church, and Bezzaz (1977). Both American and French aid efforts in West Africa are concentrated in the Sahel; this emphasis is reflected, somewhat opportunistically, in the recent literature.

16 Hogendorn (1978), McPhee (1971). Berry (1975:23) reports extreme fluctuations in the volume and price of cotton exported from Lagos in the late nineteenth century. From 1858 to 1883 annual volumes swung between 150,000 pounds and 1.5 million pounds, and prices between 6 and 19 pence per pound, with no sales at all during the periods 1862–4 and 1873–82. Between 1883 and 1899, volumes dropped from 400,000 pounds to 14,000 pounds, and prices fell from 6 to 3.5 pence per pound.

17 Suret-Canale (1971:279) says of the Office du Niger that irrigation, after producing lower-than-average yields, eventually sterilized the soil by washing it out. Labor was requisitioned to make good these deficiencies: "The colonization villages . . . were like concentration camps, with obligatory labor from 6 a.m. until sunset, restriction of movement and semi-military discipline." There were no health measures taken despite the increase in stagnant water and resulting malaria. The huge administrative staff was recruited from retired soldiers chosen for their ability to command more than for their knowledge of agronomy!

18 B. Lewis (1980:32 ff.) points out that Senegal was unable to locate *any* rice for purchase in the world market at one point during the 1973–5 drought. Food security considerations are thus paramount in the Senegalese government's promotion of rice; comparative advantage (lower prices for overseas rice, when it is available) matters less than avoidance of a repetition of this situation. It is also worth noting that rice-growing areas of West African countries (Casamance, northern Ghana) are often economically backward, so that regional equity is another reason for governments to push food production despite high local costs at this time. The Food Research Institute of Stanford University has been working on the problem of West African rice for a number of years: no papers had been published at the time of writing this book.

19 Hancock (1941:246–7) refers to early British experiments in rice growing. Sierra Leone started growing inland swamp rice around 1880, and by 1931 over 44,000 acres were devoted to the crop. Much of the rice was sold to the Gambia. The British Department of Agriculture helped out with seed, planting, mills, and the organization of cooperatives.

20 According to Shepherd (1978:65), the acreage of rice farms in Ghana's northern region leapt from 36,000 in 1970–1 to 140,000 in 1976–7. A bumper harvest in 1974–5

allowed the government to declare a state of national self-sufficiency in rice. The year of greatest expansion and hopes was 1976–7; output fell by between a third and a half overall in the following season and did not recover.

21 There is a considerable debate about the plow in West African history. See Goody (1971), A. G. Hopkins (1973).

22 Faulkner and Mackie (1933). Tiffen (1975:127) points out that, in promoting mixed farming, the colonial authorities' aim was to increase the fertility of land, whereas the farmers' was to economize on labor. It is often better to plow two acres without manuring for a yield of 300 pounds of cotton per acre than to manure one acre for a yield of 400 pounds. In any case, the official philosophy was to maintain a peasant system of agriculture. It was even proposed at one time (but not implemented) to tax farmers holding over twelve acres.

23 White and Gleave (1971:132) specify some of the difficulties of introducing mechanization under West African conditions: (1) The full costs are transferred to the farmers by a government agency; (2) cooperatives are limited by small holdings, lack of capital, and shortage of expertise; (3) plowing is liable to bring on soil degradation; (4) there are high costs of clearing and stumping woody vegetation; (5) the cost of maintaining the machinery is significant; and (6) there is no annual crop as yet capable of covering all these costs.

24 So I am informed by Allen Roberts and Jack Goody with respect to Upper Volta, at least.

25 Eric Ross (personal communication, based on his analyses of the U.S. meat industry). At least two great civilizations (not counting New Guinea's) were based to a significant degree on the pig – the French and the Chinese.

26 Hopkins (1973:250) quotes Quarcoo and Johnson (1968) to the effect that the Shai people of the Gold Coast expanded their traditional pottery business during the colonial period to the volume of half a million pots a year.

4. The state in agricultural development

1 Schumacher (1975:184), quoting one Chovard, offers this unexceptional example: "Some of the debtors were beaten or they and their wives were shut up in peanut silos or put out in the sun or sprayed with fertilizer and DDT or thrown in jail. In some cases soldiers seized their goods."

2 W. A. Lewis (1952) is a prominent early example of the emphasis on industrialization.

3 "Whether or not African settlers, even with leadership, are capable of accepting the cultivation disciplines required for intensive cultivation, which the high costs of imigration projects necessitate," is dubious in the case of the Office du Niger (Dumont 1966a:170).

4 See n. 17 to Chapter 3.

5 "At the Djebilor station in Casamance the agricultural worker who is a *décisionnaire* (one so designated by a *décision* who is given a paper stamped with a miraculous seal, which permits him to work less and earn more) hoes an average of 10 square meters a day – one percent of a Californian worker . . . He farms almost 400 CFA francs a day – one sixth of a Californian worker. The hoed square meter ends up costing sixteen times more in Casamance than in California . . . These *décisionnaires* consider themselves practically civil servants and therefore do very little work, particularly as some of them are related to deputies" (Dumont 1966a:82).

6 On Lugard and his successor, Sir Percy Girouard, see McPhee (1971:175, 178 ff.). McPhee speaks of "nationalization of the land."

7 Of the establishment of the United Ghana Farmers Council as a cocoa-buying monop-

oly, Beckman (1976:231) has observed that the incorporation of the village cocoa trade into a bureaucratic system of full-time employees, at the expense of an informal organization of part-time seasonal traders, led to many abuses and to deteriorated conditions for producers.

8 Dumont (1966*a*, 1972, 1974). Waldstein (1978*a*) contains a more recent plea on behalf of the small peasant.

9 Specifically, among the Tallensi in 1967.

10 A recent summary is Hanson (1980).

11 Comparable data are lacking for the other five countries.

12 Stedman Jones (1971) has a useful discussion of the ideological problem of the urban mob in the history of industrial capitalism.

13 For a general treatment of literacy, see Goody (1977).

14 World Bank (1978:i) reviews some rural projects in Africa as follows: "Irrigation, tree crop and livestock projects performed quite well (average rate of return: 21 percent). With one exception, rainfed annual crop projects performed poorly (average rate of return: 6 percent)." The overall rate of return on projects supported by Bank loans to agriculture was 15 percent a year.

15 There is no good account in English of Guinea Bissau's struggle for independence.

16 The five member nations of the Conseil d'Entente are all ex-colonies of France located in the eastern half of the region: Benin, Togo, Niger, Upper Volta, and the Ivory Coast.

5. The market and capital in agricultural development

1 This analysis is close to that of A. G. Hopkins (1973: chap. 2).

2 This is a great strength of the introduction to Meillassoux (1971*a*).

3 I reached these conclusions on the basis of my own unpublished researches into Gold Coast labor archives. The French colonies were rather more backward, at least before 1945.

4 Leys (1975). Hancock (1941) organizes his contrast between British colonies in West Africa and those elsewhere in the continent under the rubrics "trader's frontier" and "settler's frontier"; he makes it clear that life for Africans under the latter regime was much harsher.

5 Anthony et al. (1979) give considerable attention to this matter.

6 This account is a condensed version of the argument central to both *Capital* and *Grundrisse*.

6. The social impact of commercial agriculture

1 It is hard to document such a diffuse opinion without selecting quotations for detailed interpretation.

2 Pélissier (1966) and Dumont (1972) both refer to this problem in Senegal.

3 With the possible exception of the Ivory Coast. See Table 3, in Chapter 4.

4 Such as the interstices of traditional states in northern Ghana and Upper Volta.

5 There are, of course, other factors than nutrition involved – education, for example.

6 Hill (1977:xiii) refers to "the dire and lasting consequences of the continuing Great Inflation which (unknown to most 'Westerners') claims its chief victims in rural communities of the Third World, where earnings lag further and further behind the advancing price indices for essential manufactures and services such as transport."

7 Widespread suicides of chiefs and other leading advocates of commercial farming in the 1930s are easily forgotten by foreign specialists in West African affairs, but not by West Africans themselves.

8 M. G. Smith (1955:14–15) describes *arziki* as general good fortune, usually consisting of money, rights in land, offspring, and prestige. It is "essentially a quality of the present," easily lost and impossible to pass on to anyone. It is based on individual effort and is the gift of God. It cannot be the basis for stratification, but there are different kinds of *arziki* for the various strata and occupations.

9 This point is raised in Hart (1978), following Fortes (1945).

10 Hill's assertion (1972:18) that there are no classes in Batagarawa rests on the notion, supported for Hausaland by Nicolas (1965), that there can be no peasant aristocracy, owing to the absence of effective transmission methods and to extreme variability of personal fortune. There is no land scarcity, but many people leave the village, thereby enhancing the homogeneity of the remaining population. Many large landowners today live in towns.

11 This observation holds for the Gambia, Liberia, the Ivory Coast, Ghana, and Nigeria, to name the most obvious examples.

12 I have not yet seen authoritative studies that back up this impression, but the assumption would seem to be essential to a contemporary class analysis of African states.

13 See nn. 8 and 10 to this chapter.

14 Nadel (1942) has come in for rather extensive feminist criticism, although I have not seen his analysis and facts refuted in print.

15 Guyer (in press) provides an astute application of this principle.

16 McCormack (1979:7) shows that sex ratios vary between 1.6:1 (male to female) in fishing villages and 1.5:1 (female to male) in farming villages. There is a higher proportion of female household heads in the farming villages.

17 The magazine *West Africa* carries stories with this message on a fairly regular basis.

18 According to my own unpublished researches, gerontocratic control of marriageable women has much increased since Fortes's (1949) fieldwork.

19 The Gouro studied by Meillassoux (1974a) evolved a system of reciprocal labor called *klala;* see also Terray (1972).

20 Once again it is hard to find such an opinion documented in print by reputable scholars, but its popular currency is palpable enough.

21 McPhee (1971:130–1) quotes a Belgian author: "On peut expliquer cette conception par cette idée que la tribu irriterait les mânes ancestraux, si elle abandonnait ce qu'ils lui ont légué; enfin le sol étant par sa fécondité, sa faune et sa flore, la ressource alimentaire par excellence, n'est-ce pas une sorte de suicide que d'y renoncer?"

22 Fortes (1945) is the *locus classicus*.

7. What is to be done?

1 Those stages are reliably outlined in Kemp (1978).

2 See n. 6 to Chapter 6.

3 As the cocoa case attests: See, e.g., Hill (1963a).

4 See n. 3 to Chapter 4.

5 I am grateful to a former student, Cheng Chi-nan, for this information.

6 Stedman Jones (1971) is my source for this version of the preoccupations of Mill, Marshall, and other nineteenth-century economists.

7 James's (1963) classic account of the degeneration of this early success in the struggle for emancipation from colonialism is pregnant with analogies to postcolonial Africa.

Select annotated bibliography

Adams, A. 1977a. *Le long voyage des gens du fleuve*. Paris: Maspero. Impressive account by an anthropologist of development efforts on the Senegal River and of the experiences of indigenous peoples.

    1977b. The Senegal River Valley: What Kind of Change? *Review of African Political Economy*, no. 10, pp. 33–59. Incisive account of confrontation between government development agency and peasants who wish to control their own irrigation scheme.

Ajayi, A., and M. Crowder (eds.). 1974. *History of West Africa*. Vol. II. London: Longman. The basic historical text for the region. See Ajayi and Crowder 1976.

    1976. *History of West Africa*. Vol. I. 2nd ed. London: Longman. See Ajayi and Crowder 1974. Vol. I is the more recent, but both volumes are excellent.

Allan, W. 1965. *The African Husbandman*. Edinburgh: Oliver and Boyd. Still the best general account of African agronomy.

Amin, S. 1967. *Le développement du capitalisme en Côte d'Ivoire*. Paris: Les Editions de Minuit. In some ways Amin's best book: a trenchant case study that is not dated.

    1971. *L'Afrique de l'ouest bloquée*. Paris: Les Editions de Minuit. 1973 as *Neo-Colonialism in West Africa*. Harmondsworth: Penguin African Library. U.S. ed. (same title) 1974. New York: Monthly Review Press. Useful summary of the development histories of Francophone states, Ghana, and the Gambia. A bit superficial.

    1973. *Le développement inégal: essai sur les formations sociales du capitalisme péripherique*. Paris: Les Editions de Minuit. Translated 1976 as *Unequal Development*. New York: Monthly Review Press. Amin's general theory of Third World underdevelopment. Has a chapter on Africa. Many left-wing policy prescriptions derive from this analysis.

Amin, S. (ed.). 1974a. *Modern Migrations in Western Africa*. London: Oxford University Press, for International African Institute. Editor's introduction is masterly (French and English). Several interesting papers from a 1971 Dakar conference.

    1975a. *L'agriculture africaine et le capitalisme*. Paris: Editions Anthropos. IDEP. Important collection of articles by prominent Marxist authors, several with West African experience.

Anderson, P. 1974. *Lineages of the Absolutist State*. London: New Left Books. Synthesis of late medieval/early modern European history, emphasizing the emergence of state forms conducive to the rise of capitalism. Long essay on the Asiatic mode of production.

Anthony, K., B. Johnston, W. Jones, and V. Uchendu. 1979. *Agricultural Change in Tropical Africa*. Ithaca: Cornell University Press. Recent synthesis by Stanford economists and an anthropologist. Interesting ideas on the development of internal markets.

174

Select annotated bibliography

Augé, M. 1969. Statut, pouvoir et richesse: relations lignagères, relations de dependance et rapports de production dans la société alladian. *Cahiers d'Etudes Africaines*, 9, no. 35:461–81. Reprinted in translation in D. Seddon (ed.) 1978, *Relations of Production* (q.v.). Self-explanatory title. The Alladian are a group living in the southern Ivory Coast.

    1971. L'organisation du commerce pré-colonial en basse côte d'Ivoire et ses effets sur l'organisation sociale des populations côtières. In C. Meillasoux (ed.), *The Development of Indigenous Trade and Markets in West Africa* (q.v.), pp. 153–67. Deals with the geographical and social organization of trade, particularly in the nineteenth century at the time of the oil trade, and the importance of marriage networks.

Baier, S. 1980. *An Economic History of Central Niger*. Oxford: Oxford University Press, Clarendon Press. Traces the economic history of part of the Sahel from 1850 to 1960, paying attention to the reorientation of trade following the decline of the trans-Saharan traffic.

Balandier, G. 1969. Structures sociales traditionnelles et changements économiques. *Cahiers d'Etudes Africaines*, 9, no. 35:345–9. An insightful treatment of our general problem by a leading French social anthropologist who has worked mostly in Central Africa.

Baldwin, K. 1957. *The Niger Agricultural Project: An Experiment in African Development*. Cambridge, Mass.: Harvard University Press. Much-cited early study of irrigation at Mokwa; fairly critical of organizational failures.

Bates, R. 1978. The Commercialization of Agriculture and the Rise of Rural Political Protest in Black Africa. Social Science Working Paper no. 237, California Institute of Technology, Pasadena. Interesting treatment of a problem rarely studied by political scientists before.

Bauer, P. T. 1954. *West African Trade*. Cambridge: Cambridge University Press. A most significant book when it was published; its critique of the marketing boards and defense of indigenous market mechanisms are still required reading.

Beckett, W. H. 1944. *Akokoaso: A Survey of a Gold Coast Village*. LSE Monographs on Social Anthropology, no. 10. London: Percy Lund, Humphries and Co. Pioneering study of a cocoa-farming community. A valuable adjunct to Hill's work.

Beckman, B. 1976. *Organizing the Farmers: Cocoa Politics and National Development in Ghana*. Uppsala: Scandinavian Institute of African Studies. First-rate study by a Swedish political scientist. Based on study of the records of the United Ghana Farmers Council during the period of nationalization of the cocoa trade, 1961–6.

Berg, E. J. 1965. The Economics of the Migrant Labour System. In H. Kuper (ed.), *Urbanisation and Migration in West Africa*, pp. 160–81. Berkeley and Los Angeles: University of California Press. Clear treatment of migration by the economist who brought the backward-sloping supply curve to the study of West African labor markets.

Berry, Sara S. 1975. *Cocoa, Custom and Socioeconomic Change in Rural West Nigeria*. Oxford: Oxford University Press, Clarendon Press. Multifaceted study of the cocoa industry in Yorubaland using techniques and ideas drawn from history, anthropology, and economics.

Biebuyck, D. (ed.). 1963. *African Agrarian Systems*. Oxford: Oxford University Press. Although this volume is almost two decades old, many of the papers in it are excellent. See specific references.

Bohannan, P., and Bohannan, L. 1968. *Tiv Economy*. Evanston, Ill.: Northwestern University Press. Fine ethnography of a stateless people from Nigeria's middle belt. Comprehensive coverage of the indigenous economy.

Bohannan, P., and G. Dalton (eds.). 1962. *Markets in Africa*. Evanston, Ill.: Northwestern University Press. Still-indispensable collection of useful essays (with West Africa represented strongly by Smith, Dupire, and others). The editorial introduction was pathbreaking at the time.

Boserup, E. 1965. *The Conditions of Agricultural Growth*. Chicago: Aldine. Easily the most stimulating treatment of the problem in modern times. Stresses population dynamics.

1970. *Women's Role in Economic Development*. London: Allen and Unwin. The scope of the subject is beyond her factual grasp, but she provides many interesting ideas; African female hoe farming figures prominently in her arguments.

Boutillier, J. L. 1964. Les structures foncières en Haute-Volta. *Etudes Voltaiques*, no. 5. Discussion of customary rules of land tenure in Upper Volta. Suggests how traditional organization might be adapted to the needs of agrarian reform.

Brokensha, D., M. M. Horowitz, and T. Scudder (eds.). 1977. *The Anthropology of Rural Development in the Sahel: Proposals for Research*. Binghamton, N.Y.: Institute for Development Anthropology. Considers the sociology of Sahelian economic systems, with a view to informing development project planning and implementation.

Capron, J. 1973. *Communautés villageoises Bwa: Mali, Haute Volta*. Paris: Institut d'Ethnologie, Musée de l'Homme. Shows how an egalitarian people, surrounded by traditional states, developed a corporate strategy of social and economic organization.

Chayanov. A. V. 1966. *The Theory of Peasant Economy*. Homewood, Ill.: Irwin. Seminal work by Russian agricultural economist that has since inspired much anti-Marxist analysis of the peasantry. Early version of the "development cycle" approach.

Cipolla, C. 1978. *The Economic History of World Population*. 7th ed. Harmondsworth: Penguin. Masterly sweep of demographic history organized around the agricultural and the industrial revolutions.

Clark, C., and M. R. Haswell. 1970. *The Economics of Subsistence Agriculture*. New York: St. Martin's Press; London: Macmillan. The approach adopted by these prominent economists is not the same as this book's; but their study remains one of the best analyses available.

Cleave, J. H. 1974. *African Farmers: Labor Use in the Development of Smallholder Agriculture*. New York: Praeger. Informative discussion of labor organization and productivity; explodes several myths about African farmers in a precise way.

Clower, R. W., G. Dalton, M. Harwitz, and A. Walters, 1966. *Growth without Development: An Economic Survey of Liberia*. Evanston, Ill.: Northwestern University Press. Outspoken report on West Africa's closest approximation to Haiti; its publication was delayed. Exemplary (although unfortunately rare) case of American social scientists describing what they see.

Cohen, A. 1969. *Custom and Politics in Urban Africa: A Study of Hausa Migrants in Yoruba Towns*. Berkeley and Los Angeles: University of California Press. Seminal study that has spawned many imitators. Useful for our purposes in its treatment of traders and butchers.

Comité d'Information Sahel. 1975. *Qui se nourrit de la famine en Afrique? Le dossier politique de la faim au Sahel*. Paris: Maspero. Sometimes strident, but always stimulating "exposé," which assembles many numbers and several convincing arguments.

Copans, J. (ed.). 1975a. *Sécheresses et famines du Sahel*. 2 vols. Paris: Maspero. Indispensable collection, with a good introduction by the editor. Excellent bibliography. Covers the topic thoroughly.

Copans, J., P. Couty, J. Roch, and G. Rocheteau. 1972. *Maintenance sociale et changement économique au Sénégal*. 2 vols. *Travaux et Documents de l'ORSTOM*, no. 15. Paris: ORSTOM. Of wider significance than its focus – on the groundnut

176

farming economy of Senegal. Attacks the problem of economic inequality in a system based on kinship and religious organization.

Coquery-Vidrovitch, C. 1969. Recherches sur un mode de production africain. *La Pensée*, 144:61–78. Reprinted in translation in D. Seddon (ed.) 1978, *Relations of Production* (q.v.). Everyone reads this; but it has been surpassed by developments in the last decade. The idea of an "African" mode of production is improbable.

——— 1975. L'impacte des interests coloniaux: SCOA et CFAO dans l'ouest africain, 1910–65. *Journal of African History*, 16, no. 4:595–621. Revealing history of two large French trading companies in the colonial period.

Coquery-Vidrovitch, C., and H. Moniot. 1974. *L'Afrique noire de 1800 à nos jours*. Paris: PUF. Some matters of emphasis are disputable, but the study is invaluable for the sweep of its ideas and its historical contextualization of the present.

Cruise O'Brien, D. B. 1971. *The Mourides of Senegal: The Politics and Economics of an Islamic Brotherhood*. Oxford: Oxford University Press, Probably the best account in English of the social organization behind much of Senegal's rural groundnut economy. Fascinating story.

Curtin, P. 1975. *Economic Change in Precolonial Africa: Senegambia in the Era of the Slave Trade*. Madison: University of Wisconsin Press. America's leading West African historian gives a glimpse of the Atlantic slave trade from the African end of the story. Unique, and more localized than the title suggests.

Dalby, D., and R. J. H. Church (eds.). 1973. *Drought in Africa*. London: School of African and Oriental Studies. One of the earliest symposia aimed at illuminating the Sahelian famine/drought. Strongly geographical in emphasis.

Dalby, D., R. J. H. Church, and F. Bezzaz. 1977. *Drought in Africa II*. African Environment Special Report, no. 6. London: International African Institute. The follow-up to Dalby and Church 1973. Many interesting papers, but variable quality.

Delgado, C. L. 1979. An Investigation of the Lack of Mixed Farming in the West African Savannah: A Farming Systems Approach. In K. H. Shapiro (ed.), *Livestock Production and Marketing in the Entente States of West Africa* (q. v.), pp. 70–143. Valuable and original economic analysis of Upper Volta villagers who rejected mixed farming because they had no tradition of using cattle.

Derman, W. 1978. *Cooperatives, Initiative, Participation and Socio-Economic Change in the Sahel*. AID report. East Lansing: Michigan State University. The author takes a comprehensive view of the place of cooperatives in Sahelian development. Good bibliography. Complements this book.

Derman, W., and L. Derman. 1973. *Serfs, Peasants and Socialists: A Former Serf Village in the Republic of Guinea*. Berkeley and Los Angeles: University of California Press. Valuable ethnographic study of the evolution of a traditionally inegalitarian social structure under colonial and modern "socialist" conditions.

De Wilde, J. C., et al. 1967. *Experiences with Agricultural Development in Tropical Africa*. 2 vols. Vol. I: *The Synthesis*, Vol. II: *The Case Studies*. Baltimore: Johns Hopkins Press, for World Bank. The quality of analysis and synthesis in these volumes has not been surpassed. Nor has the truth of the authors' arguments sunk in as far as development practice is concerned. Required reading.

Dozon, J. P. 1977 Economie marchande et structures sociales: le cas de Côte d'Ivoire. *Cahiers d'Etudes Africaines*, 17, no. 68:463–83. One of the most interesting recent analyses addressed to our topic.

Dumont, R. 1966a. *False Start in Africa*. London: André Deutsch. Originally published 1962 as *L'Afrique noire est mal partie*. Paris: Editions du Seuil. See the supplementary bibliography for other Dumont classics. This one got a great deal of attention at the time. It is disjointed, but lively and provoking.

Select annotated bibliography

Dunn, J. (ed.). 1978. *West African States: Failure and Promise*. Cambridge: Cambridge University Press. A series of country case studies that complement the general argument put forward in Chapter 4 of this book.

Dunn, J., and A. F. Robertson. 1973. *Dependence and Opportunity: Political Change in Ahafo (Ghana)*. Cambridge: Cambridge University Press. Collaboration between a political scientist and an anthropologist produced this excellent study of a region heavily committed to cocoa and timber production.

Dupire, M. 1960. Planteurs autochtones et étrangers en Basse-Côte d'Ivoire orientale. *Etudes Eburnéennes*, no. 8. Abidjan: IFAN. Exceptional monograph on African export crop producers. Quite long. Great deal on social organization. Inspiring to other anthropologists.

  1962a. *Peuls nomades: étude descriptive des Wodaabe du Sahel nigérien*. Travaux et Mémoires de l'Institut d'Ethnologie, Vol. 64, University of Paris. Simply the best ethnographic account of the Fulani nomadic pastoralists, despite excellent competition (see Riesman 1977, Stenning 1959).

Dupré, G., and P-P. Rey. 1978. Reflections on the Relevance of a Theory of the History of Exchange. In D. Seddon (ed.) *Relations of Production* (q. v.), pp. 171–208. Also in *Economy and Society*, 2, no. 2 (1973); and *Cahiers Internationaux de Sociologie*, 46 (1968). Marxist rebuttal of the approach adopted in Bohannan and Dalton 1962. Emphasizes the political articulation of colonialism and lineage society in a system of economic exploitation.

Eicher, C., and C. Liedholm (eds.). 1970. *Growth and Development of the Nigerian Economy*. East Lansing: Michigan State University Press. Uneven but valuable collection of essays by economists. Some interesting papers on particular regions and problems.

Emmanuel, A. 1972. *L'échange inégal*. Paris: Maspero. Fundamental Marxist theory seeking to explain the growing gap between rich and poor nations in terms of the organization of production. Not about West Africa in particular.

Ernst, K. 1976. *Tradition and Progress in the African Village: The Non-Capitalist Transformation of Rural Communities in Mali*. New York: St. Martin's Press; London: C. Hurst. This East German sociologist has produced a synthesizing account that, although it is embedded in Marxist language, expresses much that the non-Marxist literature says less comprehensively.

Faulkner, O. T., and J. R. Mackie. 1933. *West African Agriculture*. Cambridge: Cambridge University Press. Concerned mostly with Nigeria, with some references to the Gold Coast. A timely reminder that foreigners were talking about agricultural policy in a previous period of depression.

Fieldhouse, D. K. 1973. *Economics and Empire, 1830–1914*. London: Weidenfeld and Nicholson. Excellent review of global imperialism up to World War I. Balanced assessment of economic and political factors.

Fitch, M., and Oppenheimer, R. 1966. *Ghana: The End of an Illusion*. New York: Monthly Review Press. Fiery account of Ghana's troubles published soon after Nkrumah's expulsion by coup. Stimulating, but uneven.

Forde, C. D., and R. Scott. 1946. *The Native Economies of Nigeria*. London: HMSO. No comparable work has been written since. Forde was a great anthropologist with an eye for the big picture.

Forde, D., and Kaberry P. (eds.). 1967. *West African Kingdoms of the Nineteenth Century*. London: Oxford University Press. Some of the region's most prominent anthropologists and historians present encapsulated versions of their specialties. Uniformly high quality.

Fortes, M. 1970. Time and Social Structure. In Fortes, *Time and Social Structure and*

Select annotated bibliography

Other Essays. London: LSE Athlone Press. A brilliant, original treatment of family organization in two Ashanti towns during the 1940s, when cocoa was still king.

Foster, P., and A. Zolberg (eds.). 1971. *Ghana and the Ivory Coast: Perspectives on Modernization*. Chicago: University of Chicago Press. A collection of above-average quality appearing at the apogee of the popularity of modernization theory. Looks a bit dated after the 1970s.

Frankel, S. H. 1938. *Capital Investment in Africa*. London: Oxford University Press. One of several pioneering works by an author who did much to expose the irrationality of investment patterns that persist in Africa today.

Gallais, J. 1967. *Le delta intérieur du Niger: étude de géographie régionale*. 2 vols. Mémoire no. 79. Dakar: IFAN. The best study of rural land use in Mali, with an emphasis on ethnic specialization. Also good material on regional marketing and towns.

Gallais, J. (ed.). 1977. *Stratégies pastorales et agricoles des sahéliens durant la sécheresse, 1969–74*. Bordeaux: Centre d'Etudes de Géographie Tropicale. Invaluable collection of papers outlining indigenous responses to the drought.

Galletti, R., K. D. S. Baldwin, and I. O. Dina. 1956. *Nigerian Cocoa Farmers: An Economic Survey of Yoruba Cocoa-Farming Families*. London: Oxford University Press. One of the few studies with detailed quantitative analysis of West African rural households.

Goody, J. R. 1971. *Technology, Tradition and the State in Africa,* London: Oxford University Press. Short book providing one anthropologist's synoptic view of traditional societies and their history. Thought-provoking, but thin.

Goody, J. R. (ed.). 1958. *The Developmental Cycle in Domestic Groups*. Cambridge: Cambridge University Press. This work grew out of Fortes's 1970 study. Goody's essay on the LoWiili and Stenning's on the Fulani are classic. Historians and sociologists are just now catching on that families exist in time.

1975. *Changing Social Structure in Ghana*. London: International African Insitute. Collection of original essays, mostly by Goody's students. Important comparative paper by Hill.

Gramsci, A. 1973. *Sul risorgimento*. Roma: Editori Riuniti. The relevance of Italy's national unification to African postcolonial states is palpable. Here Italy's greatest Marxist scholar provides his analysis of those nineteenth-century events.

Gugler, J., and W. Flanagan. 1978. *Urbanization and Social Change in West Africa*. Cambridge: Cambridge University Press. Useful complement to the present study. Summarizes literature on urbanization that is mostly sociological. The larger picture is a bit fragmented.

Gutkind, P., and I. Wallerstein (eds.). 1976. *The Political Economy of Contemporary Africa*. Beverly Hills: Sage. Important collection of essays sharing a variety of Marx-derived perspectives. Good bibliography; wide coverage.

Hammond, P. B. 1959. Economic Change and Mossi Acculturation. In W. R. Bascom and M. J. Herkovits (eds.), *Continuity and Change in African Culture*, pp. 238–56. Chicago: University of Chicago Press. Deals with the difficult adjustment of Mossi settlers to conditions at the Office du Niger colonization scheme. Set in the context of an account of Mossi culture.

Hancock, K. 1941. *Survey of British Commonwealth Affairs, 1919–1939*. Vol. II, Pt. 2. London: Oxford University Press. Superb treatment of colonial economic history in the interwar period, organized according to the concept of the ''trader's frontier,'' in contrast to that of the ''settler's frontier'' in central and southern Africa.

Hart, J. K. 1973. Informal Income Opportunities and Urban Employment in Ghana. *Journal of Modern African Studies*, 11, no. 3:61–89. Original formulation of the "informal sector" idea, which has been widely quoted in studies of burgeoning Third World cities.

1974. Migration and the Opportunity Structure: A Ghanaian Case Study. In S. Amin (ed.), *Modern Migrations in Western Africa* (q. v.), pp. 321–42. Largely descriptive attempt to show how diverse is the economic structure linking town and countryside. Summary of my views on the urban informal economy.

1975. Swindler or Public Benefactor? The Entrepreneur in His Community. In J. R. Goody (ed.), *Changing Social Structure in Ghana* (q. v.), pp. 1–36. An attempt to find out whether indigenous accumulators have means of coping with the social stress generated by their wealth. They do.

1978. The Economic Basis of Tallensi Social History in the Early Twentieth Century. In G. Dalton (ed.), *Research in Economic Anthropology,* I, 185–216. Greenwich, Conn.: JAI Press. A reassessment of Fortes's classic ethnography, focusing on the conditions of continuity and change in a society subject to commercialization.

1979. *The Development of Commercial Agriculture in West Africa.* Ann Arbor: USAID REDSO/WA 79–169. The ancestor of this book, missing most of the notes, Chapter 1, and several other parts of the text and text references.

Haswell, M. R. 1953. *Economics of Agriculture in a Savannah Village.* London: HMSO. The first of a unique series of studies on the Gambia covering the entire post–World War II period. The author is an agricultural economist of international renown, and each study is meticulously quantitative. Interpretations are rather low key: The facts themselves and the policy conclusions to be drawn from them are impressive enough.

1963. *The Changing Pattern of Economic Activity in a Gambia Village.* London: HMSO. See Haswell 1953.

1975. *The Nature of Poverty: A Case Study of the First Quarter Century after World War II.* New York: St. Martin's Press. See Haswell 1953.

Hawkins, E. K. 1958. The Growth of a Money Economy in Nigeria and Ghana. *Oxford Economic Papers,* no. 10, pp. 339–54. Important but neglected paper indicating that the internal commercial economy may grow faster than the export sector.

Helleiner, G. K. 1966. *Peasant Agriculture, Government and Economic Growth in Nigeria.* Homewood, Ill.: Irwin, for Yale Economic Growth Center. Since Helleiner's book was written, the notion of a "vent for surplus" (Myint's adaptation of Adam Smith) has become commonplace in West African economic studies. An important, original study.

Hicks, J. 1969. *A Theory of Economic History.* London: Oxford University Press. A fascinating, abstract account of the evolution of market and state. Appears to be theoretically naïve, but full of substantive insight.

Hill, P. 1963a. *Migrant Cocoa Farmers of Southern Ghana.* Cambridge: Cambridge University Press. Widely cited monograph, for good reasons. Her revelations about the foundation and organization of cocoa farming transformed our awareness of West Africa's indigenous economies.

1970. *Studies in Rural Capitalism in West Africa.* Cambridge: Cambridge University Press. A collection of essays on several topics; the longest is on the northern Ghanaian cattle trade. Reveals the author's varied skills as a researcher.

1972. *Rural Hausa: A Village and a Setting.* Cambridge: Cambridge University Press. Of all the books I read for the present study, this is probably the most indispensable. It is extraordinarily rich, informative, and suggestive. Together with M. G. Smith's ethnography, Norman's work, and much else, this makes the Hausa literature an outstanding source of materials on indigenous economy.

Hogendorn, J. S. 1978. *Nigerian Groundnut Exports: Origins and Early Development.*

London: Oxford University Press; Zaria: Ahmadu Bello University Press. Exciting and often funny account of how the Hausa, in 1912 and afterwards, confounded British expectations by growing groundnuts instead of cotton.

Hopkins, A. G. 1973. *An Economic History of West Africa.* New York: Columbia University Press; London: Longman. Although flawed, this is the standard work on economic history. A major synthesis that betrays lack of knowledge of the societies of the interior.

Horton, R. 1976. Stateless Societies in the History of West Africa. In A. Ajayi and M. Crowder (eds.), *History of West Africa* (q. v.), I, 72–113. Intriguing attempt to explain the variety of stateless societies as responses to pressures emanating from agriculture and warfare, as well as migration.

"J. L." 1971. New Developments in French-Speaking Africa. *Civilisations,* 21, no. 1. An informative summary for those who do not read French.

Johnston, B., and P. Kilby. 1975. *Agriculture and Structural Transformation.* New York: Oxford University Press. The arguments put forward here are a more systematic version of my own attempts. The authors have worked in West Africa: their emphasis is somewhat different.

Jones, W. I. 1976. *Planning and Economic Policy: Socialist Mali and Her Neighbours.* Washington, D.C.: Three Continents Press. Analysis of the failure of Modibo Keita's rural development policy. Sensitive integration of social organization at the village and state levels.

Jones, W. O. 1972. *The Marketing of Staple Food Crops in Tropical Africa.* Ithaca: Cornell University Press. Case studies from Nigeria, Sierra Leone, and Kenya. Mainly concerned with the determinants of market efficiency.

Kautsky, K. 1902. *Die Agrarfrage.* Stuttgart: Dietz. It is outrageous that no English translation exists of this, the best general theoretical treatment of the issues raised in my book. Frenchmen, Italians, and Russians are better served.

Kemp, T. 1978. *Historical Patterns of Industrialization.* London: Longman. Admirably brief statement of a loosely Marxist perspective on the topic. Looks at later arrivals such as Canada and India, as well as Britain and its immediate competitors.

Keynes, J. M. 1936. *The General Theory of Employment, Interest and Money.* London: MacMillan. The most general lesson of this book is how to write about interest rates in an English that entertains as it informs. Specifically, Keynes knew what was wrong with "classical theory."

Kobben, A. J. 1956. Le planteur noir. *Etudes eburnéenes.* Abidjan: IFAN. Extended piece of ethnography; complements Dupire's monograph on the lower Ivory Coast but does not rival it.

Kohler, J-M. 1971. *Activités agricoles et changements sociaux dans l'Ouest-Mossi.* Mémoires ORSTOM, no. 46. Paris: ORSTOM. Good account of Mossi rural economy, full of informative material.

Labouret, H. 1941. *Paysans d'Afrique occidentale.* Paris: Gallimard. Early work of synthesis, drawing especially on the Ivory Coast and Mali. Clearheaded analysis; useful for historical comparison with our day.

Law, R. 1978. Slaves, Trade and Taxes: The Material Basis of Political Power in Precolonial West Africa. In G. Dalton (ed.), *Research in Economic Anthropology,* I, 37–52. Greenwich, Conn.: JAI Press. Short but stimulating paper of self-explanatory title.

Le Bris, E., P-P Rey, and M. Samuel. 1976. *Capitalisme négrier: la marche des paysans vers le prolétariat.* Paris: Maspero. Looks at the social background to the rural exodus and at how village organization adapts to the absence of many young men.

Select annotated bibliography

Lele, U. 1975. *The Design of Rural Development: Lessons from Africa*. Baltimore: Johns Hopkins University Press, for World Bank. Review of World Bank projects in Africa; suffers from the anodyne jargon that passes for analysis in Bank circles.

Lenin, V. I. 1974. *The Development of Capitalism in Russia: The Process of the Formation of a Home Market for Large-Scale Industry*. Moscow: Progress Publishers. Essential reading for anyone who needs reminding why capitalism is a progressive force in backward rural areas. Devastating critique of Narodism, which lives today in development circles. Read it to find out who the Narodniks were.

Lewis, B. 1980. *Political Variables and Food Price Policy in West Africa*. New Brunswick, N. J.: AID 53/319/R-O-9. Useful summary of the food problem as tackled in literature so far. Argues that economists have missed the point, owing to their incapacity to analyze the role of politics.

Lewis, J. V. D. 1979a. Descendants and Crops: Two Poles of Production in a Malian Peasant Village. Unpublished Ph.D. dissertation, Yale University. An original and fascinating account of a corporate village's survival, from its past as a tax village in the Ségou state to its present as a supplier of labor to the Ivory Coast. Very good data on agricultural production.

Lewis, W. A. 1978a. *The Evolution of the International Economic Order*. Princeton: Princeton University Press. This very short book began life as lectures. Its author's clarity and originality stamp the whole text. Lewis is the best living example of the classical tradition of economic theory.

1978b. *Growth and Fluctuations, 1870–1913*. London: Allen and Unwin. Lewis is fascinated by the special problems of tropical exporting countries, and this is his attempt to describe the world economy at a time when many of them were definitively incorporated into the structure.

Liebenow, G. 1969. *Liberia: The Evolution of Privilege*. Ithaca: Cornell University Press. Straightforward debunking of the pretensions of the Liberian state. Some information on Firestone's rubber plantations.

Liedholm, C. 1973. *Research on Employment in the Rural Non-farm Sector in Africa*. Africa Rural Employment paper no. 5. East Lansing: Michigan State University Press. One of several works produced in the last decade by a Michigan State team that is beginning to put this neglected topic onto the map.

Lloyd, P. C. 1962. *Yoruba Land Law*. Ibadan: Oxford University Press, for the Nigerian Institute of Social and Economic Research (NISER). Very thorough account by a leading anthropologist; it deals with more than southwest Nigeria.

Lloyd, P. C. (ed.). 1966. *The New Elites of Tropical Africa*. London: Oxford University Press, for International African Institute. Results of a conference held at Ibadan in 1964. Useful sociological materials on the people who run Africa's new states.

Luxemburg, R. 1951. *The Accumulation of Capital*. London: Routledge and Kegan Paul. Luxemburg may not be the most logical of Marxist theoreticians, but she has most of the right answers. Emphasizes that capital must expand into that which it is not.

MacNamara, R. S. 1973. *Address to the Board of Governors, Nairobi, 24 September 1973*. Washington D. C.: World Bank. The key speech from which the World Bank and others derived the impetus to emphasize "equity" as a development goal.

McPhee, A. 1971. *The Economic Revolution in British West Africa*. 2nd ed. (1st ed. 1926). Introduced by A. G. Hopkins. London: Frank Cass. Astonishingly mature work that was a 1920s London School of Economics Ph.D. dissertation. The cornerstone of the region's economic history – at least for Anglophones.

Magasa, A. 1978. *Papa – commandant a jeté un grand filet devant nous: les exploités des rives du Niger, 1900–62*. Paris: Maspero. Damning account of repressive policies adopted toward sources of labor for big development projects – from the colonial government's Office du Niger to the modern Malian state.

Marx, K. 1959. *Capital*. 3 vols. London: Lawrence and Wishart. If more people read Marx instead of reading about him, much useless controversy would be cleared up. Vol. 1, Chap. 1, is extraordinarily suggestive.

  1973. *Grundrisse*. New York: Vintage Books. These are Marx's notes to himself, often difficult to penetrate. They contain the famous "precapitalist economic formations."

Mauny, R. 1961. *Tableau géographique de l'ouest africain au Moyen Age*. Dakar: IFAN. The best we have on West Africa's Middle Ages. Indispensable if we care how the region's peoples came to be what they are now from what they were before the Portuguese.

Mauss, M. 1967. *The Gift: Forms and Functions of Exchange in Archaic Societies*. New York: Norton. Enormously clarifying discussion of the contrast between gift giving and commercial contracts; opens up many new ways of thinking about the evolution of commodity economy.

Mazoyer, M. L. 1975. Développement de la production et transformation agricole marchande d'une formation agraire en Côte d'Ivoire. In S. Amin (ed.), *L'Agriculture africaine et le capitalisme* (q. v.), pp. 143–66. One of the best papers in this impressive volume; deals with the Baoulé and argues that cash cropping destroys the conditions of social reproduction.

Meillassoux, C. 1974*a*. *Anthropologie économique des Gouro de Côte d'Ivoire*. 3rd ed. (1st ed. 1964). Paris: Mouton. Classic ethnography on which a whole pyramid of Marxist theorizing once seemed to rest. Still the most important French monograph on this subject.

  1975*a*. *Femmes, greniers et capitaux*. Paris: Maspero. An attempt to generalize beyond the Gouro ethnography. The three terms of the title reflect key resources in a stages theory of social evolution. Stimulating ideas, but overall not entirely successful.

Meillassoux, C. (ed.). 1971*a*. *The Development of Indigenous Trade and Markets in West Africa*. London: Oxford University Press, for International African Institute. Very important set of conference papers. Meillassoux's introduction is wide-ranging and stimulating. Strong on the nineteenth century as a transitional era.

  1975*b*. *L'esclavage en Afrique précoloniale*. Paris: Maspero. Seventeen papers and another Meillassoux introduction. This was a successful attempt to put slavery where it belongs, at the center of West African social history.

Miers, S., and I. Kopytoff (eds.). 1977. *Slavery in Africa: Historical and Anthropological Perspectives*. Madison: University of Wisconsin Press. A useful complement to Meillassoux 1975*b*. Strong American contingent. Like its French counterpart, uneven.

Mill, J. S. 1909. *Principles of Political Economy with Some of their Applications to Social Philosophy*. 7th ed. (1st ed. 1848). New York: A. M. Kelley. The standard Victorian textbook on economics before Marshall's marginalism carried the day. Still a clearheaded, if slightly pedestrian, summary of the classical position.

Morss, E. R., et al. (Development Alternatives Inc.) 1975. *Strategies for Small Farmer Development: An Empirical Study of Rural Development Projects*. 2 vols. Vol. I: Final Report, Vol. II: *Case Studies*. Washington, D.C.: AID. These hefty volumes include a substantial West African component in vol. II. The overall assessment is judicious and worth reading.

Munroe, J. F. 1976. *Africa and the International Economy, 1800–1960*. London: J. M. Dent. Not the best summary of its topic, but a useful sketch for nonexperts and valuable background to the present book.

Nadel, S. F. 1942. *A Black Byzantium*. London: Oxford University Press. If you think

West Africa was inhabited by a homogeneous primitive peasantry, read this outstanding monograph on the Nupe of northern Nigeria. The most comprehensive ethnography that anyone has written: It is long.

Netting, R. McC. 1968. *Hill Farmers of Nigeria: Cultural Ecology of the Kofyar of the Jos Plateau.* Seattle: University of Washington Press. One of the most readable and informative anthropological accounts of an indigenous agricultural system. Highly recommended.

Netting, R. McC., D. Cleveland, and F. Stier, 1978. *The Conditions of Agricultural Intensification in the West African Savannah.* AID REDSO/WA 78–142. This should be read as a complement to the present book. Its three case studies (Northeast Ghana, the interior delta of Mali, and northern Nigeria) achieve a rounded concreteness that is entirely missing from my bird's-eye view.

Nicolas, G. 1971. Processus du résistance au "développement" au sein d'une société africaine (Vallée de Maradi, Niger). *Civilisations,* 21, no. 1:45–66. Argues that peasants resist government development initiatives, not because of "traditional" values, but because their economic interests are often infringed.

Nicolas, G., H. Doumesche, and M. Mouche. 1968. Etude socio-économique de deux villages haussa: enquête en vue d'un aménagement hydro-agricole, Vallée de Maradi, Niger. *Etudes Nigériennes, no. 22.* Niamey: Centre Nigérien de Recherche en Sciences Humaines (CNRSH). Deals with the complex effects of water projects on indigenous society, including the conflict between peasants and nomads over water use.

Norman, D. W. 1967. *An Economic Study of Three Villages in Zaria Province.* Samaru Miscellaneous Paper no. 19. Samaru, Zaria: Institute for Agricultural Research. One of the most comprehensive publications by an agricultural economist whose large output on Hausa rural economy is a major source for the region as a whole.

Ofori, I. M. (ed.). 1973. *Factors of Agricultural Growth in West Africa.* Legon: Institute of Statistical, Social and Economic Research (ISSER), University of Ghana. Interesting collection of conference papers from Legon, representing the vitality of the work done by scholars residing in West Africa.

Olatunbosun, D. 1975. *Nigeria's Neglected Rural Majority.* Ibandan: Oxford University Press, for the Nigerian Institute of Social and Economic Research (NISER). Macro account of economic factors affecting rural welfare. Sympathetic, systematic, but also rather superficial.

Pélissier, P. 1966. *Les paysans du Sénégal: les civilisations agraires du Cayor à la Casamance.* Saint-Yriex (Haute Vienne): Imprimerie Fabrègue. A monstrous tome that dominates all research on Senegal. There is really nothing like it in the West African literature. Many of his policy ideas are still valid.

Piault, C. n. d. Contribution a l'étude de la vie quotidienne de la femme Mawri. *Etudes Nigériennes,* no. 10. Niamey: CNRSH. Deals with the rapid transition from self-subsistence to commercial exchange, with notes on the condition of women and the increase in prostitution.

Polanyi, K. 1944. *The Great Transformation.* Boston: Beacon. A brilliantly original *cri de coeur,* from the depths of World War II, showing how the liberal civilization of industrial capitalism had been ruined by its own implausible assumptions. Had a big effect on economic anthropology.

Pollet, E., and G. Winter. 1978. The Social Organization of Agricultural Labor among the Soninke (Dyahunu, Mali). In D. Seddon (ed.), *Relations of Production* (q. v.), pp. 331–56. Translation of a seminal article that approaches the problem with ethnographic concreteness and analytical rigor. A model of its kind.

Raynaut, C. 1969. Quelques données de l'horticulture dans la Vallée de Maradi. *Etudes*

Nigériennes, no. 26. Niamey: CNRSH. Mostly a technical discussion of agriculture in Niger, with some interesting analytical points.

1972. *Structures normatives et relations electives: étude d'une communauté villageoise haoussa.* Paris: Mouton. Exemplary study that focuses on the circulation of commodities and cash within a village and out of it as a way of discovering how poverty is generated and maintained.

1975. Le cas de la région de Maradi (Niger). In J. Copans, (ed.), *Sécheresses et famines du Sahel* (q. v.), II, 5–43. Argues that, because groundnut farming was pursued at the expense of subsistence crops, the villagers were more vulnerable to famine when the drought came.

1976. Transformation du système de production et inégalité économique: le cas d'un village haoussa (Niger). *Canadian Journal of African Studies,* 10, no. 2:279–306. Analysis of the social changes resulting from commercialization. Shows how impoverishment is linked to the declining real value of agricultural labor.

Reboul, C. 1972. Structures agraires et problèmes du développement au Sénégal: les unités expérimentales du Siné-Saloum. Travaux de Recherche, no. 17. Paris: Institut National de la Recherche Agronomique. Also published in 1973 *Tiers Monde,* no. 54, pp. 403–16. Underlines the function of subsistence provision of food and equipment in maintaining the labor force for groundnut cultivation.

Rey, P-P. 1971. *Colonialisme, néo-colonialisme et transition au capitalisme: exemple de la Camilog au Congo-Brazzaville.* Paris: Maspero. An ambitious attempt to show how social evolution may be understood as an articulation of capitalism, petty commodity production, and the "lineage mode of production." Rey has been a persistently creative thinker in the French Marxist school, and this is his best book.

Reyna, S. P. 1942. The Costs of Marriage. Unpublished Ph.D. dissertation, Columbia University. Ethnographic study of Bagirmi Province in Chad. Links marriage to the economic structure of indigenous society.

Richards, A. I., F. Sturrock, and J. M. Fortt (eds.). 1973. *Subsistence to Commercial Farming in Present-Day Buganda: An Economic and Anthropological Survey.* Cambridge: Cambridge University Press. A collection from East Africa; of varied quality. Robertson's Bugerere case study makes some important methodological points.

Riesman, P. 1977. *Freedom in Fulani Social Life: An Introspective Ethnography.* Chicago: University of Chicago Press. Delightful monograph that, in a wholly novel way, presents the material life of the Fulani alongside their political structure and social psychology. The best ethnography of the last five years or so.

Roberts, P. 1979. The Integration of Women into the Development Process. *IDS Bulletin,* 10:60. Argues that the "animation rurale" program has been used to help women get cash for their own and their children's needs through household labor.

Robertson, A. F. 1979. Time and Class: An Examination of Cropsharing Arrangements in the Cocoa Economy of Ghana. Mimeo. Cambridge University. This unpublished paper helped me to clarify my views on rent and capital in cocoa agriculture, as well as on the development cycle phenomenon in farm growth and decline.

Schumpeter, J. A. 1954. *History of Economic Analysis.* New York: Oxford University Press. The most comprehensive intellectual history of economics available. Especially useful for presenting the thinking of preclassical philosophers and administrators and similar sources of economic ideas.

Schwimmer, B. 1976. Periodic Markets and Urban Development in Southern Ghana. In C. Smith (ed.), *Regional Analysis,* Vol. I: *Economic Systems,* pp. 123–45. New York: Academic Press. The only West African case study in an important collection. Shows the effects of government policy on a marketing structure in which rural producers originally controlled more of the situation.

Select annotated bibliography

Seddon, D. (ed.). 1978. *Relations of Production: Marxist Approaches to Economic Anthropology*. London: Frank Cass. An important set of articles translated from the French, including a whole section on Africa. Introduction by Seddon and Copans will be useful for newcomers to this body of discourse.

Seibel, H-D, and A. Massing. 1974. *Traditional Organizations and Economic Development: Studies of Indigenous Cooperatives in Liberia*. New York: Praeger. This slight study is not theoretically impressive, but it does put together a lot of material on an important topic.

Shapiro, K. H. (ed.). 1979a. *Livestock Production and Marketing in the Entente States of West Africa: A Summary Report*. Ann Arbor: Center for Research on Economic Development, University of Michigan, for AID. Four case studies, annotated bibliography, and Shapiro's introduction. Up-to-date and comprehensive.

Shepherd, A. W. 1978. The Development of Capitalist Rice Farming in Northern Ghana. Unpublished Ph.D. dissertation. Cambridge University. The definitive study so far of a development that I think has enormous implications for West African agriculture.

Smith, A. 1776. *An Enquiry into the Nature and Causes of the Wealth of Nations*. London: Everyman Library. It would be more worthwhile for West African politicians to read and ponder this work than to hire modern economists to think for them.

Smith, M. F. 1964. *Baba of Karo: A Woman of the Moslem Hausa*. New York: Praeger. Excellent, indeed unique, life history of a West African woman and ethnography of her setting. Superior to most of the literature on gender.

Smith, M. G. 1955. *The Economy of the Hausa Communities of Zaria*. London: HMSO. The first two-thirds of this is mostly about political structure and its economic effects: an invaluable corrective to mindless economism. Worth tracking down.

1978. *The Affairs of Daura: History and Change in a Hausa State, 1800–1958*. Berkeley and Los Angeles: University of California Press. Extraordinarily complex attempt to combine historical and ethnographic methods in the study of political change. Unique and thought-provoking.

Sow, F. 1972. *Les fonctionnaires de l'administration centrale sénégalaise*. Initiations et Etudes Africaines, no. 29. Dakar: IFAN. A useful discussion of a topic much referred to in my book.

1977. Quelques reflexions sur la distribution des revenus en Afrique. *Bulletin de l'IFAN*, 39, ser. B, no. 1:171–201. There are not many explicit analyses of the revenue problem in Africa's new states. This is a good beginning.

Stavenhagen, R. 1975. *Social Classes in Agrarian Societies*. Garden City, N.Y.: Doubleday, Anchor Books. A comparison of the Ivory Coast and Mexico, using secondary sources for the former. Overrated, but a readily available digest if you are not up to reading Dupire for youself.

Stenning, D. J. 1959. *Savannah Nomads: A Study of the Wodaabe Pastoral Fulani of Western Bornu Province, Northern Region, Nigeria*. Oxford: Oxford University Press, for International African Institute. Excellent field study that established the high standards maintained by modern Fulani ethnography.

Steuart, Sir J. 1767. *Principles of Political Oeconomy*. 2 vols. London: Millar and Cadell. This last of the great preclassical economists was overshadowed by Adam Smith. But his ideas may be more relevant than Smith's to present-day West Africa.

Suret-Canale, J. 1971. *French Colonialism in Tropical Africa, 1900–45*. Published in French in 1964. Translated by Till Gottheiner. London: C. Hurst. The standard text, with a strong left-wing slant. I have always found it disappointing, but others rave about it.

1972. *Afrique noire occidentale et centrale (1945–60): crise du système colonial et capitalisme monopoliste d'état*. Paris: Editions Sociales. More interesting than his earlier book, it deals with a transitional period crucial to our understanding of the modern successor states.

Swift, J. 1977. Sahelian Pastoralists: Underdevelopment, Desertification and Famine. *Annual Review of Anthropology,* 6:457–78. A digest of published materials, put together in a readable way with some thought-provoking suggestions.

Szereszewski, R. 1965. *Structural Change in the Economy of Ghana, 1891–1911.* London: Weidenfeld and Nicolson. Deals with the period of the Gold Coast's cocoa boom; this account parallels Helleiner's (1966) emphasis.

Terray, E. 1969. *L'organisation sociale des Dida de Côte d'Ivoire.* Dijon: Darantière. An excellent monograph by the French Marxist anthropologist who has been the most sensitive of his school to the requirements of empirical ethnography and historical research.

1972. *Marxism and Primitive Societies.* Pt. 2: Historical materialism and segmentary lineage-based societies, pp. 93–186. New York: Monthly Review Press. This critical review of Meillassoux's Gouro ethnography is the best single essay to have emerged from French Marxist anthropology.

Tiffen, M. 1975. *The Enterprising Peasant: Economic Development in Gombe Emirate, NE State, Nigeria, 1900–1968.* Overseas Research Publication no. 2. London: HMSO. A model study that reaches more optimistic conclusions than are usual. Mixed farming of cotton with the oxplow, it claims, has been a success!

Venema, L. B. 1978. *The Wolof of Saloum: Social Structure and Rural Development in Senegal.* Netherlands Agricultural Research Report no. 871. Wageningen: Centre for Agricultural Publishing and Documentation. Not terribly exciting, but perhaps the best introduction in English to a people and topic that have been studied intensively by French-speaking authors.

Wade, R. 1975. Irrigation and Income Distribution: Three Papers. *IDS Discussion Paper* no. 85. Nov. The sociological conclusions reached here, based on research in India, are extremely relevant to West Africa's experiment in irrigation.

Waldstein, A. S. 1978a. *Government Sponsored Agricultural Intensification Schemes in the Sahel: Development for Whom?* Abidjan: USAID REDSO/WA 78-139. The development is not for the peasants, as Waldstein makes clear. This review essay fills an important gap in the literature and emphasizes the possibilities for small irrigation schemes.

Wallace, T. 1978a. Rural Development through Irrigation: Studies in a Town on the Kano River Project. Mimeo. Centre for Social and Economic Research, Ahmadu Bello University, Zaria. Nov. I enjoyed reading this anthropological critique of development practice in the Kano River project. Perhaps it will be more widely available soon.

Weber, M. 1978. *Economy and Society.* 2 vols. Edited by G. Roth and C. Wittich. Berkeley and Los Angeles: University of California Press. The text is often tortuous and difficult; but Weber's definitions and analysis are indispensable to any serious student of matters raised in the present book.

Weil, P. 1970. Introduction of the Oxplow in Central Gambia. In P. F. M. McLoughlin (ed.), *African Food Production Systems,* pp. 229–64. Baltimore: Johns Hopkins University Press. One of several stimulating studies of the oxplow problem, this paper is a valuable contribution to Gambian research.

White, H. P., and M. B. Gleave. 1971. *An Economic Geography of West Africa.* London: G. Bell and Sons. This is the general text that I found most useful. But there are strong competitors.

Williams, G. (ed.). 1976a. *Nigeria: Economy and Society.* London: Rex Collings. Good collection of essays by a leftish group of authors.

World Bank. 1978. Rural Development Projects: A Retrospective View of Bank Experi-

Select annotated bibliography

ence in Sub-Saharan Africa. World Bank Operations Evaluation Department, Report no. 2242, Oct. 13. The World Bank's presence in rural Africa is a growing one. This is the most up-to-date review I could find. Especially interesting for figures on rates of return.

1980. *World Tables*. 2nd ed. Baltimore: Johns Hopkins University Press. The main source of figures for the present book. National economic accounts, plus a dozen comparative tables. Very convenient.

Zangheri, R. 1969. The Historical Relationship between Agricultural and Economic Development in Italy. In E. L. Jones and S. L. Woolf (eds.), *Agrarian Change and Economic Development: The Historical Problems*, pp. 23–40. London: Methuen. The communist mayor of Bologna is an economic historian. This paper clarified my ideas on the relationship between agrarian capitalism and the formation of a national home market.

Supplementary bibliography

Abbott, J. C. 1967. Agricultural Marketing Boards in the Developing Countries. *Journal of Farm Economics*, no. 49, pp. 705–22.

Adamolekun, L. 1969. Politics and Administration in West Africa: The Guinean Model. *Journal of Administration Overseas*, 8, no. 4 (Oct.).

Addo, N. O. 1974. Some Employment and Labour Conditions on Ghana's Cocoa Farms. In R. A. Kotey, C. Okali, and B. E. Rourke (eds.), *Economics of Cocoa Production and Marketing* (q. v.), pp. 204–21.

Adegboye, R. O., and A. Abidogun. 1973. Contribution of Part-time Farming to Rural Development in Ibadan Area, Western Nigeria. In I. M. Ofori (ed.), *Factors of Agricultural Growth in West Africa* (q. v.).

Afana, O. 1977. *L'économie de l'ouest africain: perspectives de développement*. Paris: Maspero.

Aghassian, M., et al. 1976. *Les migrations africaines*. Paris: Maspero.

Ahooja-Patel, K. 1969. Economic Cooperation in Africa: The Institutional Framework. *Journal of World Trade Law*, 3, no. 3 (May–June).

AID (Agency for International Development). 1978. *Agricultural Development, Policy Paper*. Washington, D.C.: AID.

Akinjogbin, I. A. 1967. *Dahomey and Its Neighbours, 1708–1818*. Cambridge: Cambridge University Press.

Allen, C. 1974. Radical Africana. *Review of African Political Economy*, no. 1, pp. 93–112.

Allunson, M. 1963. *Etude générale de la région de Man*. Vol. II: *Rapport de synthèse économique*. Vol. IV: *Etude sociologique et démographique*. Paris: Ministry of Planning (Ivory Coast), Bureau pour le Développement de la Production Agricole.

Amin, S. 1965. *Trois expériences africaines de développement: le Mali, la Guinée et le Ghana*. Paris: PUF.

1969. *Le monde des affaires sénégalaises*. Paris: Les Editions de Minuit.

1974b. *La question paysanne et le capitalisme*. Paris: Editions Anthropos, IDEP.

1975b. *La planification du sous-développement*. Paris: Editions Anthropos, IDEP.

Amselle, J-L. 1970. Les réseaux marchands Kooroko. *African Urban Notes*, no. 5, pp. 143–58.

1971. Parenté et commerce chez les Kooroko. In C. Meillassoux (ed.), *The Development of Indigenous Trade and Markets in West Africa* (q. v.), pp. 253–65.

Angey, G. 1977. Recensement et description des principaux systèmes ruraux sahéliens. *Cahiers ORSTOM*, Sér. sciences humaines, 14, no. 1:3–18.

Anschel, K., R. Brannon, and E. Smith (eds.). 1969. *Agricultural Cooperatives and Markets in Developing Countries*. New York: Praeger.

Anthonio, Q. B. O. 1968. *Fish Marketing Survey in the Kainji Lake Basin: Yelwa Area Study*. Ibadan: Nigerian Institute for Social and Economic Research.

Apter, D. 1963. *Ghana in Transition*. New York: Atheneum.

Asiwaju, A. I. 1976. Migrations as Revolt: The Example of the Ivory Coast and Upper

189

Supplementary bibliography

Volta before 1945. *Journal of African History,* 17, no. 4:577–94.

1978. Socio-Economic Integration of the West African Sub-region in Historical Context: Focus on the European Colonial Period. *Bulletin de l'IFAN,* 40, ser. B, no. 1: 160–78.

Augé, M. 1970. Les pêcheurs de requins à Pont-Bouet (Côte d'Ivoire). *Cahiers d'Etudes Africaines,* 10, no. 39:407–21.

Bachmann, H. B. (ed.). 1974. *Senegal: Tradition, Diversification and Economic Development.* Baltimore: Johns Hopkins University Press, for World Bank.

Baier, S. 1976. Economic History and Development. Drought and the Sahelian Economies of Niger. *African Economic History,* no. 1, pp. 1–16.

Barres, V. et al. 1976. *The Participation of Rural Women in Development: A Project of Rural Women's Animation in Niger, 1966–75.* Paris; IRAM.

Barth, H. 1965. *Travels and Discoveries in North and Central Africa.* (1st ed. 1857). 3 vols. London: Frank Cass.

Beales, R., and C. F. Menezes. 1970. Migrant Labor and Agricultural Output in Ghana. *Oxford Economic Papers,* n.s. 22, no. 1:109–27.

Beauvilain, A. 1977. Les Peul du Dallol Bosso. *Etudes Nigériennes,* no. 42. Niamey: CNRSH.

Behrman, L. 1967. *The Political Influence of Muslim Brotherhoods in Senegal.* Boston: Boston University Press.

Bendix, R. 1960. *Max Weber: An Intellectual Portrait.* Garden City, N.Y.: Doubleday.

Benneh, G. 1973. Small-Scale Farming Systems in Ghana. *Africa,* no. 43, pp. 134–46.

Bennoune, M. 1978. Mauritania: A Neocolonial Desert. *Dialectical Anthropology,* 3, no. 1:43–66.

Benot, Y. 1975. *Les independances africaines: idéologies et réalities.* Paris: Maspero.

Berg, E. J. 1960. The Economic Basis of Political Choice in French West Africa. *American Political Science Review,* no. 54, pp. 391–405.

1964. Socialism and Economic Development in Tropical Africa. *Quarterly Journal of Economics,* 78, no. 4.

Bergmann, H. 1974. Les notables villageois: chef de village et imam face à la coopérative rurale dans une région du Sénégal. *Bulletin de l'IFAN,* 36, ser. B, no. 2:283–322.

Bernard, G. 1970. Analyse d'un réseau social en milieu urbain. *Cahiers d'Etudes Africaines,* 10, no. 40:632–6.

Bernstein, H. 1978. Notes on Capital and Peasantry. *Review of African Political Economy,* no. 10, pp. 60–73.

Bernus, E. 1973. La sécheresse en république du Niger. In D. Dalby and R. J. H. Church (eds.), *Drought in Africa* (q.v.), pp. 140–7.

1974. L'évolution récente des relations entre éleveurs et agriculteurs en Afrique tropicale: l'exemple du Sahel nigérien. *Cahiers ORSTOM,* Sér. sciences humaines, 11, no.2:137–43.

Bernus, E., and G. Savonnet. 1973. Les problèmes de la sécheresse dans l'Afrique de l'ouest. *Présence Africaine,* no. 88, pp. 113–38.

Bienefeld, M., and M. Godfrey. 1978. Surplus Labor and Underdevelopment. IDS Discussion Paper. Sept.

Birmingham, W. B., et al. (eds.). 1967. *A Study of Contemporary Ghana.* London: Allen and Unwin.

Blanchard, F. 1977. *Une strategie des besoins essentiels pour l'Afrique.* Genève: Bureau International de Travail (ILO).

Bonnefonds, A-L. 1968. La transformation du commerce de traite en Côte d'Ivoire depuis la dernière Guerre Mondiale et l'Independance. *Cahiers d'Outre-Mer,* no. 21, pp. 395–413.

190

Supplementary bibliography

Bouche, D. 1949. Les villages de liberté en AOF. *Bulletin de l'IFAN*, nos. 3–4, pp. 524.

Bouchet, P. 1955. Le secteur expérimental de modernisation agricole des terres neuves de Boulel. *L'Agronomie Tropicale*, 8, no.2:174–216.

Boutillier, J. L. 1960. *Bongouanou, Côte d'Ivoire: étude socio-économique d'une subdivision.* Paris: Berger-Levrault.

Bradley, P., C. Raynaut, and J. Torrealba. 1977. *The Guidimaka Region of Mauritania: A Critical Analysis Leading to a Development Project.* London: War on Want.

Brasseur, P. 1964. *Bibliographie générale du Mali.* Dakar: IFAN.

  1976. *Bibliographie Générale du Mali, 1961–70.* Dakar: Nouvelles Editions Africaines.

Breton, J-M. 1978. *Le controle d'état sur le continent africain.* Paris: Libraire Générale de Droit et de Jurisprudence; Dakar: Nouvelles Editions Africaines.

Brochier, J. 1968. *La diffusion du progrès technique en milieu rural sénégalais.* Paris: PUF.

  1971. Enquête sur le mouvement cooperatif dans un arrondissement sénégalais. *Civilisations,* 21, no. 1:19–37.

Buchanan, K. M. , and J. C. Pugh. 1955. *Land and People in Nigeria.* London: University of London Press.

Bunting, A. H. (ed.). 1970. *Change in Agriculture.* London: Duckworth.

Byerlee, D., C. Eicher, C. Liedholm, and D. Spencer. 1977. *Rural Employment in Tropical Africa: Summary of Findings.* African Rural Economy Paper no. 20. East Lansing: Michigan State University.

Caldwell, J. C. 1967. Migration and Urbanisation. In W. B. Birmingham et al. (eds.), *A Study of Contemporary Ghana* (q. v.), pp. 111–46.

Carle, M. P. 1955. Le marché de l'arachide dans le Siné-Saloum (Sénégal). s.e. Dakar, fasc. 11, rapport 12.

CEDETIM (Centre Socialiste de Documentation et d'Etudes sur les Problèmes du Tiers Monde). 1974. Impérialisme français et sécheresse: la famine au Sahel. *Bulletin de liason du CEDETIM,* June.

Centre Africain des Sciences Humaines Appliquées and SEAE (Secretariat d'Etat Français aux Affairs Etrangères). 1967. *L'adaptation de la formation des cadres moyens africains.* 5 vols. Aix-en-Provence: Centre Africain des Sciences Humaines Appliquées.

Cervenka, Z. 1977. *The Unfinished Quest for Unity: Africa and the O.A.U.* London: Friedman.

Chabrolin, R. 1977. Rice in West Africa. In C. Leakey and J. B. Wills (eds.), *Food Crops of the Lowland Tropics.* Oxford: Oxford University Press.

Chambers, R. 1969. *Settlement Schemes in Tropical Africa: A Study of Organization and Development.* London: Frank Cass.

Charlick, R. 1972. Induced Participation in Nigerian Modernisation: The Case of Matameye County. *Rural Africana,* no. 18 (Fall), pp. 5–29.

Charpentier, F. 1973. Sahel nigérien en perdition. Mimeo. Niamey: CNRSH.

Chauveau, J. P. 1976. Note sur les échanges dans le Baulé précolonial. *Cashiers d'Etudes Africaines,* 17, nos. 63–4:567–602.

Church, R. J. H. 1974. *The Development of Water Resources of the Dry Zone of West Africa.* London: N.p.

Chuta, E. 1978. The Economics of the Gara (Tie-Dye) Cloth Industry in Sierra Leone. Depts. of Agricultural Economics, Michigan State University, E. Lansing; Njala University College, Njala, Sierra Leone.

Clapham, C. 1976. *Liberia and Sierra Leone: An Essay in Comparative Politics.* Cambridge: Cambridge University Press.

Supplementary bibliography

Clerc, J. 1956. *Société paysanne et problèmes fonciers de la palmeraie dahoméenne.* Paris: ORSTOM.

Cleverdon, R. The Economic and Social Impact of International Tourism on Developing Countries. *Economist Intelligence Unit, Special Report,* no. 60.

Clignet, R. 1966. Urbanization and Family Structure in Ivory Coast. *Comparative Studies in Society and History,* no. 8, pp. 385–401.

Cohen, A. 1965. The Social Organization of Credit in a West African Cattle Market. *Africa,* 35, no. 1:8–20.

1966. Politics of the Kola Trade. *Africa,* 36, no. 1:18–36.

1971. Cultural Strategies in the Organization of Trading Diasporas. In C. Meillassoux (ed.), *The Development of Indigenous Trade and Markets in West Africa* (q.v.), pp. 266–81.

Cohen, M. A., et al. 1979. *Urban Growth and Economic Development in the Sahel.* Washington, D.C.: World Bank.

Colloque International de Haifa (13–18 May, 1973). 1974. *Sociétés villageoises: autodéveloppement et intercoopération.* Recherches Coopératives no. 9. Paris: Mouton.

Coloud, R. 1958. *Evolution sociale des Agni Sanvi.* Mémoire de sociologie présenté à l'Ecole Pratique des Hautes-Etudes, Paris.

Copans, J. 1975*b.* Images, problématiques et thèmes. In J. Copans (ed.), *Sécheresses et famines du Sahel* (q.v.), I, 9–40.

Coquery-Vidrovitch, C. 1968. L'échec d'une tentative économique: l'impôt de capitation au service des compagnies concessionnaires du "Congo Francais," 1900–1909. *Cahiers d'Etudes Africaines,* 8, no. 29:96–109.

1971*a.* De la traite des esclaves à l'exportation de l'huile de palme et des palmistes au Dahomey: XIXe siècle. In C. Meillassoux (ed.), *The Development of Indigenous Trade and Markets in West Africa* (q.v.), pp. 107–23.

1971*b.* De l'impérialisme ancien à l'impérialisme moderne: l'avatar colonial. In A. Abdel-Malek (ed.), *Sociologie de l'impérialisme,* pp. 73–122. Paris: Anthropos. Reprinted in J. Bouvier and R. Girault (eds.) 1976, *L'impérialisme français d'avant 1914,* pp. 85–126.

1976. The Political Economy of the African Peasantry and Modes of Production. In P. Gutkind and I. Wallerstein (eds.), *The Political Economy of Contemporary Africa* (q.v.), pp. 90–111.

1977. La mise en dependance de l'Afrique noire: essai de périodisation, 1800–1970. *Cahiers d'Etudes Africaines,* 1–2, nos. 61–2:7–58.

Crozier, M. (ed.). 1974. *Où va l'administration français?* Paris: Collection Sociologique des Organisations.

Cruise O'Brien, D. 1967. Toward an Islamic Policy in French West Africa, 1854–1914. *Journal of African History,* 8:303–16.

1975. *Saints and Politicians: Essays in the Organization of a Senegalese Peasant Society.* Cambridge: Cambridge University Press.

Curtin, P. 1969. *The Atlantic Slave Trade: A Census.* Madison: University of Wisconsin Press.

Dalton, G. 1965. History, Politics and Economic Development in Liberia. *Journal of Economic History,* 25:569–91.

Dampierre, E. de. 1960. Coton noir, café blanc: deux cultures du Haut-Oubangui à la veille de la loi-cadre. *Cahiers d'Etudes Africaines,* 1, no. 2:128–47.

David, N. 1973. Extensive Development of the Agricultural Sector in the Semi-Arid and Northern Savannah Zones of West Africa. In D. Dalby and R. J. H. Church (eds.), *Drought in Africa* (q.v.), pp. 85–93.

Supplementary bibliography

Davis, K. 1969. *World Urbanization, 1950-1970*. Berkeley: Institute of International Studies.

Delauney, D. 1975. *Migrations et pénétration de l'économie marchande: le Waalo*. Dakar: ORSTOM.

Delbard, B. 1965. *Aspects du problème vivrier sénégalais*. Dakar: ISEA.

Devitt, P. 1973. Notes on Some Social Aspects of Drought in Pastoral Areas of Africa: An Opportunity for Radical Rethink. In D. Dalby and R. J. H. Church (eds.), *Drought in Africa* (q.v.), pp. 186-99.

Diagne, P. 1972. *Pour l'unité ouest-africaine: micro-états et integration économique*. Paris: Anthropos.

―― 1973. L'appel de l'Afrique française, un grand devoir de solidarité: le drame de l'arachide, la Grande Pihé du Sénégal. *Le Sud-Ouest Economique*, no. 234 (May).

Diarassouba, V-C. 1968. *L'évolution des structures agricoles du Sénégal: destructuration et restructuration de l'économie rurale*. Paris: Editions Cujas.

Diawara, B., and S. Traore. 1975. *Population et activité économique dans la transformation du secteur rural au Mali*. Les Annales de l'IFORD (Institut de Formation et de Recherche Démographiques), no. 1.

Dike, K. O. 1956. *Trade and Politics in the Niger Delta, 1830-1885*. London: Oxford University Press.

Diop, A-B. 1974. La famille rurale Wolof: mode de résidence et organisation socio-économique. *Bulletin de l'IFAN*, 36, ser. B, no. 1:147-63.

Dorjahn, V. R. 1962. African Traders in Sierra Leone. In P. Bohannan and G. Dalton (eds.), *Markets in Africa* (q.v.), pp. 61-88.

Dozon, J. P. n.d. Logique des développeurs/réalité des développés: bilan d'une expérience de développement rizicole en Côte d'Ivoire. Paris: ORSTOM.

Dresch, J. 1949. La riziculture en Afrique occidentale. *Annales de Géographie*, no. 58, 295-312.

Drouhin, G. 1953. The Problem of Water Resources in Northwest Africa: Arid Zone Research Programme. In *Hydrology*, vol. I. Paris: UNESCO.

Due, J. M. 1969. Agricultural Development in the Ivory Coast and Ghana. *Journal of Modern African Studies*, 7, no. 4:637-60.

―― 1973. Experience with Mechanized Agriculture in Ghana and Sierra Leone Rice Production. In I. M. Ofori (ed.), *Factors of Agricultural Growth in West Africa* (q.v.).

Dumett, R. 1971. The Rubber Trade of the Gold Coast and Asante in the Nineteenth Century: African Innovation and Market Responsiveness. *Journal of African History*, no. 12:79-102.

Dumont, R. 1962. *Reconversion de l'économie agricole des républiques de Guinée, de Côte d'Ivoire et de Mali*. Paris: PUF.

―― 1966b. The Necessity for Agricultural Development in Africa and the Practical Difficulties. FAO. UN DOC E/CN 14/342. Reprinted in J. S. Uppal and L. R. Salkever (eds.) 1972, *Africa* (q.v.), pp. 115-29.

―― 1972. *Paysanneries aux abois: Ceylan, Tunisie, Sénégal*. Paris: Le Seuil.

―― 1974. *Utopia, or Else . . .* Translated by V. Menkes. London: André Deutsch. Originally published 1973 as *L'utopie ou la mort*. Paris: Editions du Seuil.

―― 1975. *La croissance de famine: une agriculture repensée*. Paris: Editions du Seuil.

Dunsmore, J. R. n.d. *The Agricultural Development of the Gambia*. London: U.K. Ministry of Overseas Development, Land Resources Division, Land Resources Study.

Dupire, M. 1962b. Trade and Markets in the Economy of the Nomadic Fulani of Niger (Bororo). In P. Bohannan, and G. Dalton (eds.), *Markets in Africa* (q.v.), pp. 335-64.

Supplementary bibliography

1972. Les facteurs humaines de l'économie pastorale. *Etudes Nigériennes*, no. 6. Niamey: CNRSH.

n.d. La place du commerce et des marchés dans l'économie des Bororos. *Etudes Nigériennes*, no. 3. Niamey: CNRSH.

L'économie de L'Arachide au Sénégal: les problèmes humaines. 1952. *Oléagineux: Revue Générale des Corps Gras et Derivés*, no. 1 (Jan.).

Eddy, E. D. 1979. Prospects for the Development of Cattle Production on Mixed Farms in the Pastoral Zone of Niger: A Summary. In K. H. Shapiro (ed.), *Livestock Production and Marketing in the Entente States of West Africa* (q.v.), pp. 328–437.

Eicher, C. K. 1970. *Research on Agricultural Development in Five English-Speaking Countries in West Africa*. New York: Agricultural Development Council.

Eicher, C., and G. Johnson. 1970. Policy for Nigerian Agricultural Development in the 1970s. In C. Eicher and C. Liedholm (eds.), *Growth and Development of the Nigerian Economy* (q.v.).

Eighmy, T. H. 1969. Modernization in a Regional Context: Pretheory and Practice in Western Nigeria. Unpublished Ph.D. dissertation, Pennsylvania State University.

Elliot, C. M. 1969. Agriculture and Economic Development in Africa: Theory and Experience, 1880–1914. In E. L. Jones and S. G. Woolf (eds.), *Agrarian Change and Economic Development* (q.v.), pp. 123–50.

Elliott, H. 1974. Cocoa Production Prospects in the Ivory Coast. In R. A. Kotey, C. Okali, and B. E. Rourke (eds.), *Economics of Cocoa Production and Marketing* (q.v.), pp. 251–64.

Esseks, J. E. (ed.). 1975. *L'Afrique de l'independance politique à l'independance économique*. Paris: Maspero.

Etienne, P. 1968. *La diffusion de l'économie monétaire et la transformation des rapports sociaux chez les Baoulé*. Abidjan: IFAN.

Evans-Pritchard, E. 1940. *The Nuer*. London: Oxford University Press.

FAO. 1963. *Côte d'Ivoire: problèmes et perspectives de développement rural*. Enquête de la FAO sur l'Afrique.

1966. *Agricultural Development in Nigeria (1965–80)*. Rome: FAO.

1973*a*. Proposed Medium and Long-Term Programmes for the Sahelian Zone of West Africa. In D. Dalby and R. J. H. Church (eds.), *Drought in Africa* (q.v.).

1973*b*. *The Sahelian Zone: A Selected Bibliography for the Study of Its Problems*. FAO Library Occasional Bibliographies, no. 9. Rome: FAO, Library and Documentation Division.

FAO (United Nations Food and Agriculture Organization) and World Bank (IBRD). 1975. Economic Development of Areas Freed from Onchocerciasis in Ghana. Informal country paper, Rome. Oct.

Fauvre, C. 1978. *L'agriculture et le capitalisme*. Paris: Editions Anthropos.

Fieloux, M. 1976. Les migrations Lobi en Côte d'Ivoire: archaisme ou création sociale? In M. Aghassian et al., *Les migrations africaines* (q.v.), pp. 43–61.

Flores, X. 1971. *Agricultural Organizations and Development*. Geneva: ILO.

Fogg, C. D. 1965. Economic and Social Factors Affecting the Development of Smallholder Agriculture in Eastern Nigeria. *Economic Development and Cultural Change*, 13, no. 3 (Apr.): 278–92.

Forde, C. D., and P. Kaberry (eds.). 1967. *West African Kingdoms of the Nineteenth Century*. Cambridge: Cambridge University Press.

Fortes, M. 1945. *The Dynamics of Clanship among the Tallensi*. London: Oxford University Press.

1949. *The Web of Kinship among the Tallensi*. London: Oxford University Press.

Fortes, M., and D. Mayer. 1966. Psychosis and Social Change among the Tallensi of N.

194

Supplementary bibliography

Ghana. *Cahiers d'Etudes Africaines,* 6, no. 21:5–40.

Franco, M. 1978. La rentabilité, critère du développement rural en Afrique? *Revue Tiers-Monde* 19, no. 73:139–48.

Frank, A. G. 1969. *Latin America: Underdevelopment or Revolution.* New York: Monthly Review Press.

Fréchou, H. 1958. Les plantations européens en Côte d'Ivoire. *Cahiers d'Outre Mer,* no. 8, pp. 269–70.

Freyssinet, J. and A. Mounier. 1975. *Les revenues de travailleurs agricoles en Afrique centrale et occidentale.* Geneva: Bureau International de Travail (ILO).

Froelich, J-C. 1969. Les structures sociales traditionelles et le développement. *Genève-Afrique,* 8, no. 2:36–46.

Fuglestad, F. 1974. La grande famine de 1931 dans l'ouest nigérien: reflexions autour d'une catastrophe naturelle. *Revue Française d'Histoire d'Outre-Mer,* 61, no. 222:18–33.

Gallais, J. 1972. Essai sur la situation actuelle des relations entre pasteurs et paysans dans le Sahel ouest-africain. In *Etudes de Géographie Tropicale Offertes à Pierre Gourou.* Le Monde D'Outre-Mer Passé et Présent, Etude 36, pp. 301–13. Paris: Mouton.

1975. *Pasteurs et Paysans du Gourma: la condition sahélienne.* Bordeaux: Editions du Centre National de la Recherche Scientifique; Paris: Centre d'Etudes de Géographie Tropicale.

Galloy, P., Y. Vincent, and M. Forget. 1963. *Nomades et paysans d'Afrique noire occidentale.* Annales de l'Est, Mémoire no. 23. Nancy: Université de Nancy.

Gatin, A. 1968. Foreign Aid: What It Is, How It Works, Why We Provide It. *Bulletin of State Department,* 59, no. 1537 (Dec.).

Gilbert, E. H. 1969. *The Marketing of Staple Foods in N. Nigeria.* Unpublished Ph.D. dissertation, Stanford University.

Gleave, M. B., and M. F. Thomas. 1968. The Bagango Valley: An Example of Land Utilization and Agricultural Practice in the Bamenda Highlands. *Bulletin de l'IFAN,* ser. B, no. 30, pp. 655–81.

Goddard, A. D. 1970. Land Tenure and Economic Development in Hausaland. *Agricultural Newsletter* (Samaru, northern Nigeria), no. 2, pp. 30–3.

1973. Changing Family Structures among the Rural Hausa. *Africa,* no. 43, pp. 207–18.

Goddard, A. D., J. C. Fine, and D. W. Norman. 1971. *A Socio-Economic Study of Three Villages in the Sokoto Close-Settled Zone.* Samaru Miscellaneous Paper no. 33. Samaru, Zaria: Institute for Agricultural Research.

Gonidec, P-F. 1974. *Les systèmes politiques africains.* 2 vols. Paris: Libraire Générale de Droit et de Jurisprudence.

Goody, J. R. 1962. *Death, Property and the Ancestors.* Stanford: Stanford University Press.

1977. *The Domestication of the Savage Mind.* Cambridge: Cambridge University Press.

1979. The Resettlement of Oncho Freed Areas in Northern Ghana. Ms. U.K. Ministry of Overseas Development.

1980. Rice-burning and the Green Revolution in Northern Ghana. *Journal of Development Studies,* 16, 2:136–55.

Gosselin, G. 1970. *Développement et tradition dans les sociétés africaines.* Geneva: Bureau International de Travail (ILO).

Goulet, D. 1978. Looking at Guinea-Bissau: A New Nation's Development Strategy. Overseas Development Council, Occasional Paper no. 9, Washington, D.C.

Goussault, Y. 1970. *L'animation rurale dans les pays de l'Afrique francophone.* Geneva: ILO.

Supplementary bibliography

Green, R., and S. Hymer. 1966. Cocoa in the Gold Coast: A Study in the Relations between African Farmers and Agricultural Experts. *Journal of Economic History* 26:299–319.

Greigert, J., and C. Sauvel. 1970. *Modernisation de la zone pastorale nigérienne: étude hydrogéologique.* Niamey: République du Niger, BRGM, Ministère de l'Economie Rurale, Direction de l'Elevage.

Guillaume, M. 1960. Les aménagements hydro-agricoles de riziculture et de culture de décrue dans la vallée du Niger. *L'Agronomie Tropicale,* 15, nos. 1–4:73–91, 133–87, 273–324, 390–413.

Guiraux, X. 1937. *L'arachide sénégalaise.* Paris: Libraire Technique et Economique.

Gurmu, T. 1975. Le développement du capitalisme agraire au Ghana avec mention spéciale du district d'Ejura. In S. Amin (ed.), *L'agriculture africaine et le capitalisme* (q.v.), pp. 349–77.

Guyer, J. 1980. *The Provident Societies in the Rural Economy of Yaounde, 1945–1960.* Boston University Working Paper no. 37. Boston: African Studies Center.

In press. Food, Cocoa and the Division of Labor by Sex in Two West African Societies. *Comparative Studies in Society and History.*

Haeringer, P. Structures foncières et création urbaine à Abidjan. *Cahiers d'Etudes Africaines,* 9, no. 34:219–70.

Hammond, P. B. 1960. Management in Economic Transition. In W. E. Moore and A. S. Feldman (eds.), *Labor Commitment and Social Change in Underdeveloped Areas* (q.v.), pp. 109–22.

1966. *Yatenga: Technology in the Culture of a West African Kingdom.* New York: Free Press.

Hanson, J. 1980. *Is the School the Enemy of the Farm? The African Experience.* African Rural Economy Paper no. 22. East Lansing: Michigan State University.

Harris, G. R. 1974. *The Government, Agricultural Institutions and Farmers in Ghana, 1966–72.* Unpublished Ph.D. dissertation, Boston University.

Hart, J. K. 1969. *Migrants and Entrepreneurs: A Study of Modernization among the Frafras of Ghana.* Unpublished Ph.D. dissertation, Cambridge University.

1970. Small-Scale Entrepreneurs in Ghana and Development Planning. *Journal of Development Studies,* July, pp. 103–20.

1971. Migration and Tribal Identity among the Frafras of Ghana. *Journal of Asian and African Studies* 6:21–36.

Hartwig, G. W., and W. M. O'Barr. 1974. *Student Africanist's Handbook: A Guide to Resources.* New York: Schenkman Publishing Co., Halstead Press.

Haswell, M. R. 1973. *Tropical Farming Economics.* London: Longman.

Hecht, R. 1978. Review Article: The Rise of Radical African Studies. *Journal of Development Studies,* 15:120–6.

Hervouett, J-P. 1977. Stratégies d'adaptation différenciés à une crise climatique: l'exemple des éleveurs agriculteurs du centre sud-mauritanien, 1969–74. In J. Gallais (ed.), *Stratégies pastorales et agricoles des sahéliens durant la sécheresse, 1969–1974* (q.v.).

Hiernaux, C. R. 1950. Notes sur l'évolution des Gagou. *Bulletin d'IFAN.* 12, no. 2:488–512.

Hill, P. 1956. *The Gold Coast Cocoa Farmer: A Preliminary Survey.* London: Oxford University Press.

1957a. *Obomofo-Densua: A Company of Cocoa Farmers.* Cocoa Research Series, no. 9. Legon: University of Ghana.

1957b. *Kofi Pare: An Aburi Family Land.* Cocoa Research Series, no. 18. Legon: University of Ghana.

Supplementary bibliography

1962. Social Factors in Cocoa Farming. In J. B. Wills (ed.), *Agriculture and Land Use in Ghana* (q.v.).

1963b. Three Types of Southern Ghanaian Cocoa Farmer. In D. Biebuyck (ed.), *African Agrarian Systems* (q.v.).

1966. Landlords and Brokers: A West African Trading System (with a note on Kumasi Butchers). *Cahiers d'Etudes Africaines*, 6, no. 27: 349–66.

1969. Hidden Trade in Hausaland. *Man* 4, no. 3:392–409.

1977. *Population, Prosperity and Poverty: Rural Kano, 1900 and 1970*. Cambridge: Cambridge University Press.

1978. Food Farming and Migration from Fante Villages. *Africa* 48:220–9.

HMSO. *What Is British Aid?* London: HMSO.

Hogendorn, J. S. 1970. The Origins of the Groundnut Trade in Northern Nigeria. In C. Eicher and C. Liedholm (eds.), *Growth and Development of the Nigerian Economy* (q.v.).

Hopkins, E. 1974. "Operation Groundnuts": Lessons from an Agricultural Extension Scheme. *IDS Bulletin*, 5:59–66.

Horowitz, M. M. 1972. Ethnic Boundary Maintenance among Pastoralists and Farmers in the Western Sudan (Niger). *Journal of Asian and African Studies*, 7:105–14.

1978. *An Analysis of the Sociological Assumptions of Livestock Sector Projects with Particular Reference to Niger, Upper Volta, Ivory Coast, Togo, Benin, Sudan and Somalia*. Washington, D.C.: IDA, for USAID.

Howard, R. 1978. *Colonialism and Underdevelopment in Ghana*. New York: Africana.

Hugon, P. 1968. *Analyse du sous-développement en Afrique noire: l'exemple de l'économie du Cameroun*. Paris: PUF.

Hunter, G., A. H. Bunting, and A. Bottrall. 1976. *Policy and Practice in Rural Development*. London: Croom Helm, for ODI.

Hymer, S. H. 1971. The Political Economy of the Gold Coast and Ghana. In G. Ranis (ed.), *Government and Economic Development*, pp. 129–80. New Haven: Yale University Press.

ICA. 1960. *Questions and Answers on the Mutual Security Program*. Washington, D.C.: Publications of the State Department no. 7027.

Igbozurike, M. 1976. *Problem Generating Structures in Nigeria's Rural Development*. Uppsala: Scandanavian Institute of African Studies.

Jackson, M. 1977. *The Kuranko: Dimensions of Social Reality in a West African Tribe*. London: C. Hurst.

Jalee, P. 1971. *Le tiers monde en chiffres*. Paris: Maspero.

James, C. L. R. 1963. *The Black Jacobins: Toussaint L'Ouverture and the San Domingo Revolution*. 2nd ed. New York: Vintage Books.

James, M. 1973. Drought Conditions: A Note on the Response of Farmers and Livestock Owners to the Dry 1972–73 Season on the Sandy Plains and Dune Fields and the Clay Plains of the Pressure Water Zone in N.E. Nigeria. In D. Dalby and R. J. H. Church (eds.), *Drought in Africa* (q.v.).

Johnson, R. 1967. Conception du travail dans le milieu traditionnel africain. *Revue Psychopathologique Africaine*, 3, no. 2.

Jones, E. L., and S. L. Woolf (eds.). 1969. *Agrarian Change and Economic Development: The Historical Problems*. London: Methuen.

Jones, G. I. 1963. *The Trading States of the Oil Rivers*. London: Oxford University Press.

Joseph, R. 1976. The Gaullist Legacy: Patterns of French Neo-Colonialism. *Review of African Political Economy*, no. 6, pp. 4–13.

Kamara, L. 1971. Integration fonctionelle et développement accéléré en Afrique. *Revue Tiers-Monde*, 12, no. 48.

197

Supplementary bibliography

Kane, F., et al. 1977a. Femmes prolétaires du Sénégal, à la ville et aux champs. *Cahiers d'Etudes Africaines,* 17, no. 65:77–94.

1977b. Des femmes sur l'Afrique des femmes. *Cahiers d'Etudes Africaines,* 17, no. 65:77–94.

Kaye, G. 1972. *The Political Economy of Colonialism in Ghana: Documents and Statistics, 1900–1960.* Cambridge: Cambridge University Press.

Keita, F. 1972. *Etude sur la fiscalité (Sénégal).* Dakar: Institut Africain de Développement Economique et de la Planification.

Keita, M. 1975. Interventions en milieu rural et capitalisme agraire dans la region de Tilaberi. In S. Amin (ed.), *L'agriculture africaine et le capitalisme* (q.v.), pp. 167–84.

Kilby, P. 1969. *Industrialization in an Open Economy: Nigeria 1945–1966.* Cambridge: Cambridge University Press.

Kimba, N. 1973.La coopération. *Nouvel Africasia,* no. 1 (Jan.).

King, R. 1976. *Farmers' Cooperatives in N. Nigeria: A Case Study Used to Illustrate the Relation between Economic Development and Institutional Change.* Mimeo. Dept. of Agricultural Economics, Reading University.

Klein, M. 1968. *Islam and Imperialism in Senegal, Siné-Saloum (1847–1914).* Palo Alto: Stanford University Press.

1977. Servitude among the Wolof and Sereer of Senegambia. In S. Miers and I. Kopytoff (eds.), *Slavery in Africa* (q.v.).

Klein, M. (ed.). 1980. *Peasants in Africa: Historical and Contemporary Perspectives.* Beverly Hills: Sage.

Kohler, J-M. 1974. *Les Mossi de Kolongtomo et la collectivisation à l'Office du Niger.* Travaux et Documents no. 37. Paris: ORSTOM.

Kotey, R. A., C. Okali, and B. E. Rourke (eds.). 1974. *Economics of Cocoa Production and Marketing.* Legon: Institute for Statistical, Social and Economic Research (ISSER).

Kowal, J. M., and A. H. Kassam (eds.) 1978. *Agricultural Ecology of Savannah: A Study of West Africa.* Oxford: Oxford University Press, Clarendon Press.

La Anyane, S. 1963. *Ghana Agriculture: Its Development from Early Times to the Mid-20th Century.* Accra: Oxford University Press.

Lacombe, M. 1969. *Contribution à l'étude de l'emploi du temps paysan dans la zone arachidière.* Dakar: ISEA.

Lacoste, Y. 1976. *Géographie du sous-développement: géopolitique d'une crise.* Paris: PUF.

Latour Dejean, E. de. 1975. La transformation du régime foncier, appropriation des terres et formation de la classe dirigeante en pays Mawri (Niger). In S. Amin (ed.), *L'agriculture africaine et le capitalisme* (q.v.), pp. 185–232.

Laurent, S. 1970. Formation, information et développement en Côte d'Ivoire. *Cahiers d'Etudes Africaines,* 10, no. 39:422–68.

Lawson, R. M. 1971a. *The Changing Economy of the Lower Volta, 1954–67.* London: Oxford University Press, for International African Institute.

1971b. The Supply Response of Retail Trading Services to Urban Population Growth in Ghana. In C. Meillassoux (ed.), *The Development of Indigenous Trade and Markets in West Africa* (q.v.), pp. 376–98.

Laya, D. 1973. Recherche et développement: le projet de mise en valeur des cuvettes de Kutukalé et Karma en pays Songhay. *Etudes Nigériennes,* no. 24. Niamey: CNRSH.

Le, T. K. 1972. *L'éducation; facteur ou frein au développement.* Colloque IDEP sur les Stratégies du Développement Economique, Afrique et Amérique Latine Comparées, Sept. 4–17, 1972. Dakar: IDEP.

Leach, E. R. 1961. *Rethinking Anthropology.* London: Athlone Press.

Supplementary bibliography

Lefebvre, Y., M. Lefebvre, et al. 1974. *L'association des paysans, moyen de formation et d'animation dans les villages africains: le cas des maisons familiales rurales au Sénégal et au Tchad*. Paris: Union Nationale des Maisons Familiales Rurales d'Education et d'Orientation, Institute d'Etude du Développement Economique et Social.

Lefevre, R. 1948–49. Cacao et café, cultures revolutionnaires. *Revue de Géographie Humaine et d'Ethnologie*, 1.

Le Houérou, H. N. 1973*a*. *The Sahelian Zone: A Selected Bibliography for the Study of Its Problems*. Rome: FAO.

1973*b*. *Contribution à une bibliographie des phénomènes de desertification, de l'écologie végétale, des pâturages et du nomadisme dans les régions arides de l'Afrique et de l'Asie du sud-ouest*. Rome: FAO.

Leon, M., and J. Shier (eds.). n.d. *International African Bibliography: Current Books, Articles and Papers in African Studies*. Quarterly. London: Mandell.

Léricollais, A. 1973. *La sécheresse et les populations de la vallée du Sénégal*. Mimeo. Contribution au Colloque sur la Désertification, Nouakchott, Dec. 17–19.

Levitzion, N. 1976. The Early States of the Western Sudan to 1500. In J. F. A. Ajayi and M. Crowder, *History of West Africa* (q.v.), Vol. 1, pp. 114–51.

Lewis, J. V. D. 1979*b*. Small Farmer Credit and the Village Production Unit in Rural Mali. *Social Sciences and African Development Planning*.

Lewis, O. 1951. *Life in a Mexican Village: Tepoztlan Restudied*. Urbana: University of Illinois Press.

Lewis, W. A. 1952. *Industrialization in the Gold Coast*. London: HMSO.

Leynaud, E. 1961. *Les cadres sociaux de la vie rurale dans la haute-vallée du Niger*. 3 vols. Paris.

Leynaud. E., and Y. Cisse. 1978. *Paysans malinke du haut Niger*. Bamako: Editions Populaires de Mali.

Leys, C. 1975. *Underdevelopment in Kenya*. London: Heinemann.

1976. The "Overdeveloped" Post-Colonial State: A Re-Evaluation. *Review of African Political Economy*, no. 5, pp. 39–48.

Liniger-Goumaz, M. 1969. L'URSS, La Chine Populaire et l'Afrique. *Genève-Afrique*, 8, no. 2:69–78.

Little, K. 1973. *African Women in Towns: An Aspect of Africa's Social Revolution*. Cambridge: Cambridge University Press.

Lloyd, P. C. 1974. *Power and Independence: Urban Africans' Perceptions of Social Inequality*. London: Routledge and Kegan Paul.

Lofchie, M. F. 1968. Political Theory and African Politics. *Journal of Modern African Studies*, 6, no. 1:3–15.

1975. Political and Economic Origins of African Hunger. *Journal of Modern African Studies*, 13, no. 4:551–68.

Lovejoy, P. 1978. Plantations in the Economy of Sokoto Caliphate. *Journal of African History*, 19, no. 3:341–68.

Luabeya-Kabeya, B. 1970. Le concept d'économies externes dans la pensée économique. *Cahiers Economiques et Sociaux* (Institute de Recherches Economiques et Sociales, Kinshasa), 8, no. 1 (Mar.):29–47.

McCormack, C. P. 1972. Mende and Sherbro Women in High Office. *Canadian Journal of African Studies*, 6, no. 2:151–64.

1977. Wono: Institutionalized Dependency in Sherbro Descent Groups. In S. Miers and I. Kopytoff (eds.), *Slavery in Africa* (q.v.).

1979. Control of Land, Labour and Capital in Rural Southern Sierra Leone. Ms. Cambridge University.

Supplementary bibliography

McGee, T. 1971. *The Urbanization Process in the Third World*. London: Bell.

McIlroy, R. J. 1963. *An Introduction to Tropical Cash Crops*. Ibadan: Oxford University Press.

McKeown, T. 1976. *The Modern Rise of Population*. London: Edward Arnold.

McLoughlin, P. F. M. (ed.). 1970. *African Food Production Systems*. Baltimore: Johns Hopkins Press.

Madsen, M. R., and J. Morley. 1973. The Present Drought Situation in Mauritania, Senegal, Mali, Upper Volta, Niger and Chad. In D. Dalby and R. J. H. Church (eds.), *Drought in Africa* (q.v.).

Mainet, G., and G. Nicolas. 1964. La vallée du Gulbi de Maradi: enquête socio-économique. *Etudes Nigériennes*, no. 16. Niamey: CNRSH.

Mair, L. 1953. African Marriage, Social Change. In A. Phillips (ed.), *Survey of African Marriage and Family Life* (q.v.).

Marchal, J-Y. 1974. L'Office du Niger: ilôt de prospérité paysanne ou pôle de production agricole? *Revue Canadienne des Etudes Africaines*, 8, no. 1:73–90.

Martin, A. 1956. *The Oil-Palm Economy of the Ibibio Farmer*. Ibadan: University of Ibadan Press.

Martin, D., and T. Yannapoulos (eds.). 1973. *L'Afrique noire*. Fondation National des Sciences Politiques, Bibliographies Françaises de Sciences Sociales: Guide de Recherches no. 5. Paris: Armand Colin.

Maton, G. 1969. Enquêtes sur le développement: la mise en valeur des polders du Lac Tchad. *Coopération et Développement*, no. 27 (Sept.-Oct.), pp. 28–34.

1974. La politique des grandes barrages hydro-agricoles. *Actuel-Développement*, no. 3.

Meillassoux, C. 1960. Essai d'interpretation du phenomène économique dans les sociétiés traditionnelles d'auto-subsistence. *Cahiers d'Etudes Africaines*, 1, no. 4:38–61.

1963. Economie des échanges pré-coloniaux en pays Gouro. *Cahiers d'Etudes Africaines*, 3, no. 12:551–76.

1970. A Class Analysis of the Bureaucratic Process in Mali. *Journal of Development Studies*. 6:97–110.

1971*b*. Le commerce pré-colonial et la développement de l'esclavage à Gubu du Sahel (Mali). In C. Meillassoux (ed.), *The Development of Indigenous Trade and Markets in West Africa* (q.v.), pp. 182–95.

1973. The Social Organization of Peasantry: The Economic Basis of Kinship. *Journal of Peasant Studies*, no. 1.

1974*b*. Development or Exploitation: Is the Sahel Famine Good Business? *Review of African Political Economy*, no. 1, pp. 27–33.

Mellor, J. W. 1966. *The Economics of Agricultural Development*. Ithaca: Cornell University Press.

1976. *New Economics of Growth*. Ithaca: Cornell University Press.

1978. Basic Human Needs: A Development Perspective. Paper given at International Development Conference, Feb. 8. International Food Policy Research Institute Reprint.

Mellor, J. W., and U. Lele. 1972. *Growth Linkages of the New Food Grain Technologies*. Occasional Papers, no. 50, Dept. of Agricultural Economy. Ithaca: Cornell University Press.

Mende, T. 1972. *De l'aide à la recolonisation: les leçons d'un échec*. Paris: Editions du Seuil.

Menezes, C. F. 1966. *Agricultural Migration and Rural Development in Ghana*. Unpublished Ph.D. dissertation, Northwestern University.

Merlin, P. 1958. L'équipement hydraulique de l'AOF. *Marchés Tropicaux du Monde*,

Supplementary bibliography

special number, Mar. 22, pp. 766–75.

Mesnil, J. 1970. *Connaissance du milieu et vulgarisation agricole: les cas de l'opération Centre-Mossi.* Paris: SATEC (Société d'Aide Technique et de Coopération).

Meunier, R. 1975. L'aide d'urgence et les nouveaux projects de développement. In J. Copans (ed.), *Sécheresses et famines du Sahel* (q.v.), I, 109–30.

Miège, J. 1951. L'agriculture baoulé. In *Conference internationale des africanistes de l'ouest, Dakar, comptes rendus,* II, 47–59.

Miner, H. 1953. *The Primitive City of Timbuctoo.* Garden City, N.Y.: Doubleday.

Ministère du Plan et du Développement, Sénégal. 1964. Le role de l'arachide dans la croissance économique du Sénégal. July.

Miracle, M. P. 1961. Seasonal Hunger: A Vague Concept and an Unexplored Problem. *Bulletin de l'IFAN,* 23, ser. B, no. 1/2:272–83.

——— 1972. The Elasticity of Food Supply in Tropical Africa during the Pre-Colonial Period. *Ghana Sociological Science Journal* (Legon), 2, no. 2:143–4.

Miracle, M. P., and B. Fetter. 1970. Backward-Sloping Labour Supply Functions and African Economic Behaviour. *Economic Development and Cultural Change,* no. 18, pp. 240–51.

Montgomery, J. D. 1962. *The Politics of Foreign Aid.* New York: Praeger, for Council on Foreign Relations.

Moore, W. E., and A. S. Feldman (eds.). 1960. *Labor Commitment and Social Change in Underdeveloped Areas.* New York: Social Science Research Council.

Morgan, L. H. 1877. *Ancient Society.* New York: Henry Holt.

Morgan, W. B., and R. P. Moss. 1965. Savanna and Forest in Western Nigeria. *Africa,* 35. no. 3:286–94.

Morris, W. H. M., and T. K. White. 1979. Summary of Workshop, Purdue University, Dept. of Agricultural Economics, AFT/SFWA/SDP.

Mortimore, M. J. 1973. Famine in Hausaland, 1973. In D. Dalby and R. J. H. Church (eds.), *Drought in Africa* (q.v.).

Moyer, R., and S. Hollander. 1968. *Markets and Marketing in Development Economies.* Homewood, Ill.: Irwin.

Murdock, G. P. 1959. *Africa: Its Peoples and Their Culture History.* New York: McGraw-Hill.

Murray, R. 1967. Second Thoughts on Ghana. *New Left Review,* no. 42.

Myint, H. 1971. The "Classical Theory" of International Trade and the Underdeveloped Countries. In Myint, *Economic Theory and Underdeveloped Countries.* London.

Ndongko, W. A. 1975. *Planning for Economic Development in a Federal State: The Case of Cameroon, 1960–71.* Afrika-Studien no. 85, IFO-Institut für Wirtschaftsforschung, Munchen; Afrika-Studienstelle. Munich: Weltforum Verlag.

N'Dongo S. 1975. *Voyage forcé: itinéraire d'un militant.* Paris: Maspero.

Nelson, G., and F. M. Tilestone. 1977. *Irrigation: A Paradox for Sahelian Development.* Mimeo. USAID, REDSO/WA, Abidjan, Ivory Coast.

Niang, M. 1975. Reflexions sur le régime des terres au Sénégal. *Bulletin de l'IFAN,* 37, ser. B, no. 1:137–53.

——— 1976. L'évolution du statut juridique, politique et social de la femme en Afrique traditionelle et moderne. *Bulletin de l'IFAN,* 38, ser. B, no. 1:52–66.

Nicolas, G. 1965a. *Budgets collectifs de groupements domestiques en republique du Niger.* Bordeaux: Université de Bordeaux.

——— 1965b. *Circulation des richesses et participation sociale dans une société hausa du Niger (Canton de Kantche).* Bordeaux: CUP-AGEB.

——— 1967. Une forme atténuée du potlach en pays hausa (République du Niger): le Dubu. *Cahiers de l'ISEA, Economies et Sociétés,* no. 2 (Feb.).

Supplementary bibliography

1968*a*. La société africaine et ses reactions à l'impact occidental. *L'Afrique Noire Contemporaine*. Paris: A. Colin, Collection U.

1968*b*. Processus oblatifs à l'occasion de l'intronisation de chefs traditionnels en pays hausa (République de Niger). *Tiers Monde*. no. 33 (Jan.–Mar.):43–94.

1969*a*. Processus oblatifs à l'occasion de la "courtication" des jeunes filles au sein d'une société africaine (vallée de Maradi). *Cahiers de l'ISEA, Economies et Sociétés*.

1969*b*. Développement rural et comportement économique traditionnel au sein d'une société africaine. *Genève-Afrique*, 8, no. 2:18–35.

1975. *Dynamique sociale et apprehension du monde au sein d'une société hausa.* Travaux et Mémoires de l'Institut d'Ethnologie, no. 76. Paris: Museum National d'Histoire Naturelle.

Nicholas, J. n.d. Les juments des dieux. *Etudes Nigériennes*, no. 21. Niamey: CNRSH.

Nkrumah, K. 1963. *Africa Must Unite*. London: Heinemann.

Norman, D. W. 1977. Economic Rationality of Traditional Hausa Dryland Farmers in the North of Nigeria. In R. D. Stevens (ed.), *Tradition and Dynamics in Small-Farm Agriculture*, pp. 63–91. Ames: Iowa State University Press.

1978. Farming Systems and Problems of Improving Them. In J. M. Kowal and A. H. Kassam (eds.), *Agricultural Ecology of Savannah* (q.v.), pp. 318–47.

November, A. 1965. *L'évolution du mouvement syndical en Afrique occidentale*. Geneva: L'Institut African de Genève.

Nukunya, G. K. 1975. The Effects of Cash Crops on an Ewe Community. In J. R. Goody (ed.), *Changing Social Structure in Ghana* (q.v.), pp. 59–72.

OECD (Organization for Economic Cooperation and Development). 1970. *Development Assistance, 1970 Review*. Paris: OECD.

Okali, C. 1976. *The Importance of Non-Economic Variables in the Development of the Ghana Cocoa Industry*. Unpublished Ph.D. dissertation, Legon.

Okali, C., and R. A. Kotey. 1971. *Akokoaso: A Resurvey*. Technical Publications Series, no. 15. Legon: Institute of Statistical, Social and Economic Research, University of Ghana.

Olivier de Sardan, J-P. 1969*a*. *Système des relations économiques et sociales ches les Wogo du Niger*. Paris: Institut d'Ethnologie.

1969*b*. Les voleurs d'hommes (notes sur l'histoire des Kurtey). *Etudes Nigériennes*, no. 25. Niamey: CNRSH.

Olowusani, H. A. 1966. *Agriculture and Nigerian Economic Development*. Ibadan and London: Oxford University Press.

Olowusani, H. A., I. S. Derna, et al. 1966. *Uboma: A Socioeconomic and Nutritional Survey of a Rural Community in Eastern Nigeria*. Edited by D. Stamp and B. Cox World Land Use Survey, Occasional Paper no. 6. Ebbingford.

Opoku, K. T. 1972. Le mariage africain et ses transformations. *Genève-Afrique*, II, no. 1:3–37.

Ormières, J-L. 1975. Les consequences politiques de la famine. In J. Copans (ed.), *Sécheresses et famines du Sahel* (q.v.), I, 131–45.

ORSTOM. (Office de la Recherche Scientifique et Technique Outre-Mer) 1977. *Essais sur la reproduction de formations sociales dominées (Caméroun, Côte d'Ivoire, Haute-Volta, Sénégal, Madagascar, Polynésie)*. Travaux et Documents, no. 64. Paris: ORSTOM.

Paden, J. N., and E. W. Soja. 1970. *The African Experience*. Evanston, Ill.: Northwestern University Press.

Papy, L. 1951. La vallée du Sénégal: agriculture traditionelle et riziculture mechanisée. *Cahiers d'Outre-Mer*, no. 4, pp. 277–324.

Supplementary bibliography

Paulme, D. 1940. *Organisation sociale des Dogon (Soudan français)*. Paris: Domat-Moutchrestion.

Peacock, A., and G. K. Shaw. 1971. *Politique budgetaire et problème de l'emploi dans les pays en voie de développement*. Etudes sur l'Emploi, no. 5. Paris: Centre de Développement de l'OCDE (OECD).

Péhaut, Y. 1970. *L'arachide au Niger*. Etudes d'Economie Africaine. Bordeaux: Centre d'Etudes d'Afrique Noire.

Person, Y. 1970–1. *Samori: une revolution dyula*. 3 vols. Dakar: IFAN.

Phillips, A. (ed.). 1953. *Survey of African Marriage and Family Life*. London and New York: Oxford University Press, for International African Institute.

Porgès, L. 1974. *Bibliographie des régions du Sénégal: complement pour la période des origines à 1965 et mise à jour 1966–1973*. Paris: Mouton.

Post, K. 1972. Peasantization and Rural Political Movements in Western Africa. *Archives Européennes de Sociologie*, 13, no. 2:223–54.

Purvis, M. J. 1970. New Sources of Growth in a Stagnant Smallholder Economy in Nigeria: The Oil Palm Rehabilitation Scheme. In C. Eicher and C. Liedholm (eds.), *Growth and Development of the Nigerian Economy* (q.v.).

Quarcoo, A. K., and M. Johnson. 1968. Shai Pots: The Pottery Industry of the Shai People of Southern Ghana. *Baessler-Archiv*, 16:47–88.

van Raay, H. G. T. 1975. *Rural Development Planning in a Savannah Region*. Rotterdam: Rotterdam University Press.

Raulin, H. n. d. *Problèmes fonciers dans les régions de Gagnoa et Daloa*. ORSTOM, Mission d'Etudes des groupements immigrés en Côte d'Ivoire.

Raynaut, C. 1973. La circulation marchande des céréales et les mécanismes d'inégalité économique. *Cahiers du Centre d'Etudes et des Recherches Ethnologiques*. Bordeaux, no. 2, pp. 1–48.

1977a. Lessons of a Crisis. In D. Dalby, R. J. H. Church, and F. Bezzaz (eds.), *Drought in Africa II* (q.v.), pp. 3–29.

1977b. Aspects socio-économiques de la préparation et de la circulation de la nourriture dans un village hausa (Niger). *Cahiers d'Etudes Africaines*, 17, no. 68:569–98.

Reboul, C. 1973. La crise de l'agriculture sénégalaise. *Le Monde Diplomatique*.

1975. Causes économique de la sécheresse au Sénégal: systèmes de cultures et calamités "naturelles." INRA, Document de travail.

Redfield, R. 1930. *Tepoztlan, a Mexican Village: A Study of Folk Life*. Chicago: University of Chicago Press

Reissman, L. 1964. *The Urban Process: Cities in Industrial Societies*. New York: Free Press.

Remy, G. 1972. Les leçons d'un échec: la culture atelée en pays Mossi (Haute Volta). *Cahiers d'Etudes Africaines*. 12, no. 47:512–19.

Renninger, J. P. 1979. *Multinational Cooperation for Development in West Africa*. New York: Pergamon.

République du Niger. 1972. *Avant-project de développement du département de Maradi*. Niamey: République du Niger, CAD.

Reverdy, J-C. 1969. La formation des cadres moyens en Afrique francophone: facteurs d'inadaptation et perspectives d'avenir. *Genève-Afrique*, 8, no. 2:3–17.

Rey, P-P. 1969. Articulation des modes de dependance et des modes de reproduction dans deux sociétés lignagères. (Punu et Kunyi du Congo-Brazzaville). *Cahiers d'Etudes Africaines*, 9, no. 35:415–40.

1973. *Les alliances des classes*. Paris: Maspero.

1975. Les formes de la décomposition des sociétés précapitalistes au nord Togo et le mécanisme des migrations vers les zones de capitalisme agraire. In S. Amin (ed.), *L'agriculture africaine et le capitalisme* (q.v.), pp. 233–56.

Reynolds, L. G. (ed.). 1976. *Agriculture in Development Theory*. New Haven: Yale University Press.

Richards, A. I. 1952. *Economic Development and Tribal Change*. Cambridge: W. Heffer, for East African Institute of Social Research.

Roch, J. 1975. Les migrations économiques de saison sèche en bassin arachidier sénégalais. *Cahiers ORSTOM*, Sér. sciences humaines, 12, no. 1:55–80.

Roch, J., and G. Rocheteau. 1971. Economie et population: le cas du Sénégal. *Cahiers ORSTOM*, Sér. sciences humaines, 8, no. 1.

Rocheteau, G. 1970. Pionniers mourides au Sénégal: changement technique et transformation d'une économie paysanne. Mimeo. ORSTOM, Dakar.

Rodts, R. 1971. *Etude économique de la SAED*. Paris: SAED.

Salamu, P. 1972. *Le procès de "sous-développement."* Paris: Maspero.

Salifou, A. 1974. *Crise alimentaire au Niger: les leçons du Passe*. Doc. no. CS/2576-22. Dakar: IDEP.

Sandbrook, R., and Cohen, R. (eds.). 1975. *Towards an African Working Class*. London: Longman.

Saylor, R. G. 1967. *The Economic System of Sierra Leone*. Durham, N.C.: Duke University Press.

Schultze, W. 1973. *A New Geography of Liberia*. London: Longman.

Schumacher, E. J. 1975. *Politics, Bureaucracy and Rural Development in Senegal*. Berkeley and Los Angeles: University of California Press.

SEAE (Secretariat d'Etat Français aux Affaires Etrangères). 1972. Structures et statistiques de l'emploi pour 14 états africains et malgache, éléments de statistiques rétrospectives. *Statistiques décennales de l'emploi salarié, 1960–1970* (SEAE), ser. b, No. 1.

1974. L'aide française aux pays sahéliens victimes de la sécheresse. SEAE. Feb.

SEDES (Société d'Etudes pour le Développement Economique et Social). 1972. *La commercialisation de produits vivriers: étude économique*. 2 vols. Paris: République de Côte d'Ivoire.

Service de la Statistique de Dakar (SSD). *Situation économique du Sénégal*. Dakar: SSD. 1961 ff. (Annually).

Shapiro, K. H. 1979*b*. The Livestock Economies of West Africa: An Overview. In K. H. Shapiro (ed.), *Livestock Production and Marketing in the Entente States of West Africa* (q.v.), pp. 4–69.

Sheets, H., and R. Morris. 1974. *Disaster in the Desert: Failures of International Relief in the West African Drought*. Washington, D.C.: Carnegie Endowment.

Shepard, C. Y. 1936. Report on the Economy of Peasant Agriculture in the Gold Coast. *Gold Coast*, no. 1.

Shepherd, A. W. 1979. Agrarian Change in Northern Ghana: Public Investment, Capitalist Farming and Famine. Mimeo. London.

Sidikou, A. H. 1974. Sédentarité et mobilité entre Niger et Zgaret. *Etudes Nigériennes*, no. 34. Niamey: CNRSH.

Skinner, S. W. 1964. *The Agricultural Economy of the Ivory Coast*. Washington, D.C.: AID.

Sleeper, J. A. 1978. An Economic Analysis of the Role of Ox-Plowing and Cattle-Feeding in the Stratification of West African Livestock Production. Unpublished master's thesis, University of Maryland.

Smelser, N. 1959. *Social Change in the Industrial Revolution: An Application of Theory to the British Cotton Industry*. Chicago: University of Chicago Press.

Supplementary bibliography

Sohn, L. B. (ed.). 1971. *Basic Documents of African Regional Associations*. New York: Oceana Publications, for the Inter-American Institute of International Legal Studies.

Souleymane, D. 1972. Les civilisations paysannes face au développement en Afrique occidentale. *Cahiers d'Etudes Africaines*, 12, no. 47:342–52.

Sow, F. 1973. Les diplomes sénégalais de l'Université de Dakar. *Bulletin de l'IFAN*, 35, ser. B, no. 2:380–432.

Spittler, G. 1977. Traders in Rural Hausaland. *Bulletin de l'IFAN*, 39, no. 2.

Stebbing, E. P. 1935. The Encroaching Sahara: The Threat to West African Colonies. *Geo-Journal*, no. 85, pp. 506–24.

Stedman Jones, G. 1971. *Outcast London*. Oxford: Oxford University Press, Clarendon Press.

Steedman, C., T. Davis, M. Johnson, and J. Sutter. 1976. *Mali: Agricultural Sector Assessment*. Ann Arbor: Center for Research on Economic Development, University of Michigan.

Surroca, C. 1970. Plantations speculatives et cultures vivrières en pays Agni. *Etudes Rurales*, no. 39, pp. 501–30.

Swift, J. 1973a. Le nomadisme pastoral en tant que forme d'utilisation des terres: les Touareg de l'Adrar des Iforar. *Etudes Maliennes*, no. 5, pp. 35–44.

1973b. Disaster and a Sahelian Nomad Economy. In D. Dalby and R. J. H. Church (eds.), *Drought in Africa* (q.v.), pp. 71–8.

1979. West African Pastoral Production Systems. AID/afr-c-1169. Working Paper No. 3, CRED, University of Michigan.

Tardits, C. 1963. Développement du régime d'appropriation privée des terres de la palmeraie du Sud-Dahomey. In D. Biebuyck (ed.), *African Agrarian Systems* (q.v.), pp. 297–314.

Taussig, M. 1980. *The Devil and Commodity Fetishism in South America*. Chapel Hill: University of North Carolina Press.

Taylor, W. C. 1956. *The Firestone Operations in Liberia*. Washington, D.C.: National Planning Association.

Terray, E. 1971. Commerce pré-colonial et organisation sociale chez les Dida de Côte d'Ivoire. In C. Meillassoux (ed.), *The Development of Indigenous Trade and Markets in West Africa* (q.v.), pp. 145–52.

1974. Long Distance Exchange and the Formation of the State: The Case of the Abron Kingdom of Gyaman. *Economy and Society*, 3, no. 3.

1976. Classes and Class Consciousness in the Abron Kingdom of Gyaman. In M. Bloch (ed.), *Marxist Analyses and Social Anthropology*, pp. 85–135. New York: John Wiley.

Thomas, L-V. 1964. Acculturation et nouveaux milieux socio-culturels en Afrique noire. *Bulletin de l'IFAN*, 36, sér. B, no. 1:164–215.

Thomas, R. 1973. Forced Labour in British West Africa: The Case of the Northern Territories of the Gold Coast, 1906–27. *Journal of African History*, 14:79–103.

Thompson, D'A. 1917. *On Growth and Form*. Cambridge: Cambridge University Press.

Tims, W. (ed.). 1974. *Nigeria: Options for Long-Term Development*. Baltimore: Johns Hopkins University Press for World Bank.

Tocqueville, A. de. 1863. *Democracy in America*. Cambridge, Mass.: Sever and Francis.

Tuinder, B. A. den. 1978. *Ivory Coast: The Challenge of Success*. Johns Hopkins University Press for World Bank.

UNCTAD (United Nations Commission on Trade and Development). 1970. *Review of International Trade and Development, 1969/70*. UNCTAD TD/B/309, 1st pt., 7/8/70. Geneva: UNCTAD.

UNDP/FAO (United Nations Development Program/Food and Agriculture Organization).

Supplementary bibliography

1977. *Etude hydro-agricole du bassin du fleuve Sénégal, organisation pour la mise en valeur du fleuve Sénégal: rapport de synthèse des études et travaux.* AG:DP/RAF/65/061. Rome: UNDP/FAO.

Union Générale des Travailleurs Sénégalais en France. 1975. *Qui est responsable du sous-développement?* Paris: Maspero.

Uppal, J. S., and L. R. Salkever (eds.). 1972. *Africa: Problems in Economic Development.* New York: Free Press.

Vanhaeverbeke, A. 1970. *Rémuneration du travail et commerce intérieur.* Louvain.

Vianes-Bernus, S. n. d. Mouvements de marchandises au Ghana. *Etudes Nigériennes,* no. 4. Niamey: CNRSH.

Vigo, A. H. S. 1958. *A Survey of Agricultural Credit in the Northern Provinces of Nigeria.* Kaduna: Ministry of Social Welfare and Coops.

Viguier, P. 1961. *L'Afrique de l'ouest vue par un agriculteur: problèmes de base en Afrique tropicale.* Paris: La Maison Rustique.

Wade, A. 1964. *Economie de l'ouest africain.* Paris: Présence Africaine.

Waldstein, A. S. 1978*b*. Peasantization of Nomads and Nomadization of Peasants: Responses to State Intervention in an Irrigated Agricultural Development Scheme in the Senegal River Delta. Prepared for a Conference on the Sahel, University of New Hampshire.

Wallace, T. 1978*b*. *Gandu: How Useful a Concept for Understanding the Organization of Labour in Rural Hausa Society?* Zaire: Center for Social and Economic Research, Amadu Bello University.

Wallerstein, I. 1976. The Three Stages of African Involvement in the World Economy. In P. Gutkind and I. Wallerstein (eds.), *The Political Economy of Contemporary Africa* (q.v.), pp. 30–57.

Weinberg, W. R. 1971. The Costs of Foreign Private Investment. *Civilisations,* 21, nos. 2–3:207–21.

Weiskel, T. 1979. Labor in the Emergent Periphery: From Slavery to Migrant Labor among the Baule Peoples, 1880–1925. In W. Goldfrank (ed.), *The Capitalist World System: Past and Present,* pp. 207–33. Beverley Hills: Sage.

Wells, J. C. 1974. *Agricultural Policy and Economic Growth in Nigeria, 1962–68.* Ibadan: Oxford University Press, for Nigerian Institute of Social and Economic Research.

White, H. P. 1956. Internal Exchange of Staple Foods in the Gold Coast. *Economic Geography,* no. 32, pp. 115–25.

Widstrand, C. (ed.). 1975. *Multinational Firms in Africa.* Uppsala: Nordiska Afrika-Instituten.

Wilks, I. 1975. *Asante in the Nineteenth Century.* Cambridge: Cambridge University Press.

Williams, G. 1976*b*. Taking the Part of the Peasants: Rural Development in Nigeria and Tanzania. In P. Gutkind and I. Wallerstein (eds.), *The Political Economy of Contemporary Africa* (q.v.), pp. 131–54.

Wills, J. B. 1962. *Agriculture and Land Use in Ghana.* London and New York: Oxford University Press, for Ghana Ministry of Food and Agriculture.

Wisner, B. 1973. Global Interdependence of Drought Response and the Struggle for Liberation. *Journal of the Geographical Association of Tanzania,* no. 8, 86–122.

Wittfogel, K. 1957. *Oriental Despotism.* New Haven: Yale University Press.

World Bank. 1973. *A Report on Development Strategies for Papua New Guinea.* Port Moresby: IBRD, for UNDP.

1975. Rural Development. Sector Policy Paper, Washington, D.C. Feb.

1976. Appraisal of Upper Regional Agricultural Development Project, Ghana. Document of the World Bank, no. 106a-GH (Annex 10, Appx 1). June.

Supplementary bibliography

1977. *Atlas: Population, Percapita Product and Growth Rates*. Washington, D.C.: World Bank.

Yudelman, M., G. Butler, and R. Banerji. 1971. *Evolution technologique de l'agriculture et emploi dans les pays en voie de développement*. Etudes sur l'emploi no. 4. Paris: Centre de Développement de l'OCDE (OECD).

Zahan, D. 1963. Problèmes sociaux posés par la transplantation des Mossi sur les terres irriguées de l'Office du Niger. In D. Biebuyck (ed.), *African Agrarian Systems* (q.v.), pp. 392–403.

Zajaczkowski, A. 1960. La famille, le lignage et la communauté villageoise chez les Ashanti de la période de transition. *Cahiers d'Etudes Africaines*, 1, no. 4:99–114.

Zell, H. M. (ed.). 1978. *African Books in Print*. 2 vols. 2nd ed. London: Mansell.

Ziegler, J. 1971. *Le pouvoir africain: élément d'une sociologie politique de l'Afrique noire et de sa diaspora aux Amériques*. Paris: Editions du Seuil.

Index

Abidjan, 21, 22, 122
Abron, the, 168
abusa, 62, 63
  see also caretakers; sharecropping
Accra, 2, 22, 56, 66, 96, 122
accumulation, 37–38, 40, 41, 55, 62, 77, 110,
  111, 116–117, 139, 141, 144, 157,
  180, 182
acephalous peoples, *see* stateless societies
Adams, A., 73, 90, 174
Adegboye, R., and A. Abidogun, 61, 139
administrators, 30, 33, 45, 46, 47, 69–70, 81,
  85, 88, 92, 93, 98, 102, 103, 104,
  106, 112, 121, 128, 135, 148, 149, 157,
  169, 170, 185, 186
  see also bureaucracy; civil service; government
Africa Economic Digest, 167
Africanization, 139
age, 35–36, 54, 122, 132, 144
age grades, 9, 145
agrarian revolution, 11, 13, 73, 97, 98,
  110, 113, 117–120, 176
agronomy, 66, 75, 98, 170, 174
aid, 47, 65, 71, 86, 87, 105–107, 135, 137,
  151, 152–153, 154, 160, 165, 170
  officials, 14, 17, 137
  see also donor agencies, international
AID (U.S. Agency for International
  Development), 3, 105, 106–107, 135,
  180
Ajayi, A., and M. Crowder, 30, 168, 175,
  181
Akan, the, 170
Akokoaso, 170
alcohol, *see* liquor
alienation, 37, 85, 141, 156, 160
Alladian, the, 175
Allan, W., 174
Almoravids, the, 19
aluminum smelter, 55

Amazonia, 152
amenities, 125, 133
Americans, 4, 26, 39, 131, 136, 176, 183
  blacks, 152, 153
  see also United States, the
Americas, the, 20, 32
Americo-Liberians, 107, 139–140
Amin, S., 1, 7, 15–16, 17, 45, 66, 84, 112,
  118, 122, 124, 169, 174, 180, 183
Anderson, P., 17, 83, 174
Anglophone, 21, 138, 168, 182
Angola, 102
animals, 20, 34, 53, 55, 56, 74, 75, 78,
  112
  by-products, 77
  husbandry, 34, 35, 37–38, 76, 77, 79
  see also livestock; pastoralism
animation rurale, 98, 185
annual cycle (of agriculture), 54, 61, 157
Anthony, K., et al., 17, 45, 172, 174
anthropology, 2, 4, 6, 7, 14, 16, 106, 119,
  146, 149, 156, 167, 174, 175, 176, 178,
  179, 183, 184, 187
AOF (Afrique occidentale française), 21,
  43–46, 84–85, 107
Apter, D., 168
Arabs, and Arabic, 19, 21, 29, 30, 32, 114,
  138
arboriculture, 7, 29, 34, 59
  see also trees and tree products
archaeology, 6, 19, 20
Argentina, 77
aristocracy, 30, 32, 33, 34, 41, 42, 58, 76,
  85, 110, 143, 173
aristocratization, 38
armed camp, 32
army, 30, 31, 34, 44, 54, 70, 94, 100, 101,
  103, 113, 124, 140
  see also military; soldiers; warfare
artisan, *see* crafts

Index

Index

capital, capitalism, 8, 11, 13, 15, 16, 17, 26, 29, 34, 35, 40, 41, 44, 45, 49, 61, 62, 66, 68, 70, 73, 77, 83, 84, 85–86, 87, 89, 91, 92, 94, 102, 104, 105, 106, 107, 110, 113, 115, 116, 117, 118, 120, 125, 131, 139, 140, 143, 147, 149, 154, 157, 158–161, 164, 165, 170, 171, 174, 179, 180, 181, 182, 183, 185, 186, 188
  industrial, 8, 40, 51, 113, 118, 164, 172, 184
  Marx's, 19, 172, 183
  merchant, 113, 169
  noncapitalist, 178
capital cities, 2, 39, 48, 122–123, 125, 140, 155
  see also primate urbanization
capital-intensive enterprise, 49, 64, 87, 88, 93, 154, 156, 162, 165
Capron, J., 176
caravans, 33, 38
caretakers, 61
  see also abusa
Caribbean, the, *see* West Indies
cartel, 60, 108
  see also OPEC
Casamance, 66, 72, 170, 171, 184
cash, cash economy, *see* money
cash crops, 8, 16, 38, 56, 61, 62, 70, 71, 79, 81, 112, 141, 143, 144, 148, 154, 156–158, 161, 183
  see also commerce; exports
cassava, 48, 64, 65, 160
caste, 30, 34, 53, 54, 78, 140
cattle, 36, 37, 53, 55, 67, 68, 73, 75, 76, 103, 105, 115, 144, 152, 177, 180
cattle cake, 57
Cayor, 184
Central Africa, 175, 179, 186
centralization, 14–15, 25, 27, 30, 31, 34, 35, 41, 45, 73, 90, 92, 140
  see also government; state, the
cereals, 48, 66, 70, 71, 72–73, 160
  see also grain
ceremonial expenditures, 148
Ceylon, 42, 155
CFAO (Compagnie Française de l'Afrique Occidentale), 114, 177
Chad, 21, 127, 187
Chad, Lake, 20, 21, 22, 30, 102
Chambers, R., 93
Chayanov, A., 15, 167, 176
cheap-food policy, 160
  see also food
chiefs, 31, 32, 35, 39, 46, 54, 61, 67, 91–92, 124, 139, 140, 143, 147, 148, 149, 172

children, 36, 40, 53, 55, 56, 76, 78, 97, 118, 126, 127, 130, 136, 139, 143, 144, 145, 149
China, 5, 10, 23, 171
Chi-nan, Cheng, 173
Christianity, 21, 29, 32, 149
Churchill, W., 69
Cipolla, C., 4, 48, 132, 176
circulation of labor, 123–124, 134, 140, 141, 146, 163
  see also migration; mobility
cities, 29, 30, 32, 33, 45, 48, 51, 52, 54, 61, 62, 65, 68, 73, 76, 77, 81, 87, 97, 102, 107, 112, 117, 121, 122–123, 125, 129, 130, 142, 146, 151, 153, 154, 155, 157, 159, 162, 163, 164, 168, 173, 176, 179, 180
  see also towns; urbanization
civilization, 4, 20, 26, 30, 31, 35, 52, 80, 101, 105, 136, 138, 154, 171, 184
civil service, 47, 104, 139, 140, 171
  see also administrators; bureaucracy; government
Clapham, C., 59
Clark, C., and M. Haswell, 176
class, 30, 39, 40, 43, 46, 85, 109, 111, 117, 118, 121, 137, 138–139, 140–141, 144, 155, 167, 173, 185, 186
  consciousness, 140
  structure, 13, 137
  see also middle class
clearing of land, 55, 61, 65, 76, 128, 145, 169, 171
Cleave, J., 55, 169, 176
clientship, 131, 148
climate, 26–27, 30, 56, 66, 131, 138, 139, 146, 150, 152, 156
  see also ecology
cloth, 34, 37, 38, 44, 53, 68, 69, 80, 115, 144
clothing, 53, 54, 78, 130, 134
Clower, R., et al., 92, 96, 107, 119, 139, 176
coast, the, 19, 20, 21, 24, 26, 28, 29, 31, 32, 33, 35, 40, 42, 43, 45, 50, 52, 56, 58, 65, 68, 72, 74, 77, 84, 91, 93, 101, 107, 111, 112, 114, 122, 123, 130, 133, 138, 143, 160, 163, 169, 175
cocoa, 13, 17, 44, 56, 58, 59–63, 65, 96, 98, 111, 125, 143, 147, 152, 158, 165, 170, 171, 173, 175, 178, 179, 180, 185, 187
coercion, *see* force
coffee, 44, 63
cognatic kin groups, 53, 143
Cohen, A., 33, 63, 68, 176
Cold War, the, 47, 151

Index

Index

Index

economics (*cont.*)
  see also world, economic system of
économie de traite, see trade
Economist Intelligence Unit, the, 167, 170
ECOWAS (Economic Community of West
  African States), 25, 108–109, 161
Ecuador, 60
education, 30, 32, 47, 54, 80, 87, 97, 99,
  100, 101, 126, 134, 139, 144, 156, 172
  higher, 86, 97, 98, 139, 144.
EEC (European Economic Community), 82,
  108, 161
  see also Europe
egalitarianism, 31, 38, 39–40, 135, 141,
  176
eggs, *see* poultry
Egypt, 20, 58, 69
Eicher, C., and C. Liedholm, 178
elders, 32, 35, 38, 41, 55, 110, 136, 144,
  145, 146
  see also older and younger men
electricity, see utilities
elite, 30, 32, 45, 67, 84, 97, 107, 112, 135,
  139, 156, 182
Elliot, C., 169
embeddedness, 77–81, 118, 129
emigration, rural, *see* exodus, rural
eminent domain, 91
Emmanuel A., 169, 178
employment, 38, 61, 64, 87, 90, 95, 97,
  107, 125, 133, 139, 144, 179, 181
  off farm, 77, 81, 182
  see also labor; wages
enclosures, 159
energy, 54, 71, 86, 120, 155
  crisis, 47, 76
England, 5, 10, 14, 17, 69, 108, 133, 140,
  167, 169
  see also Britain
English-speaking, *see* Anglophone
Entente states, *see* Conseil d'Entente
enterprise, entrepreneurs, 55, 61, 62, 63,
  73, 104, 114, 120, 131, 157, 162, 180,
  187
  see also business; capital
environment, 11, 12, 20, 26, 37, 41, 55,
  56, 89, 94, 119, 126, 128, 138, 160
  see also climate; ecology
epidemiology, *see* disease
epigraphs, ix
equipment, *see* machines; tools
equity, 105, 135, 136, 137, 155, 170, 182
Ernst, K., 178
estates, 34, 35, 57–58, 70, 89, 118,
  139–140, 154, 158–161
ethics, *see* morality
Ethiopia, 134

ethnic groups, 21, 30, 32, 33, 38, 53, 67,
  68, 74, 79, 110, 115, 138–139, 141,
  146, 179
ethnocentric, 156
ethnography, 6, 7, 16, 17, 28, 31, 58, 141,
  167, 175, 177, 180, 181, 183, 184, 185,
  186, 187
Eurasia, 34, 35
Europe, 1, 2, 3, 7, 14, 19, 20, 29, 31, 32,
  33, 41, 42, 50, 53, 57, 58, 60, 63, 75,
  76, 97, 111, 112, 114, 116, 126, 127,
  138, 152, 156, 167, 174
  medieval, 28
  northwest, 168
  southern, 23
  western, 5, 25, 108
  see also EEC
Evans-Pritchard, E., 167
exchange, 52, 68, 70, 112, 115, 145, 146,
  153, 162, 178, 183
employment, 97
excise duties, 47, 87
exodus, rural, 17, 44, 47–48, 49, 97, 102,
  121–125, 134, 145, 153, 154, 159,
  162–164, 181
  see also migration; urbanization
expenditure patterns, 46, 48, 49, 80,
  99–102, 125
  see also government
experimentation, 72, 73, 75, 98, 120
exploitation, 16, 39, 47, 59, 66, 96, 103,
  108, 112, 113, 120, 138, 163, 178, 182
exports, 20, 21, 28, 40, 45, 47, 50, 55,
  57, 67, 69, 71, 73, 77, 78, 86, 107, 125,
  156, 167, 169, 180, 182
  agriculture, 13, 46, 48, 49, 91, 92, 102,
  116, 153, 165
  boom, 7, 44, 56, 63, 118, 155
  crops, 8, 12, 16, 42, 44, 45, 56–63,
  66–70, 81, 84, 86, 92–93, 97, 111, 112,
  114, 118, 122, 125, 127, 134, 143,
  146, 152, 158, 160, 161, 178
expropriation, *see* alienation
extension services, 72, 80, 95, 98

factionalism, 148
family, 39–40, 53, 61, 64, 117, 123, 126,
  127, 131, 136, 139, 145, 148, 157, 170,
  179
  labor, 35, 38, 61, 117–118, 145
  see also domestic groups; kin
famine, 48, 49, 66, 71, 124, 126–127, 133,
  149, 150, 155, 156, 176, 177, 185,
  187
  relief, 127, 137, 152
Far East, the, *see* Asia
Faulkner, O. T., and J. R. Mackie, 75, 98,

Index

119, 171, 178
fertility, natural, 10–11, 55, 67, 158
fertilizer, 73, 93, 95, 115, 146, 157, 159, 161, 171
feudalism, 67, 90
fee simple, 92
fiber, 57, 70
Fieldhouse, K., 27, 43, 178
finance, 30, 35, 40, 43, 47, 83, 87, 93, 115–116
Firestone Tire and Rubber Company, 59, 92, 107, 182
fishing, 20, 53, 79, 161, 173
Fitch, M., and R. Oppenheimer, 45, 60, 63, 178
Fogg, C. D., 169
food, 9–10, 12, 17, 30, 34, 35, 37, 38, 45, 48, 53, 54, 55, 61, 62, 64–65, 66, 69, 70–73, 74, 75, 78, 80, 92–93, 102, 118, 120, 125, 126, 127, 129, 130, 131, 133, 134, 142, 143, 144, 151, 153, 155, 156, 157, 158, 159, 160, 161, 162, 163, 168, 169, 170, 181, 182, 185
Food Research Institute, Stanford University, 169, 170, 174
force, 28, 32, 34, 39–40, 44, 48, 84, 85, 88, 92, 93, 103, 105, 112–113, 114, 116, 124, 146, 160, 168, 170, 171
see also corvee; power
Forde, D., and P. Kaberry, 31, 178
Forde, D., and R. Scott, 178
foreign enterprises, see multinational corporations
foreign-exchange, 64, 69, 87, 160, 161
forest, the, 7, 10, 12, 16, 20, 21, 26, 29, 31–32, 33, 34, 35, 38, 40, 42, 44, 45, 48, 52, 54, 55, 56–65, 70, 71, 74, 79, 91, 112, 118, 122, 123, 128, 130, 133, 138, 143, 147, 152, 157, 158, 160, 163, 168
Fortes, M., 16, 91, 167, 168, 173, 178, 179, 180
forts, 28, 31, 32, 42, 111
fortune, good, 136, 141, 173
Foster, P., and A. Zolberg, 86, 179
Fouta Djallon, 31
fowls, see poultry
France, 14, 16, 21, 26, 42, 43–46, 49, 59, 63, 66, 67, 84–85, 86, 94, 98, 103, 104, 106, 108, 112, 114, 133, 138, 140, 148, 151, 162, 169, 170, 171, 172, 177, 185, 186
Francophone, 21, 49, 138, 169, 181, 187
Frank, A. G., 168
Frankel, S. H., 89, 93, 179
Freetown, 22, 44
free-trade area, 103

frontier, 56, 61, 102, 172, 179
fruits, 44, 63, 65, 70
fuel, 54, 78, 130
  prices, 50
Fulani, the, 17, 31, 53, 85, 169, 178, 179, 185, 186
Fulbe, see Fulani
functionalism, 166
funerals, 126, 148

Gallais, J., 179
Galletti, R., et al., 179
Gambia, the, 21, 22, 23, 93, 99, 100, 101, 103, 122, 132, 138, 170, 173, 180, 187
gandu, 168
Gao, 29
gasoline, see oil
Gaud, W. S., 107
gentile constitution, the, 92
geography, 4, 20, 26, 29, 31, 35, 49, 168, 175, 177, 179, 183, 187
Germany, 15, 42, 49, 108, 162, 168
  East, 178
gerontocracy, 37, 173
Ghana, 13, 21, 22, 23, 24, 25, 49, 56, 57, 60, 63, 64, 73, 86, 93, 94, 96, 99, 100, 101, 108, 112, 115, 122, 132, 138, 160, 170, 173, 175, 178, 179, 180, 185, 186
  ancient, 20
  northern, 2, 73, 76, 96, 140, 169, 170, 172, 180, 184, 186
  see also Gold Coast, the
Gill and Duffus, 169
gin, 65
Girouard, Sir P., 171
global economy, the, see industrialization; world, economic system of
GNP (Gross National Product), 23, 24, 66, 137, 138
  per capita, 23, 24
goats, 37, 53, 54, 76
gold, 20, 32, 41, 111, 152
Gold Coast, the, 7, 44, 45, 46, 59, 60, 85, 103, 138, 169, 171, 172, 175, 178, 187
  see also Ghana
Gombe emirate, 70, 76, 187
B. F. Goodrich Company, 59
Goody, E., 167
Goody, J., 16, 104, 133, 140, 149, 167, 171, 172, 179, 180
Gouro, the, 168, 173, 183
Goussault, Y., 98
government, 11, 14, 15, 21, 34, 45, 46, 49, 57, 68, 72, 73, 83, 85, 87, 88, 90, 91, 95, 103, 106, 113, 114, 115, 116,

215

Index

Index

217

Index

Index

Maghreb, the, 19, 29, 77
  see also North Africa
maize, *see* corn
malaria, 128, 170
Malaysia, 57
Mali, 21, 22, 23, 24, 66, 68–70, 86, 99,
  100, 101, 122, 131, 132, 137, 151,
  176, 178, 179, 181, 182, 183, 184
  ancient, 20, 30
malpractices, trading, 67
Malthusian, 134
"mammy," market, 36, 111, 143, 144
Manchester, 5, 69
Mande, Manding, 21, 30, 33, 111
manganese, 152
manioc, *see* cassava
Mansa Musa, 20
manufacturing, 5, 29, 31, 32, 34, 41, 44, 46,
  52, 55, 57, 60, 70, 78, 80, 107, 117,
  143, 152, 161, 172
manure, 53, 66, 74, 171
  green, 75
Maradi, 148, 184, 185
marginalism, *see* neoclassical theory
markets, marketing, 8, 9, 17, 26, 27, 37,
  38, 41, 44–45, 48, 53, 55, 58, 60, 63,
  65, 70, 71, 73, 77, 79, 80, 81, 84,
  90, 93, 95, 104, 107, 110–115, 119,
  125, 126, 127, 128, 129, 130, 131,
  133, 134, 138, 142, 145, 146, 150, 151,
  152, 155, 156, 157, 159, 160, 162,
  175, 177, 179, 180, 181, 183, 185
market, home (national), 26, 64, 66, 69,
  70, 87, 88, 103, 108–109, 115, 116,
  120, 125, 134, 143, 152, 158, 159,
  161, 162, 164, 188
market, internal, 45, 87, 114, 153, 174,
  180
  see also commerce; merchants; trade;
  world, economic system of
market demand, 12–13, 37, 38, 42, 53,
  60, 65, 69, 71, 73, 80, 110, 120, 129,
  144, 153, 159, 162
market gardening, 7, 37, 65, 71, 111, 142,
  165
marketing boards, 45, 60, 63, 79, 84, 86,
  92–93, 99, 114, 139, 175
  see also monopsony
marriage, 9, 36, 53, 54, 78, 110, 123,
  144–145, 146, 173, 175, 185
  breakdown of, 145
Marshall, A., 164, 173, 183
Marx, K., 3, 13, 15, 18, 19, 40, 117,
  158, 167, 170, 172, 183
Marxism, ix, 13–14, 16, 17, 18, 107, 167,
  169, 174, 178, 179, 181, 182, 183, 185,
  186, 187

anti-Marxist, 176
neo-Marxist, 15
matrilineal, 36, 55, 170
Mauny, R., 20, 183
Mauritania, 21, 22, 23, 45, 88, 122, 132, 152
Mauss, M., 121, 167, 183
Mazoyer, M., 183
meat, 74, 76, 77, 171
Mecca, pilgrimage to, 20
mechanization of agriculture, 8, 10, 12,
  72, 73, 76, 93, 104, 118, 143, 144, 158,
  160, 171
  see also machines
medicine, 43, 53, 71, 78, 127, 130, 133,
  152
medieval West Africa, 19–20, 28, 30, 32,
  35, 41, 183
Mediterranean Sea, the, 19, 20, 29, 30,
  50, 138
Meillassoux, C., 16, 34, 36, 144, 167,
  168, 169, 172, 173, 175, 183
Mellor, J., 135, 155, 162
men, 17, 36, 39–40, 53, 55, 56, 64, 121,
  142–145
  see also older and younger men; young men
Mende, T., 107
mercantilism, 4, 28, 40, 44, 50, 103, 160,
  167
merchants, 8, 28, 29, 30, 31, 32, 33, 34, 38,
  42, 43, 47, 53, 58, 59, 61, 64, 68,
  79, 85, 88, 92–93, 110–112, 114, 116,
  140, 143, 176
  houses, 44, 50, 68, 85, 112, 114, 115, 176
  princes, 43
  tradition, 138
  see also commerce; markets; trade
metal, metal products, 34, 41, 45, 53, 111,
  115, 152
Mexico, 148, 186
Mexico City, 5
Michigan State University, 81, 182
middle class, 156
Middle East, the, 19, 29, 50, 151
middlemen, 103, 111
Miers, S., and I. Kopytoff, 34, 168, 183
migration, 2, 56, 61, 62, 67, 69, 71, 85,
  97, 112, 118, 121–125, 138, 146, 147,
  154, 157, 159, 163, 164, 168, 175,
  176, 180, 181
  see also circulation of labor; exodus,
  rural; mobility; *navetanes*
military, 15, 26, 31, 32, 34, 41, 42, 43,
  46, 49, 57, 74, 86, 87, 101, 104, 113,
  162, 163, 170
  see also army; soldiers; warfare
milk, 74
Mill, J. S., 13, 18, 158, 164, 167, 173, 183

219

Index

millet, 68, 71, 127
  beer, 37
Miner, H., 168
minerals, 20, 21, 87, 152, 161
  see also mining
mining, 29, 32, 34, 44, 46, 60, 64, 84, 85,
  88, 92, 107, 112, 152, 161
  see also minerals
mixed farming, 53, 74, 75–76, 171, 177,
  187
mobility, 43, 45, 103, 121–125, 140, 141,
  148, 163
  social, 139
  see also circulation of labor; migration
modernization, 26, 155, 156, 164, 168,
  179
Mokwa, 175
money, 9, 11, 14, 17, 35, 41, 46, 47, 49, 61,
  66, 67, 68, 69, 78, 86, 87, 88, 90,
  93, 94, 96, 105, 106, 112, 115–117,
  118, 124, 126, 129, 130, 131, 137,
  138, 142, 143, 145, 147, 153, 173, 181,
  185
money economy, 156, 180
moneylending, *see* usury
monocropping, 56, 60
monopoly, 32, 33, 34, 44, 57, 73, 85, 88,
  90, 95, 110, 114, 136, 142, 143, 144,
  158, 172
  state monopoly capitalism, 186
monopsony, 47, 63, 68, 69, 79, 84, 86,
  87, 88, 92–93, 95, 114
  see also marketing boards
Monrovia, 22, 122
morality, 121, 135, 137, 149–150
Morgan, L. H., 92
Morocco, 41, 77
Morss, E. R., et al., 183
mortality rates, 26, 127, 132–133, 156
  infant, 25
  see also death
Mossi, the, 21, 31, 69, 179, 181
motor vehicles, *see* trucks
Mourides, the, 67, 87, 118, 147, 177
multinational corporations, 46, 65, 87, 89,
  94, 98, 115, 120, 150, 161
Munroe, J., 43, 183
Murdock, G. P., 36
Muslim, *see* Islam
Myint, H., 167, 180

Nadel, S. F., 30, 118, 131, 140, 142, 146,
  169, 173, 183
Nairobi, 135, 182
Naples, 48
Narodism, 182

nation-state, 9, 15, 21, 30, 46, 49, 50, 83,
  86, 105, 108–109, 126, 159, 161, 166
  see also state, the
navetanes, 67, 168
  see also migration
Near East, the, *see* Middle East, the
necessities, 37, 54, 72, 80
needs, 89, 101, 126, 130, 143, 155, 156, 158,
  161
  see also basic human needs
neoclassical theory, 13, 167, 183
Netting, R., 184
Netting, R., et al., 71, 184
New England, 165
Niamey, 22, 122
Nicolas, G., 148–149, 169, 173, 184
Nicolas, G., et al., 74, 169, 184
Niger, 21, 22, 23, 24, 47, 88, 99, 100, 101,
  103, 122, 148, 151, 172, 175, 184, 185
Niger river, 20, 22, 52, 57, 69, 175, 182
  bend, 29
  Delta, 32
  Inner Delta, 89, 179, 184
  Project, 175
Nigeria, 21, 22, 23, 24, 25, 41, 44, 45, 47,
  49, 50, 56, 66, 68, 86, 108, 122,
  132, 133, 137, 138, 151, 154, 178, 180,
  181, 184, 187
  eastern, 57, 58, 169
  middle belt, 175
  northern, 9, 13, 17, 33, 44, 52, 57, 66, 68,
  70, 76, 77, 85, 88, 91, 93, 99, 100,
  101, 103, 114, 118, 140, 142, 173, 184,
  186, 187
  southern, 57, 59, 63, 138
  southwest/western, 60, 124, 143, 175,
  179, 182
Nile river, 20, 30
nineteenth century, the, 14, 27, 28, 29, 33,
  34, 40, 41, 42–43, 45, 53, 56, 57,
  58, 67, 69, 90, 102–103, 108, 111, 113,
  128, 131, 133, 134, 146, 148, 163,
  164–165, 168, 170, 173, 175, 178, 179,
  183
Nkrumah, K., 60, 166, 178
nomads, 29, 30, 73, 123, 178, 184, 186
  see also pastoralism
Norman, D., 169, 180, 184
North Africa, 19, 58
  see also Maghreb, the
Norway, 24
Nouakchott, 22
Nukunya, G. K., 71
numbers, *see* statistics
Nupe, the, 118, 142, 184
nutrition, 17, 25, 48, 57, 64, 65, 71, 72,

220

Index

rhetoric, 96, 104, 155, 167
Rhodesia, 112
rice, 45, 48, 65, 66, 70, 71, 72–73, 88, 93, 95, 104, 107, 119, 140, 143, 152, 157, 160, 161, 169, 170, 171, 186
Richards, A. I., et al., 185
rich men, 73, 131, 135, 136, 149
  see also wealth
Riesman, P., 17, 178, 185
riots, 160
Risorgimento, 11, 15, 179
ritual, 32, 34, 35, 54, 55, 136, 148
rivers, river valleys, 20, 26, 29, 30, 66, 72, 84, 94, 101, 114
road gang, 89
roads, 44, 47, 80, 81, 87, 92, 102, 106, 114, 128, 161, 162
Roberts, A., 171
Roberts, P., 185
Robertson, A. F., 62, 167, 170, 185
Rome, ancient, 19, 164
root crops, 48, 56, 64, 70
Ross, E., 171
rotation, long fallow, *see* shifting cultivation
rubber, 42, 44, 56, 58–59, 61, 107, 111, 143, 152, 169, 182
  vulcanization, 42, 58
rulers, ruling class, 14, 30, 33, 34, 41, 42, 45, 46, 47, 52, 83, 84, 85, 86, 88, 91, 102, 105, 107, 108, 109, 125, 127, 139–140, 153
rural industry, *see* crafts
Russia, 15, 17, 46, 86, 108, 149, 151, 176, 182

Sahara desert, the, 19, 20, 21, 22, 29, 30, 63, 66, 69, 74, 126
Sahel, the (Sahelian countries), 17, 21, 24, 25, 29, 47, 49, 66, 73, 77, 86, 89, 100, 106, 126, 127, 133, 136, 137, 150, 152, 163, 170, 175, 176, 177, 179, 187
salaried workers, *see* wage
salt, 37
Samory, 43
Sandbrook, R., and R. Cohen, 117
savannah, the, 4, 10, 12, 16, 20, 21, 27, 28, 29, 30, 31, 32, 33, 35, 36, 37, 38, 40, 42, 44, 45, 48, 52, 53, 54, 55, 56, 57, 61, 62, 63, 65–73, 76, 77, 85, 91, 111, 112, 114, 118, 122, 123, 125, 127, 130, 133, 134, 136, 138, 139, 143, 145, 146, 157, 158, 160, 163, 168, 169, 177, 180, 186
savings, 115, 131, 142
schistosomiasis, 101, 128
schooling, *see* education
Schumacher, E. J., 171

Schumpeter, J., 167, 185
Schwimmer, B., 185
SCOA (Société Commercial de l'Ouest Africain), 114, 177
Scotland, 24, 82
Scottish Enlightenment, the, 13, 160
seasonality, 10, 123, 124, 146
secret societies, 31, 148
security, 26, 35, 37, 99, 100, 117, 118, 130, 131, 149, 150, 155, 163, 170
Seddon, D., 175, 177, 178, 184, 186
sedentary agriculturalists, 30, 67, 74
Ségou, 68, 182
Seibel, H- D., and A. Massing, 95, 146, 186
self-sufficiency, 8–10, 16, 20, 35–39, 60, 64, 71, 90, 107, 108–109, 110, 118, 128–129, 130, 131, 134, 135, 147, 149, 150, 154, 155, 156, 162, 164, 167, 170, 171, 176, 184, 185
  see also individualism
Senegal, 13, 17, 21, 22, 23, 66–68, 72, 84, 85, 86, 93, 100, 101, 103, 104, 111, 112, 122, 127, 132, 138, 146, 147, 170, 172, 176, 177, 184, 185, 186, 187
Senegal River, 19, 20, 22, 23, 52, 90, 174
Senegambia, 44, 66, 67, 68, 147, 177
servants, 118
services, 52, 61, 78, 80–81, 99, 100, 101, 102, 117, 125, 126, 128, 129, 130, 142, 151, 156, 165, 172
  center, 162
  see also social services
settlement patterns, 56, 103, 123, 134, 163
settlers, 56, 123, 124, 170, 172, 179
Shai, the, 171
Shapiro, K., 73, 77, 177, 186
sharecropping, 62, 117, 118, 141, 185
  see also abusa; caretaker
shea butter, 70
sheep, 37, 53, 54, 76
shelter, *see* housing
Shepherd, A., 140, 170, 186
Sherbro, 143
shifting cultivation, 7, 36, 55, 64, 123, 169
shipping, 43, 114
Sierra Leone, 21, 22, 23, 25, 56, 81, 88, 93, 100, 101, 103, 122, 132, 138, 143, 170, 181
Siné-Saloum, 185, 187
slavery, 16, 20, 27, 28, 30, 31, 32, 33, 34, 35, 38, 39–40, 41, 42, 43, 50, 52, 59, 61, 64, 67, 68, 88, 110, 111, 112, 115, 117, 123, 127, 133, 136, 140, 145, 163, 168, 181, 183
  abolition of, 42, 67
  estates, 9, 30–31
  see also force

223

Index

slave trade, *see* Atlantic slave trade
Sleeper, J., 75
slums, 2, 123, 130
smallholders, 8, 13, 46, 47, 48, 62, 63, 70, 72, 77, 85, 86, 87, 89, 95, 154, 155, 156–158, 159, 165, 171, 172, 176, 183
  see also: peasants; production
Smelser, N., 5
Smith, A., 14, 158, 160, 167, 180, 186
Smith, M. F., 168, 186
Smith, M. G., 9, 53–54, 141, 169, 173, 176, 180, 186
smuggling, 73, 87, 93, 103, 104
soap, 42, 57, 77, 80, 143, 161
"soapboilers," 85
socialism, 104, 107, 177, 181
social order, *see* social organization
social organization, 6, 9, 17, 21, 27, 29, 30, 31, 35, 37, 38, 39–40, 41, 49, 50, 54, 60, 61, 67, 68, 72, 74, 75, 95, 118, 121, 124, 127, 128, 135, 136, 141, 145–150, 155, 156, 157, 159, 163, 175, 176, 177, 178, 180, 181, 187
social sciences, 4, 6, 13, 15, 16, 29, 59, 176
social services, 47, 80, 99, 100, 101, 155
social structure, *see* social organization
sociology, 149, 179, 182
soft drugs, 63, 137
soil, 26, 55–56, 67, 69, 70, 72, 75, 76, 98, 127, 169, 171
soldiers, 30, 67, 73, 87, 102, 109, 139, 140, 170, 171
  mercenaries, 30, 38
  see also army; military; warfare
Songhay, 30
Soninke, the, 184
sorghum, 70, 71
Southern Africa, 139, 151, 179
Sow, F., 186
soya beans, 57
Spain, 14
Spearman's *rho*, 168
specialization, *see* division of labor
special-purpose currency, 115
  see also money
stabilization funds, *see* marketing boards
standard of living, 17, 46, 60, 66–67, 94, 101, 112, 126–135, 140, 154, 155
staple crops, 37, 44, 47, 63, 64, 65, 69, 70, 72, 152, 158, 181
starvation, 126, 127, 130, 134
  see also famine; hunger
state, the, 11, 13, 14–15, 17, 20, 25, 26, 30, 32, 40, 45, 46, 50, 53, 60, 63, 64, 67, 68, 71, 73, 83–109, 110, 115, 117, 119, 120, 123, 125, 127, 128, 131, 136, 138, 139, 141, 142, 147, 153, 157, 160, 161, 164, 165, 166, 167, 172, 174, 176, 179, 180, 181, 186
  as entrepreneur, 46, 88–90, 113
  formation, 31, 33–35, 43, 133
  see also colonies; government; postcolonial
state farms, 89, 118
stateless societies, 31, 33, 34, 40, 136, 163, 168, 175, 181
states, successor, 14, 27–28, 29, 45, 46–50, 67, 106, 116, 119, 140, 153, 169, 178, 182, 187
statistics, 104–105, 121, 125, 126, 130, 167, 169, 176, 179, 180, 188
Stavenhagen, R., 170, 186
Stedman Jones, G., 172, 173
Stenning, D., 17, 178, 179, 186
Steuart, Sir J., vi, 14, 18, 158, 160, 186
storage, 10, 30, 37, 64, 70, 79
strangers, 33, 35, 61, 64, 92, 136, 139, 147, 178
strategic significance, 47, 106, 151, 153
stratification, 12, 29, 30, 33, 36, 136, 137, 138, 141, 147, 173
  see also class
sub-Saharan Africa, 23, 25, 60, 107, 132, 133, 138, 175, 188
subsidies, 48, 69, 97, 102, 130, 140
subsistence, *see* self-sufficiency
successor states, *see* states, successor
Sudan, the, 20, 21, 29, 52–54, 76, 111, 136
  the country, 69
sugar, 45, 65, 72, 89, 140
Sumatra, 57
Suret-Canale, J., 16, 17, 67, 84, 94, 112, 115, 126, 128, 169, 170, 186
surpluses, 10, 15, 30, 35, 37, 45, 68, 73, 84, 88, 94, 107, 125, 131, 139, 142, 144, 151, 153, 155, 156, 162
survival, 126, 127
Swift, J., 30, 187
Switzerland, 140
Syrians, *see* Levantines
Szereszewski, R., 187

Taiwan, 5, 72
Tallensi, the, 31, 169, 172, 180
tariffs, 103, 158, 160, 161
Taussig, M., 141
taxes, 11, 30, 33, 34, 35, 45, 47, 52, 53, 60, 67, 83, 84, 87, 90, 91, 97, 103, 104, 105, 112, 124, 127, 128, 135, 142, 169, 171, 181, 182
tea, 45, 65, 72
technology, 8, 12, 13, 26, 28, 42, 50, 53, 55, 62, 67, 70, 88, 105, 120, 125, 128,

Index

Index

usury, 96, 116, 117, 141, 142
  see also banking
utensils, 34, 37
utilities, 94, 100, 101, 128, 130

vegetable oils, export of, 1, 3, 5, 27, 42,
  57, 66, 111, 112, 152
  see also export
vegetables, 65, 70, 71
Venema, L. B., 187
vent-for-surplus, 12–13, 167, 180
villages, 9, 17, 30, 35, 36, 38, 39–40, 52,
  53, 58, 65, 68–69, 75, 78, 79–81, 95,
  96, 97, 108, 110, 118, 121, 123, 124,
  125, 127, 129, 131, 135, 137, 139, 140,
  141, 142, 145, 146, 147, 149, 155,
  156, 160, 163, 170, 172, 173, 175, 176,
  178, 180, 181, 182, 184, 185
virgin lands, 12, 13, 56, 61, 153, 158
Volta river, 22, 23, 32, 94
  lake, 94
  Voltaic area, 53

Wade, R., 73, 187
wages, 8, 11, 13, 38, 49, 53, 61, 62, 65, 73,
  78, 87, 88, 89, 95, 111, 117–118,
  124, 129, 141, 142, 159, 160, 164
  see also labor
Waldstein, A., 172, 187
Wallace, T., 187
warfare, 10, 28, 30, 32, 33, 34, 41, 42, 43,
  45, 49, 52, 53, 54, 64, 83, 86, 100,
  123, 133, 153, 156, 163, 181
  see also army; military; soldiers
warriors, *see* warfare
water, 76, 78, 88, 89, 102, 129, 157, 170,
  184
  courses, 128
  diseases borne by, 101, 128
  drainage, 56
  projects, 94
  rights, 74
  supply, 10, 66, 71, 73, 80, 162
wealth, 12, 20, 24, 35, 37, 38, 49, 63, 64,
  74, 86, 102, 104, 111, 115–117, 119,
  135, 136, 137, 140, 153, 159, 180,
  186
  see also accumulation; capital; rich men
Weber, M., ix, 3, 13, 17, 83, 90, 99, 168,
  187

weeding, 55, 76
Weil, P., 187
Weiskel, T., 59
welfare, 15, 17, 78, 84, 89, 94, 100, 106,
  121, 133, 161, 165, 184
  state, 105
West Africa, 170, 173
westernized, 138
West Indies, 42, 85, 155
wet season, the, 66, 71
wheat, 70
White, P., and M. Gleave, 168, 171, 187
Wilks, I., 168
Williams, G., 187
Wittfogel, K., 169
Wolof, 31, 67, 168, 187
women, 17, 36, 37, 38, 39–40. 53, 54, 55,
  64, 79, 110, 115, 123, 129, 142–145,
  173, 176, 183, 184, 185, 186
  feminism, 173
workers, *see* labor; proletariat; wages
world, economic system of, 1–2, 4, 7, 9,
  14, 15, 21, 23, 25, 26, 27, 28, 40, 42,
  45, 49–50, 57, 60, 63, 66, 80, 85,
  86, 105, 108–109, 110–113, 120, 126,
  132, 134, 151, 152, 155, 158, 160,
  162, 165, 170, 182, 183
  capitalism, 83, 150
  gap between rich and poor nations, 137, 178
  population, 162, 176
  prices, 72, 93
  production, 60
  recession, 47, 107, 124, 155
World Bank, the, 3, 23, 24, 46, 50, 57,
  66, 82, 87, 99, 100, 105–106, 132, 135,
  144, 161, 167, 172, 182, 187, 188
World Tables, 188

yams, 64, 65, 70
yields, 11, 75, 88, 157, 170
  per acre, 72, 171
Yoruba, the, 79, 143, 175, 176, 179, 182
young men, 37, 38, 39, 64, 68–69, 92, 97,
  110, 118, 122, 124, 125, 145, 146,
  168, 181
  see also older and younger men

Zambia, 86
Zangheri, R., 15, 188
Zaria, 53, 184, 186

226

CAMBRIDGE STUDIES IN SOCIAL ANTHROPOLOGY

General Editor: Jack Goody

*Also published as a paperback